THE TRUTH ABOUT CRUISE SHIPS

A Cruise Ship Officer Survives the Work,
Adventure, Alcohol, and Sex of Ship Life

JAY HERRING

See pictures from my time at sea, and watch video of what happened inside the ship during the hurricane. Just go to Facebook and search for "The Truth About Cruise Ships."

www.TheTruthAboutCruiseShips.com

Published by:
SaltLog Press
5621 Bedford Lane
The Colony, TX 75056

ISBN: 0981843611
ISBN-13: 978-0-9818436-1-2

Library of Congress Control Number: 2010901750
Salt Log Press, The Colony, TX

Third Revision
Printed in the United States of America

CONTENTS

Acknowledgements

I am lucky to have had so much help throughout this project. The following people made the book much better than it otherwise would have been.

Dorrie O'Brien was my first editor, and she had the unfortunate task of working with a very raw manuscript. She helped me restructure the content so that it became more of a story with a timeline, rather than a collection of facts.

Next was Mike Foy, who was an invaluable resource. For the last four years, I have constantly pestered him for his insightful feedback.

Ryan Shopp suggested using the flashback style intro, and now I can't imagine the opening any other way. Ryan was also a source of positive energy throughout the project.

Dave Gibson helped talk me through the content and how to present it.

Natalie Lynch was next. Though not an editor by trade, she was as thorough as any editor could be, and provided invaluable tweaks and insight from a much needed female perspective.

Scott Kincaid was also unbelievably thorough and fast with his improvements for the text. He has a unique gift for making things easier to understand and follow, and the rescue-the-cat moments are there because of him.

Craig Haveman helped me appreciate the need to cut the boring content.

Risa Barnes went out of her way to help on multiple occasions, and I always look forward to our conversations.

David Brian Bruns generously took the time to explain the importance of when to reveal certain content. He also taught me the benefits of doing a systematic breakdown of a manuscript.

Michael Allinder can tell a great story, and he reminded me that some details don't need to be shared.

Ms. Valiant Effort proofread and gave some perspective on how the story was told.

Deirdre Kennerson purchased the pre-release eBook on the first day it was available and gave me some much needed positive feedback.

Scott Zaleski purchased the pre-release eBook and reminded me to avoid deviating from the subject.

Next was my mother, to whom I cannot apologize enough. The stories in here are not the things that mothers are supposed to know, and she would have preferred I not tell them.

And finally, my loving wife Mirka. She helped me with the content and details from the very beginning, and I could not ask for a more understanding and supportive life partner.

WHY TELL THE STORY?

When people find out that I worked on a cruise ship, they always ask the same questions.

"Did you live on the ship?"

Yes.

"Could you get off in port?"

Usually.

"Can you get me a discount?"

Not anymore.

But conversations have a short attention span and the topic shifts after only a few questions. Nevertheless the subject resurfaces with people who see me often.

"Did you ever sail in rough seas?"

Yes. And then I tell them about the damage my ship took from the hurricane.

"Did your ship ever get infected with the Norovirus?"

Yes. And then I talk about how infected crewmembers were quarantined and how we decontaminated the ship.

"Was there a lot of sex?"

Big time. And then I tell them about the Lithuanian girl.

Again the dialogue ends, but most people want to know more. The problem is that what I saw and experienced would never fit into the time restrictions of a conversation. There's just too much to tell. Ship life was so unique that it's hard to describe to anyone who hasn't lived it.

My job onboard was to fix the computers. Through socializing—a given when it came to ship life—I knew plenty of people, but I also knew all the senior officers because they had computers. In fact, every department had computers, and this gave me access to the entire ship.

Of course I saw things that passengers could never see, but as the I/S manager, I saw things that crewmembers in other departments could never see. While on the bridge, I observed as the captain maneuvered the ship away from the pier. While at the information desk, also called the purser's desk on Carnival's ships, I listened to passengers complain about their cruise. While in the back of the purser's office, I listened to the pursers complain about the passengers. It was like a backstage pass to everything.

I worked for Carnival Cruise Lines from 2002 to 2004. Different cruise lines have different rules for their crew, and these change over time. Living conditions change over time. In the early '80s, some crewmembers slept in cabins with eight to ten bunks and no closet space or ventilation.

During my time with Carnival, we got paid less than crewmembers who worked for Royal Caribbean, but they had more restrictions than we did. Royal's crew bars served only beer and wine, and being drunk was grounds for disciplinary action. Carnival's crew bars had beer, wine, and liquor, and we could get hammered every night. And did.

I wrote this for those who have ever been interested in cruising, but this is not a book about the passenger experience. You can simply take a cruise for that. This is a book about my crew experience and the person I became while onboard. It's also my coming-of-age story as it happens within the culture of a cruise ship, which, as you'll see, is completely different than the culture most people live in on land.

If you don't like stories of romance and alcohol, then this book is not for you. But otherwise, you'll get answers to all the questions that people have asked or didn't think to ask over the years, and more importantly, you'll get the behind-the-scenes story that conversations never have time for.

If you take the time to learn about your destination before you travel there (for example, reading a guide book or reading up on the history of a place you intend to visit), it can help you better enjoy your trip. What many people don't realize when it comes to cruises, is that the ship *is* the destination. You spend more time on the ship than you do in port.

So I hope that the story of my time on ships will help you enjoy your cruises more, and if you haven't cruised yet, I hope it will help you decide if it's something you would like to try.

Jay Herring
Dallas, Texas

CHAPTER 1

HOW EASY IS ROMANCE
ON A CRUISE SHIP?

I had been onboard my first ship for five days when I went to the crew bar and met a woman from Trinidad and Tobago. She was a black woman and she was overweight, maybe even a little flabby, but such a sweetheart. I saw her the next night in the crew bar and she looked upset so I went over and sat down.

"What's wrong?" I asked.

"I just had an argument with the chief purser," she said with her Caribbean accent.

"That's too bad."

"Yes, I do not get along with the pursers on this ship very well," she said, starting to tear up a little. "I do not have many friends onboard."

Although I liked her, I could understand why others might shy away. She had slow, almost voodoo-like mannerisms that bordered on creepy. But she was so easy to talk to and, like me, perfectly content to sit and talk one on one.

"So do you have a girlfriend?" she asked, changing the subject.

"No."

"Have you been with anyone on the ship yet?"

"Nope. It's actually been twelve years since I slept with someone."

"Come on now."

"It's true." I said, and then told her why (more on that later).

"Hmm. That's fascinating. You know, I used to sleep with a skinny white guy from England on my last ship. You remind me of him."

"Oh, yeah?"

"He and I had lots of fun, and I never left him unsatisfied. I may not look it, but I'm actually a really good lover."

"You don't say."

"I've been with lots of men in my day. I'm forty-one, after all. And in my years, I've learned exactly what men like and how to please them. And now"—she took a sip of her drink— "and now all the men I sleep with are extremely satisfied."

I had always imagined athletic girls—especially flexible athletic girls—to be the best lovers. But this lady from Trinidad had me rethinking that assumption. Maybe it was just another one of the after effects of abstinence, but those voodoo mannerisms were now bordering on sensual.

"Would you like to have sex with me?" she asked, taking another sip of her drink. "We could go to my cabin right now."

Woodrow.

I couldn't believe how quickly the opportunity had presented itself. "I might be interested in that."

"Might?"

"Yeah."

"But not right now?"

"Yeah, not just yet."

"Okay, well, you think about it and I'll call you later this week." She got up and left me at the table, alone with my thoughts.

My cabin phone rang at 8:00 p.m. two days later.

"Hi, it's me," she said. "How are you?"

"I'm good. How are you?" I responded.

"Good, good. Are you ready to do what we talked about the other night?" she asked, wasting no time on idle chit-chat.

Before I get into what happened next, let's step back and talk about how I got to this point.

*** GETTING READY TO CRUISE? HERE ARE A FEW TIPS ON ENJOYING YOUR TIME AT SEA ***

*** TIPS FOR ENJOYING YOUR CRUISE ***

1. Sail with your age group. If it's cold, they're old. Alaskan cruises often have an older crowd and in general, any cruise longer than seven days will have an older crowd. Younger passengers usually can't afford longer cruises nor do they have vacation time to take them. Three and four day cruises are party cruises and typically have a younger crowd, especially in the Caribbean. Two day cruises to nowhere are especially popular with the party crowd. If you are looking for an older more relaxed crowd, look for longer voyages especially in colder climates. If you want to party with a younger crowd, look for shorter voyages especially in warmer climates.

2. If you have assigned seating in the dining rooms, then the secret about the people you sit with is that they are likely very similar to you. The Maitre'd intentionally seats similar people together. Couples with couples, singles with singles, seniors with seniors. Realize that these people may become your new best friends on the cruise.

3. Remember to set your watch to "ship time" which may or may not change when you cross time zones.

4. Don't be late. The ship will only wait about fifteen minutes after its scheduled sailing time. Each cruise line has a port agent that can help if you do miss the ship. Most people fly to the next port to meet the ship there, but you'll pay for all extra expenses.

5. Remember that the captain has.."

These are a few of the tips included in the companion ebook called *"Cruise Like a Master: How To Save Money And Be Completely Prepared For Your Cruise Without All The Stress!"* It's a result of the research in the writing of *The Truth About Cruise Ships*.

Available now at: www.CruiseLikeaMaster.com

CHAPTER 2

How to Get a Cruise Ship Job

I love computers and all of the great things they do, but I never much enjoyed fixing them. After four years as the Information Technology, or IT, Manager at a small consulting company, I realized that, in fact, I hated fixing them. I started looking for another job and mentioned it to my boss. He respected my honesty and then promptly laid me off two months later. At first I was bitter, very bitter, but then I realized my mistake: You should never be too forthcoming with an employer.

I had lived with my parents for a few months following graduation, and now without a job, I was back mooching off them for the second time since college. After three months of job hunting, I had no leads. While driving home one night, I said to myself out loud and out of the blue, "I could be a bartender on a cruise ship."

I had never been on a cruise. In fact, I had never even seen a cruise ship in person. Dallas was far enough inland that I rarely even saw the ocean. I don't know what made me think of it.

I went to Carnival.com and while reading about the onboard bartenders, I noticed an opening for a shipboard I/S manager. Not that it mattered, and not that I could describe the difference, but I found the title "I/S manager" a bit antiquated. It had been generally replaced with the title "IT manager" years ago—in my mind, at least.

No matter what they called it, it was exactly what I needed. I would leave the nine-to-five corporate life. I would get to travel. I would not have to live with my parents. Within two hours it had become my dream job and I wanted nothing in this world more than to work on a cruise ship. I still hated computers, but I'd tolerate them in this case. I applied for the

I/S manager position only because I thought it would pay better than bartending.

I filled out the online application and submitted my résumé. I called the corporate office throughout the week and, after speaking to several operators, found out the name and email address of the hiring manager. I sent my résumé again, this time directly to him. I also left him a voicemail. A few days later he emailed me to schedule a five-minute phone interview.

"If you were to get hired," he said over the phone, "your time with the company would be measured in what we call contracts. A typical contract is eight months of work followed by a mandatory eight-week vacation."

I would later find out that captains, chief engineers, and a few other high-level positions worked a four-month contract followed by eight weeks of vacation.

I didn't understand the need for such a long vacation, especially since these were not paid vacations. Every day of vacation was a day without pay. A week or two might be nice, I thought, but eight weeks? I knew that I wouldn't need a vacation and if I did take one, it certainly wouldn't be eight weeks long.

"Are you still interested?" he asked after talking a little more about the job.

"Yes I am." So we scheduled an onsite interview in Miami.

The corporate office had a six-foot replica of the red funnel or smoke stack that brands every Carnival ship. The funnel is supposed to resemble a whale's tail folded over on its way back into the water, but I never made that connection until years after I left Carnival.

The lobby was spacious and clean and had two model ships on display. Each one was a perfect replica, built to a scale of 1:200 and complete with miniature pieces of furniture visible through cabin windows. It had deck chairs next to the pools and miniature mannequins standing all around. The model was so detailed and precise that to commission one brand new would cost over $15,000.

I'd never seen a ship up close, and after looking at the mannequins—each was about the size of an ant, compared to the ship, which was six feet long—I got an idea of just how massive a cruise ship is.

"If you drink or smoke," the hiring manager said during the interview, "then you will probably do more of that on ships."

"Well, I don't smoke, but I do drink," I said. "And if I end up having an extra beer here and there, then no big deal."

"Yeah, well, for most people, it ends up being more than just an extra beer here and there."

"Okay," I said, willing to see where being agreeable would get me.

"You'd carry a pager that could go off at any time, day or night, and you'd have to respond to it. After some time, you will get tired of being on the ship."

"Really?" I asked. Such a notion sounded strange.

"Yes. You get to where you feel trapped, with no way to escape."

I knew this wouldn't happen to me, but I didn't argue. I just made sure he knew that I was excited.

The interview went well, but it could have gone better. I could have been better. Speaking is a skill that deteriorates with inactivity, and after three months of lying around my parents' house, I was rusty.

The hiring manager told me that he had whittled some 600 résumés down to twenty-five site visits and would hire up to five people. I had doubts about my interview and figured I wasn't his first choice, but at least my foot was in the door.

I mailed a thank you letter the next day. I wanted him to know my determination, so I called or emailed every ten days.

He always recognized me but kept saying things like, "Not sure what we're doing yet," or "I'll be out all next week."

"It would just be so awesome," I said to my parents one night over dinner. "I would get to work on a ship and be at the beach with people from all over the world."

"Yes, well," my stepfather had to chime in, "if you want to work on a cruise ship just to meet lots of girls, I wouldn't count on it."

That actually hadn't occurred to me until he said it. I was excited because working on a cruise ship sounded so different from anything I had done. And now I was excited about meeting lots of girls, too.

✲ ✲ ✲

After two agonizing months of waiting for an answer from Carnival, I finally received an incoming call from a Miami area code. I answered. It was the hiring manager.

"I'd like to hire you if you're still available," he said.

I took a nanosecond to consider and stumbled over my words as I wholeheartedly accepted. "How many people did you hire on this round?" I asked.

"You're one of three."

That felt good. Actually, out of 600 applicants, it felt lucky. The conversation ended and I hung up. "I'm going to work on a cruise ship," I said to no one.

I did a celebratory dance that had me looking like a wounded duck, and for the rest of the day I felt happier than ever.

Included with the offer letter was a list of shipboard rules and regulations: No fishing from the ship. No gambling in the ship's casino. No fraternizing with the passengers. My mom read it over and added a rule of her own.

"You are not the captain," she said, "and you do not go down with the ship."

When my manager said I had the job, I was too excited to think about anything besides getting on a plane. Two hours later I calmed down and thought, *What now?* I was to start in one week and had some questions so I called him back.

"How do I receive mail and pay bills?" I asked.

"The crew can receive mail," he said, "but it goes to the corporate office first and from there it gets forwarded to the ship. The delay could be up to two months or longer if you transfer ships. Most crewmembers handle their bills online or have someone at home do it for them."

I later found out that the delay in receiving mail was generally only a couple of weeks.

"Should I keep my cell phone?"

"I would, but keep in mind that it will only work when the ship is close to U.S. soil."

I set my cell phone and credit card to bill automatically, and my parents agreed to open anything else that looked important.

"How much stuff should I bring?"

"However much you are willing to carry on and off the ship. I'd suggest that you pack light for the first contract."

I packed only clothes, books, and toiletries and was able to fit everything in one large suitcase and one carry-on.

My new salary was almost half of what I'd made at my last job, but I didn't care because I was going to be on a cruise ship. My manager justified the salary by explaining that crewmembers had few living expenses. They didn't pay for food or rent or utilities.

I said goodbye to my friends, and most of them were as excited and curious about the new gig as I was.

"This is the perfect time for you to end your abstinence," one of my friends told me. "You'll never get a chance like this again."

"A chance like what?" I asked.

"A chance to learn how to become a good lover. What better way than to practice with women from all over the world? In fact," he went on, "your future wife will hold it against you if you don't take this opportunity to sleep with all these women."

For the next few days I thought about it, and he was right. A cruise ship probably was the best place to lose my second virginity. I was past my prime and had nothing to show for it. I had never been in love. I had never dated anybody longer than two months. Something had to change, so enough of this "I have to love you first" crap.

I was almost twenty-eight years old and decided that at my next opportunity, I was going to have sex for the third time in my life, which would be the first time in nearly twelve years.

✳ ✳ ✳

Carnival sent me a one-way plane ticket to Miami and paid for a hotel room that was walking distance from the office. I slept on the most comfortable portion of a hotel mattress: the side that was farthest away from the TV. Since everyone sits directly in front of the TV, that spot is always more worn out than anywhere else on the bed.

On my first day, they sent me to a clinic for a drug test and a physical that included a mandatory HIV test. Those who fail the HIV test are not able to work onboard, and I would soon understand the business sense behind this. The drug test was easy because I had never used anything harder than alcohol and nicotine. I later met crewmembers who used a detoxifying drink to beat the drug test even though they had smoked pot a couple of weeks earlier.

The one-story clinic was on a pier, and behind it was a massive white wall covered with windows. It was my first glimpse of a ship, and it blew me away. To see the top of the ship from inside the shuttle, I had to hunch over in my seat and twist my head to look up. I got out and stood there, staring upwards. I approached the ship to get a better look. A security fence kept me from getting too close, and looking to the right, I could see the bow or the front of ship. But when I looked left I couldn't see the stern, the back of the ship, because the ship stretched out behind a building, making it impossible for me to tell how big it was.

And let there be no mistake—cruise ships can be truly massive. Some can hold over 8,000 passengers and crew. A Boeing 747 has a wingspan that is slightly wider than the Royal Caribbean's *Allure of the Seas*, but remove twenty-one feet from each wing and you could fit ten of those jumbo jets inside the ship with lots of room to spare. The ship has ten acres of walking space and there is enough steel in the *Allure of the Seas* to stretch around Earth five times. Every day the ship's engines generate the equivalent daily electrical consumption of 50,000 American homes. For a freight train to weigh as much as the *Allure of the Seas*, it would have 900 fully loaded rail cars and be 18 miles long.

Amenities onboard Royal's *Voyager of the Seas* include an ice skating rink, a miniature golf course, and a rock climbing wall. The *Norwegian Pearl* has a four-lane bowling alley. The biggest cabin with Norwegian Cruise Lines is what they call a "Garden Villa." Yes, it's a cabin, but it's a 5,000-square-foot cabin. It has three bedrooms, three bathrooms, a private terrace and sundeck, a hot tub, and enough room for 100 people to party. Ship designs haven't even reached their limit yet. In fact, every few years the record is broken as a new ship claims the title of being the largest cruise ship in the world.

On the second day of the job, I was shuttled to a company called Action Uniform, where they issued me three white officer uniforms and two formal navy-blue uniforms that included a jacket, a dress shirt, pants, and a standard gold tie. I would later meet an I/S manager who used to wear a tie he found in Italy that was identical to the ties Carnival issued, except it had a naked girl woven into the back side of the tie.

* * *

I had a friend who lived in Fort Lauderdale. We never dated, as in we never went on an actual date, but she was a kissing buddy and for an entire semester we had done everything short of intercourse.

"I have some condoms on the dresser if you want to get one," she said one night back in college while we were in the middle of one of our late night make-out sessions.

She knew my thoughts on sex, and it was the first time she'd brought it up.

"I'm not ready."

"Okay."

We continued making out as usual and she never mentioned it again.

So before my ship assignment, while I was staying in Miami, she drove down from Fort Lauderdale one Saturday night and we went to South Beach. It had been a few years since we'd seen each other. We ate dinner and walked to a couple of clubs and went back to my hotel room. Game on. We started kissing, and after a few minutes she pulled away.

"This isn't really doing it for me," she said.

"What do you mean?"

"Well, it's like . . . been there, done that."

She was right. A person's kissing style is as unique and identifiable as their handwriting, and the best kisses come from unfamiliar lips. To this day, I still think the best kiss I've ever had with my wife Mirka was our first kiss.

But it had been a long time since my first kiss with this girl in the Miami hotel. After countless nights together, we were so familiar with each other that our kissing was boring. Very boring. There was no emotion, of course, but there wasn't even any passion. I wasn't going to bring it up because I was hoping to break my twelve-year streak, but after she said it, I had to agree with her.

"Well, we could have sex if you want," I said. "We haven't been there or done that. There are some condoms in my suitcase if you want to go get one."

"Are you serious?" She seemed taken aback.

"Yeah. You could be the first girl I've been with in twelve years."

I don't know if she believed that or not, but she declined my offer and left. I haven't talked to her since.

☆ ☆ ☆

I spent the rest of my two weeks in Miami talking to folks in the office and going through some boring computer-based training exercises. There were two other new I/S managers with me in Miami. One was a guy from Nicaragua and the other was a guy I'll call JB, an American. The three of us went out for beers one night with another I/S manager, a veteran from Brazil named Fonzo, who'd been on ships for five years.

The new guys bombarded Fonzo with questions about ship life. We asked about the hours and the workload. We asked about dealing with the other departments. We asked if you could really get fired for sleeping with a passenger. My hiring manager took this topic very seriously and said someone had just been fired for sleeping with a passenger. I assumed it was an isolated incident, but Fonzo told us that it happened all the time—crewmembers just didn't get caught every time, and when they did get caught, they didn't necessarily get fired. It depended on the circumstances and whether or not the staff captain liked you. Then he taught us how to get away with it. Here's what he said:

"Never take a passenger to your cabin. Don't even take them into a crew area. A hidden spot on the ship will work, but the best place is in the passenger's cabin. If you can get in and out without being seen by security, then you're home free. If security does see you, then you just have to say that you were fixing the TV. It is part of our job. You could even get the passenger to call the purser's desk to request that the TV get fixed. The pursers would then page you about it and you'd have a purser who could verify that you had a reason to be in the cabin. Your pager would also show that the purser paged you."

"Have you ever done this?" I asked.

"Of course I have," Fonzo said.

JB and I kept asking questions, but the Nicaraguan got bored and left. I finished three pints of beer. Fonzo was on his fourth pint and JB had just started his sixth pint when I said goodbye and headed back to the hotel.

Time crept in Miami. It was like those nights before Christmas when I couldn't sleep because I was so anxious to open presents. I just couldn't wait to get on a ship and see the inside of it. I wanted to know how it all worked. Words like "captain," "bridge," and "chief engineer" always made me think of *Star Trek*. I wanted to meet a chief engineer and a captain and ask them a million questions. I wanted to see the engine room and the bridge.

After two weeks, I finally had a ship assignment—the *Fantasy*. I left on an early morning flight and landed in Orlando, Florida. At the airport, I found a woman wearing a Carnival shirt and holding a Carnival sign. Her job was to direct passengers arriving by plane to a shuttle bus that would take them to the ship at Port Canaveral. I told her I was a crew member, and she said I would ride in the same shuttle bus that the passengers used to get to the ship. It was a 45-minute drive, and as we neared the pier I saw the giant NASA Vehicle Assembly Building. Then I saw three cruise ships parked next to one another: a Disney ship, a Royal Caribbean ship, and Carnival's *Fantasy*. The *Fantasy* is a big boat, but it was much smaller than the other two and it had the most weathered paint job. It looked downright shoddy next to the others, and one passenger called it the red-headed step-ship.

Conversation flowed easily among the passengers on the shuttle as they talked about the ports and the other ships they had cruised on. I turned in my seat to face the conversation. I was the only person traveling alone and since I wasn't wearing a uniform, I looked like a passenger.

"Are you meeting anybody onboard?" one woman asked.

"No."

"Have you ever cruised before?"

"No."

"So what made you decide to cruise?"

"I just wanted to try it," I said.

I didn't want them to know that I was a crew member. I didn't want to face the wow-you're-going-to-be-a-crewmember-so-let's-ask-you-a-million-questions conversation. No, I'd just fade into the crowd when we got to the ship and they'd never know. Then the bus stopped.

"Crewmembers get off here," the driver said.

My stomach churned. I had deceived these people and was dreading having to stand. I prolonged it, rising slowly and looking back at a group of offended faces.

"This is my stop," I said with a weak voice as I raised both eyebrows. "See you later."

There was no response. They just stared as I turned around and walked off the bus. One other crew member was on the bus, but I didn't know until she stood up, too. She'd been smart and kept a low profile. She'd been on ships for a couple of years and had no interest in the conversations of passengers.

I walked up the crew gangway and was met by a security officer from India. There would be two I/S managers on the *Fantasy* while I was there: Dipsu, who was the senior I/S manager from India, and me, a trainee. Security paged Dipsu and asked me to wait. There I waited, standing on a cruise ship for the first time.

CHAPTER 3

THE PROS AND CONS OF
THE HIGHEST RANK ONBOARD

While standing just inside the hull door, I reached over and touched the hull of the ship. White is the chosen color for most cruise ships because it reflects the sun's heat, and because they just look great in white. The paint was a quarter-inch thick on the hull to protect the steel from the corrosive saltwater.

The average cruise ship dedicated sixteen crewmembers to do nothing but paint. Day in, day out, all they did was paint both the inside and outside of the ship. Combined, they slopped on eighty gallons of paint every week. Because the paint flaked off unevenly and was reapplied with rollers and brushes, it was practically textured and came nowhere close to matching the smoothness of an airplane's aerodynamic paint job. The paint insulated the ship's steel and gave it a dull coolness that was in contrast to the sharp cold you feel from touching the metal when you board an airplane.

Crewmembers walked up the gangway every couple of minutes, carrying handfuls of shopping bags. They slid their ship IDs into the security machine, which gave a loud beep of acceptance. The ceiling was low, and because there wasn't much space, I was in the way. So were my suitcases. I was perpendicular to (and had a narrow view of) a wide corridor that ran from the front of the ship to the back. I watched as an endless flow of crewmembers marched in both directions.

Dipsu arrived and led me to my cabin. We were in a crew area, but I didn't know it at the time. My suitcases bounced along a diamond-plated metal floor, and it was then I noticed how much painted steel I was surrounded by. The floor, the walls, the ceiling – everything was metal, and with the exception of the red floor, everything was painted white. Voices and footsteps pinged off the metal, and the air smelled of scratched steel and paint and cigarettes. It was an odd sight for me to see people smoking indoors at work.

When my cabin door swung open, I was astounded by what I saw. It was absurdly small. I couldn't believe that it had bunk beds and that two people were expected to live in such a tiny space. I had to turn my suitcase sideways to fit it through the door. Dipsu said he'd used his connections to get me a cabin to myself, adding that it was temporary and he didn't know how long it might last. He left me to unpack and returned in an hour to give me a tour of the ship.

From my cabin on Deck 0, we went to a door with stairs that went up to the passenger areas. We walked past a few passenger cabins and then hopped on an elevator up to Deck 4 and walked past the information desk, the shore excursion desk, the photo gallery, then up to Deck 5, where we walked from the bow to the stern. I saw the main showroom, the gift shop, the arcade, Dining Room One, the galley, Dining Room Two, and the children's playroom. From the stern we went up to Deck 6 and worked our way to the bow, passing the kiddy pool, a number of bars (each with its own name), the disco, the casino, and the second level of the main lounge.

Then we moved on to Deck 7, where we stepped into the crew area for a look at the crew bar, which was empty because it wasn't open yet, and then reentered the passenger areas for a stroll through the pool area and the snack bars and the pizza bar at the stern of the ship. The next few decks consisted mostly of passenger cabins so Dipsu led me to Deck 10 to see the passenger gym, the spa, and the beauty salon. Then we stepped back into the crew area and went down a few decks to see the computer room. After a cursory glance at the machines crowded in the tiny space, he said I was done working for the day and asked if I had any questions.

"Yeah," I said. "Which way is my cabin? I have no idea how to get back there."

"Sure," he said patiently. "It's on Deck 0 at the front of the ship."

Blank stare.

"Okay, follow me," he said, and led me around a couple of corners to the crew elevator. "Take the elevator down to Deck 0, walk out of the elevator, turn the corner, and take a left turn to the cabin corridors."

At that point my head started spinning and I was off balance. The ship had just pushed away from the pier. Had I been on an open deck I probably wouldn't have felt the movement of the ship, but here in this confined space, with low ceilings and no windows, there was no mistaking it. The dizziness felt like a nicotine buzz. A new and fun way to catch a buzz. I described it with enthusiasm to Dipsu, but the movement was so commonplace for him that he simply smiled with indifference.

I returned to my cabin and thought about how cool it was to see everything that was available to the passengers. During the tour I had been totally lost. I didn't know if I was at the front of the ship or at the back. I didn't know if I was facing the front or the back. I couldn't distinguish the starboard or right side from the port or left side of the ship. We hopped back and forth between passenger and crew areas using doors that were hidden around corners. From the passenger side, the doors are marked "Crew Only," but they aren't marked on the crew side. So it's harder to find a portal to the other world when you're in a crew area.

There were so many decks, each with a name like Empress or Upper or Lido—labels that meant nothing to me. I couldn't associate the deck name with its numeric value. I couldn't tell where the decks were in relation to one another. Was the Upper Deck above the Empress Deck? What deck was below the Riviera Deck? What was the name of Deck 5? I had no idea. And more importantly, why didn't they just use deck numbers instead of goofy names like "Empress?"

There was so much space to learn. Passengers got lost all the time, and they only navigated *half* the ship. I had to find my way in the passenger areas and in the crew areas. Also, passengers had "You Are Here" diagrams at every elevator and even color handouts of the deck plan. I kept one of those in my pocket. It helped for the passenger areas, but it didn't tell me where the crew training center was or where the revenue accountant's office was. Color-coded, pocket-sized crew area deck plans just didn't exist.

Add to everything my horrible sense of direction. Without a map, I always get lost, and when I walk into an unfamiliar building, I lose my orientation and don't know which way is north. The same thing happens with elevators. When the doors open I cannot instinctively walk out and take a left toward the parking garage. I first have to reorient myself by looking around.

So, during the first week I was lost constantly. Dipsu carried a pager, and after beeping him he would call me back and I would ask, "Where is the dining room?" or "How do I get to the computer room from the spa?" He was always patient and never annoyed at helping me find my way. I also had to approach a window to see which way the water was passing before I knew which direction was the front of the ship.

All I could judge for certain was whether I was in a crew area or a passenger area. Passenger areas were splashed with color and loaded with lavish decorations and neon lights. Different lounges had different themes. Lots of giant windows flaunted the ocean, and turning a corner might leave you gaping up at a nine-story atrium that blew you away if for no other reason than because it was inside a boat.

The crew areas blew you away, too, but only because they were so bland. No polished tile floors. Only a few cabins had carpet. Otherwise the crew walked on white or tan linoleum or on painted steel that was red or maybe blue. Most walls were white. There were almost no decorations. No themes. Only a few windows in certain areas. No atrium. In the crew areas, crewmembers wore honest expressions instead of the manufactured service smiles they put on for the passengers.

In the passenger areas, cabin corridors not only provided access to the cabins, they also added to the splendor of the ship. The floor was carpeted to match the wall coverings. Quality light fixtures were used. Sometimes indirect lighting was used to give off a warm glow. If you stood at one end of the ship and faced the other, the parallel walls of the corridor appeared to converge to a single vanishing point, like the example of train tracks from science class.

But in the crew areas, cabin corridors served only as pathways to the cabins. No splendor. They were half the width of passenger corridors, and you had to turn sideways when you walked past someone. Overhead, fluorescent tubes gave off direct light that was uncomfortable because of the low ceilings. Years of foot traffic had loosened the glue and rippled the linoleum in some areas. Some spots were mushy and collapsed to the solid metal beneath, and I frequently stumbled when my shoe caught a raised linoleum ripple. The crewmembers weren't supposed to smoke in the cabins, so they did it in the corridors. The ventilation was good enough that the smoke didn't linger, but so many of the crew smoked that I constantly walked through fresh clouds of it. Ashtrays were bolted to the walls and added their ashy stench to the air. The only decorations were the pictures or dry erase boards that the girls taped to their cabin doors.

✳ ✳ ✳

Dipsu told me not to worry about wearing my uniform the first day onboard. Good thing, too, because I wasn't ready. He asked me to wear it the second day, but I still wasn't ready. I wasn't a ship's officer. And it wasn't a uniform. It was a Halloween costume, and I felt stupid in it. It was crisp with starch and almost perfectly monotone. It had a white shirt, white pants, white belt, white socks, and white shoes. I didn't have my epaulettes yet - those black shoulder pieces that have the gold stripes on them - so the only color to be found was the gold belt buckle and a little splash of red and blue on my nametag.

Besides the insignia and the number of stripes on the epaulettes, all officer uniforms looked the same. The white uniform was worn during the day. After 5:00 p.m., officers wore a formal navy blue suit that looked more normal and less like Halloween. Each department had its own insignia that was worn on the epaulettes of the white uniform, and on the jacket cuffs of the evening uniform.

Passengers had some dress requirements as well. Shorts were generally not allowed in the dining rooms during dinner, and every cruise had at least one formal night. Ladies were to wear formal dresses while the men were to wear a coat and tie, maybe even a tuxedo. The formal nights added fun for the passengers, but it was also another way to generate revenue. More pictures from formal night were purchased than any other.

Crewmembers were broken out into three ranks: officers, staff, and crew. Cruise ships these days carry about 1,000 crewmembers. Some carry more, some carry less, but 1,000 is a good round number to work with. Each rank had different privileges that I didn't understand until much later. All I knew was that I was an officer and that officers wore the white uniforms.

Turns out that only 10% or about 100 of the crew were officers. Examples included department heads like the housekeeping manager, the food and beverage manager, and the chief of security. Assistant managers to these positions were also officers. The three most senior officers onboard were the captain, the chief engineer, and the hotel director. Career paths that led to these senior positions were also officers and included the bridge officers, the engineering officers, and the pursers, respectively.

Only 15% or about 150 crewmembers were staff, the next rank below the officers. Examples included musicians, dancers, social hosts, casino staff, shoppies, which was crew lingo for the gift shop employees, and Steiners, which was crew lingo for the spa employees. (The company that ran the spas on Carnival's ships was called Steiner Leisure Limited.) Even the cruise director was considered staff, but the position carried with it more prestige and privilege than many of the officer positions.

The word "crew" was used interchangeably for two sets of employees: one, for any shipboard employee, and two, for an employee with the specific rank of crew. From here on, I'll use "crew" to mean any shipboard employee, and though I rarely said it on the ship, I'll use "crew-ranked" to mean employees with that specific rank.

So, 75% or the remaining 750 crewmembers were crew-ranked, which was the lowest rank. Examples included cabin stewards, restaurant servers, cocktail waitresses, bartenders, chefs, painters, fire patrolmen, and garbage handlers.

In all, over 200 unique job titles existed within roughly ten different departments. Each department had a career path that ended with the department head. The housekeeping manager, for example, was a department head who managed a couple of assistant housekeeping managers, who in turn managed the cabin stewards and other cleaning personnel.

The division of labor was more apparent on a cruise ship than just about anywhere else. On land, people usually work with others that have similar positions or working conditions. Construction folks work next to construction folks. Office personnel work next to other white-collar office personnel. But ships cram blue-collar, white-collar, and nearly everyone in between into a small space. Mechanics wearing coveralls soaked in engine grime live within walking distance of a doctor with ten years of post-high school education. The production singer, who works an average of two hours a day, would often walk past the guy who shreds garbage ten hours a day.

Staff and crew-ranked employees had uniforms unique to their department. They also had day uniforms that were more casual than the formal evening uniforms. None of their uniforms resembled the all-white officer uniforms. Staff employees had a higher rank and thus more privilege than the crew-ranked employees, but their uniforms didn't distinguish this the way the officer uniforms did. Even if you knew nothing of the ship's ranking system, the white uniform told you that officers were at the top. The rest of the uniforms didn't do this, and unless you already knew, you couldn't look at a cocktail waitress and a casino dealer and tell which one was ranked higher than the other.

It's interesting how attire affects one's confidence. I didn't realize it at the time, but that white uniform changed me. A few years after I quit ships, I actually wore it for Halloween, and though I wasn't conscious of it at the time, I felt more confident. My wife, Mirka, saw the change. It reminded her of the way I carried myself in that uniform on the ship. I had more bounce in my step and more confidence my actions. It had the opposite effect the first time I put it on.

On my first day in costume, Dipsu led me to the ice cream machine in the crew mess hall. It was during the early dinner hours and there were a lot of people in there. The contrast was striking. There were two white uniforms among a hundred multi-colored crew-ranked uniforms, and all eyes were on me, the new guy.

Even though there were about a thousand of us, crewmembers took notice of new crewmembers. This was especially true for cute girls and officers. Everywhere I went crewmembers looked at me and read my nametag to find out where I was from and what my position was.

I was walking down a corridor when a crew-ranked crewmember I didn't know motioned to me for a special handshake. He was leaning against a wall and held out a closed fist with the palm facing the floor at stomach level. I didn't know this handshake. The distance between us closed fast, and I only had a couple of seconds to guess a response. I couldn't leave him hanging because refusing a handshake was one of the most disrespectful things you could do. There was only one handshake in my repertoire that involved a fist. It was the over-and-under fist tap I had learned in the '80s.

I made a fist with my palm facing to the side and tapped the top of his hand. It was like putting a square block in a round hole. Few things make you feel more antiquated than botching a handshake. Maybe I was just out of touch with pop culture, then again maybe this handshake hadn't made it to Dallas yet. For the rest of the day I watched everyone interact until I finally saw the knuckles-to-knuckles fist bump handshake properly executed. I got to redeem myself a couple of days later when the same guy, leaning against the same wall, extended his fist again.

One day I walked into a crew elevator that was stuffed with Steiners, all of whom were female, and cute.

"What's your name?" one of them named Jess asked.

"Jay."

"What's your position?"

"I'm an I/S manager."

"Is this your first contract?"

"Yeah."

Then the elevator stopped at my deck. "All right, well, I'm sure we'll see each other around," I said as I walked out. I looked back and saw Jess poke her head out.

"I'm *sure* we will," she said with a raised eyebrow. The rest of the girls giggled and shushed each other, and I felt the flush in my cheeks. Comments like that can make your day.

Apart from those kinds of interactions, I just wanted to go unnoticed while I got comfortable with the environment, but my costume prevented that completely. It was the most conspicuous uniform onboard, which meant, among other things, that passengers cornered me and the other officers more than the staff or crew-ranked crewmembers. Because of this, shore-side management didn't give the new hires their epaulettes because it made them look experienced. But even without epaulettes, I was constantly confronted with questions that I could not answer.

"Where's the gym?"

"I don't know."

"How fast is the ship going right now?"

"I don't know."

"Can I take a tour of the bridge?"

"I don't know."

It was awful. I thought it was my duty to know everything, and it felt so uncomfortable to constantly respond with, "I don't know."

So sometimes I made stuff up.

"I see that the purser's desk is closed right now," one lady said at 2:00 a.m. "What time does it open?"

"It opens at 6:00 a.m.," I said without hesitation.

Dipsu later told me that the purser's desk was always open and only closed late at night whenever the one person on duty took a restroom break. After asking him all the other questions I had received, I could answer with confidence.

"Bridge tours are not allowed. The max speed of the ship is thirty miles per hour. We're currently going about twenty miles per hour." Sometimes I'd give the speed in knots just to make them ask, "What is that in miles per hour?" so I could pretend to approximate it in my head and come off looking really smart.

On my third day, I went to the bridge and met a captain for the first time. This was not something that most crewmembers did, but since there were computers on the bridge, it was part of my domain. The captain was about 75 years old with stringy white hair. He was six-foot-two and 300 pounds of hobbling heart disease and not at all what I expected. He didn't look anything like the captains from *Star Trek*. I would later meet captains that did fit Starfleet's TV profile, namely younger and better kept, but this guy was one broken hip away from a nursing home.

The captain shook my hand with disinterest and barely made eye contact before turning his body, his entire massive body, away from me. His mannerisms matched his supreme rank. He beamed authority like I had never seen, and everyone around acted respectful and almost afraid of him. My body language, on the other hand, displayed the over-eagerness that comes with inexperience.

Following that, I met a couple of bridge officers whose mannerisms also matched their lesser rank. They held eye contact longer and were a little more approachable, though not much more. One officer, however, was very friendly, and when I asked how the navigational equipment worked he spent the next twenty minutes showing and explaining every piece of equipment on the bridge. This private tour was exactly what I had been dreaming about in Miami.

Dipsu invited me to the crew bar that night. I was a bit nervous and didn't know what to expect, and it was probably why I hadn't gone there sooner. As in most crew areas, decorations were sparse and there were no windows. It was purely functional—a space for people to drink and socialize. There was one dart board crowded between two pillars, and a ping-pong table that was in use most of the night.

I noticed that unless they were there to buy a quick drink and leave, most of the staff and crew-ranked crewmembers did not wear their work uniforms in the crew bar. I wore regular clothes that night, but Dipsu had on his white uniform.

"It's a nice status symbol, so wear the uniform next time," Dipsu advised.

A door at the front of the crew bar led outside to the forward-most part of the ship, which, like all cruise ships, was designated "Crew Only." This drove the passengers crazy, I later learned, because they wandered all over trying to get there and were always disappointed to find it off limits. The reason for this was that the bridge was at the front of the ship and looked out over the bow, and at night any lights at the front of the ship were turned off so that the bridge officers could maximize visibility by getting their eyes adjusted to the dark. It was okay to let the crew walk around a dark deck because it was their home and they knew the area, but for safety reasons, passengers were not allowed.

When Dipsu led me out there I was greeted by a cool rush of night sea air that was unpolluted and downright invigorating. There were more stars in the sky than I ever saw in Dallas. The sound of waves splashing away from the bow was the kind of stuff that was recorded and sold as "Soothing Nature Sounds." I couldn't believe that there were only six people out there. Inside the crew bar, sixty people were breathing thick bar smoke under a low ceiling and harsh fluorescent lighting and I didn't understand why people chose the less pleasing environment. We drank a couple of beers and I met a few people before heading back to my cabin pretty early in the night.

✲ ✲ ✲

At the end of the first four-day cruise, the ship was back at home port and I began my first embarkation day which is when a new cruise begins. I/S managers were on and off the ship throughout the day because they supported computers both on the ship and in the embarkation terminal. Dipsu said that, because we went back and forth so much, gangway security wouldn't make me scan my ID every time. I looked on as he nodded to the security officer and walked off the ship. A few paces behind him, I nodded as well and kept walking.

"What are you doing!" the security guy yelled as he stopped me in a panic. "You must scan ID anytime you exit the ship."

Later, when I was the I/S manager of my own ship and the security guys knew who I was, it was just like Dipsu had said and the security staff almost never asked me to scan my ID during embarkation day.

There was one main artery in the crew area and we called it the I-95. Just like the interstate that runs from Miami all the way up the east coast into Maine, the I-95 on the ship ran all the way from bow to stern. It was the widest crew corridor and ran one deck beneath the lowest passenger deck on every ship. Every crewmember used it multiple times a day to get from their cabins to the mess halls or to their work station or to the crew bar or to just about anywhere on the ship.

Like all crew areas, the I-95 was built for utility, not appearances. The floor was either smooth metal or diamond-plated steel, and the painted areas were always scratched up from everything that rolled over it. Where it was bare, the metal oxidized into a dark gray, but the constant foot traffic kept it from looking rusty. You never realized how nicotine-stained the walls were until a fresh coat of white was rolled on. Crowded pipes and bundled wires ran the length of the ceiling, and smaller pieces of this mass would bend at ninety-degree angles and disappear through walls at random points along the way. Everything along the ceiling was brush-painted in the same thick white that coated the walls. Paint seeped into the wire bundles and fused them into a unified mass that looked like it was ready to molt.

The I-95 was a multipurpose highway with traffic at all hours, and it played a big role in embarkation day. The marshaling area, a section of the I-95 that was as wide as the ship and had double hull doors on either side, filled up with items to be offloaded the day before embarkation. When the marshaling area was full, extra pallets were lined up along the corridor and made the narrow walking space even more congested. The crew slid past one another as they navigated around broken pieces of the engine, giant blocks of compacted aluminum cans, and 55-gallon drums of used engine oil. Cabin stewards pushed trolleys back and forth along the corridor and into the marshaling area as they loaded passenger luggage into giant metal cages that would be offloaded the next day.

Embarkation day itself was an impressive operation. The last passenger from the previous cruise was off the ship around 9:30 a.m., and just three hours later at 12:30, the entire ship had been cleaned and was ready for the first new passenger to board. Zero downtime maximizes profits, so this is how all cruise ships work.

While the sheets on every bed were changed and each of the 1,000+ cabins was vacuumed, countless pallets passed through the hull doors of the marshaling area as multiple forklifts raced around with precision and went *beep-beep* for hours. Once off the ship, the luggage-filled cages were emptied, refilled with luggage from the new passengers, and brought back onboard. Pallets of refuse and spent items were offloaded. Pallets of new merchandise for the gift shop were loaded and set the shoppies in motion with trolleys that rolled up and down the I-95 to restock the gift shop.

Fresh food was loaded. And I mean lots of food. Lots and lots of food. For a seven-day cruise, the *Carnival Conquest*, for example, brought on no less than:

23,000 pounds of beef
12,000 pounds of fish
3,000 pounds of lobster
18,000 pounds of fruit
23,000 pounds of vegetables
108,000 individual eggs
200 bottles of champagne
11,000 beers

And I'm being conservative. It seemed like an obscene amount of food, but when you did the math, it was perfectly reasonable. On average, each person, all 4,000 passengers and crew, was served about a pound of meat, a pound of vegetables, and half a beer each day. After everything was loaded, the forklifts were parked in the marshalling area and remained on the ship until they were needed again.

✳ ✳ ✳

During my second cruise, I sat in my cabin one night and considered the schedule. Dipsu had me working 9:00 to 6:00 every day. We had done a four-day cruise and then a three-day cruise. That was our cycle, and it would repeat, beginning with the next four-day cruise. We did two cruises a week, with one cruise ending on the same day that the next cruise began.

It added up to something, but I couldn't tell what.

Then it hit me. One cruise ended on the *same day* that a new cruise began. I had a seven-day work week. I would not have a day off for eight months. It was a detail my hiring manager had failed to mention. Not that I remembered anyway. I used this revelation to start conversations in the crew bar that night and held firm that an eight-week vacation was completely unnecessary.

The next night in the crew bar I met the woman from Trinidad and Tobago. Two days later, she called me at 8:00 p.m.

"So are you ready to do what we talked about the other night?" she said, propositioning me for sex.

Now I had two problems with this. One was that clandestine sex was very hard to pull off on the ship. I had only been there a week and already I could tell that much. I had my own cabin, but there was always someone in the corridor. The chances of her walking in and out of my cabin without being seen were very low, especially at 8:00 p.m., which was a time of high traffic in the corridor. I didn't know the ship culture yet and thought that it would hurt my chances with the other girls—the other more attractive girls—if they found out I had been with this woman who was apparently disliked by many. My second problem was that she had openly admitted to having slept with lots of guys, which meant a greater risk of STDs.

I was ready for this and wanted to give it a try, I really did, but I turned her down, saying, "Yeah, you know, I'm sorry, but I don't think so." It was a strategic decision.

"Can I ask why?" she asked, confused.

"Well, I just arrived on the ship and I'm not quite ready yet."

"Do you want to wait a couple days before we get together?"

"Actually, no, I don't think we would be a good match." She'd forced me to say it.

"Okay, well, I'll talk to you later, then." The pain of rejection was in her voice.

Because I had essentially said yes when we talked about it in the crew bar, I felt bad about it. It was one of the few times I ever felt bad about saying no.

✻ ✻ ✻

There was a tall girl from Croatia who lived in the cabin right across from me. The prospect of being with her was part of the reason I turned down the girl from Trinidad. The Croatian used to sit on the floor in the corridor to smoke, and I would sit next to her and we'd chat. This girl was unbelievable. A perfect 10. She had dark hair, and she was tall and skinny, with light blue eyes, pouty lips, and a gorgeous face. She could easily have been a model. One night she told me that she had a boyfriend who worked in the casino and that he would be arriving on the ship in a couple of weeks.

So much for going out with her. Since she was taken, I sat with some Steiners in the crew bar the next night. The Croatian sat with her group of friends, and we kept watching each other across the room. Out of the corner of my eye, I saw her walking toward my table, but when I looked up at her, she flipped her head away. I didn't understand. She had a boyfriend, and yet acted as if she missed my attention.

Whatever the reason, I let it go and mostly hung out with the Steiners on the *Fantasy*. There were no rules when it came to dating or socializing with people of different ranks, and if

I was not eating with Dipsu I sat down at their table in the staff mess. One of the Steiners was a cute girl from Slovakia. Her smile could put you at ease and was not diminished by her uneven teeth.

Now, I have an obsession when it comes to oral hygiene. I floss after every meal and keep packages of floss throughout the house so it's always close at hand. There's a package of floss by the couch, in the kitchen, and of course the mandatory car floss in the glove box. I prefer to brush after every meal. I have a habit of wiping my mouth frequently when I eat, and if I am eating something messy like a juicy hamburger or salad with big pieces of lettuce, then I may dab my mouth after every bite.

But this Slovak girl didn't do that. When she ate, she always had a shiny blotch of wetness or some sort of crumb somewhere around her mouth. One night it was just the two of us at a table, with me sitting across from her, and I looked up to see a giant glob of ranch in the corner of her mouth. I tried to ignore it, but after three seconds, I just couldn't take it anymore.

"You have something here," I said, pointing to the corner of my mouth.

She looked right in my eyes without blinking and continued to chew with her mouth mostly open. "Yeah, I know it's there," she said with a slight grin as she continued to stare.

Don't ask me why, but I found that incredibly attractive. With her seductive confidence she's the only person I've met who could make sloppy eating look sexy.

Confidence was attractive to me, and power was attractive to the Bulgarian waitress who worked in the staff mess. She was gorgeous, with one of the prettiest faces you've ever seen. She was barely twenty and full of smiles and innocence. I sat in the crew bar one night watching her accept—even become enamored with—the advances of an old, overweight, unattractive food and beverage (F&B) manager.

I couldn't believe it. He was old enough to be her father. But he was a senior officer and the head boss of her department. He had status. Power. And within thirty minutes he had her. They left the bar together to do what I'm sure was just about anything he wanted.

✳ ✳ ✳

Before ships I was accustomed to hearing only a handful of accents. Growing up in Texas, I was familiar with the Mexican accent, and while studying computer science in college, I got used to Indian and Asian accents. Every other accent, especially the ones from Europe, was foreign to me.

One of the first times I heard a European accent was before I worked for Carnival and when I called the British airline easyJet to book a flight. English was not the operator's first language, and listening to her was like having phone sex. The flight I booked was part of a two-week trip in Europe. One day while I was London I rode the Tube, and as the train was arriving at one of the stops, the girl in the window seat got up, looked me in the eye, and with that delicious British accent, said, "I'm getting off at this stop." I smiled and thought, *me too*.

On the ship, I got to listen to delightful accents every day. And like walking into a house with fresh baked banana nut muffins, I indulged in the accents as sensory experience. Only a handful of the crew, maybe ten to twenty people, were American.

Another handful were Canadian—although to my ears they didn't have an accent, they just said "aboot" instead of "about." The remaining 97% fell into one of two categories: native English speakers and non-native English speakers. If English was their first language then they spoke with a regional accent. This was the case with people from places like England, Wales, Scotland, Ireland, Australia, and South Africa.

Then there were those whose first language was not English. These people displayed varying levels of proficiency in sentence structure and vocabulary. Each accent was slightly different and was based on what country they came from and how long they had been speaking English. This was the case with people from places like the Czech Republic, Italy, Romania, Slovakia, Bulgaria, Macedonia, Slovenia, Hungary, and Poland.

Unless you're in a culturally diverse place like New York City, you rarely meet a first-generation specimen from Europe or South Africa. But everywhere I went onboard, in every department and every day, I met people from all over the world. With no exposure, it's hard for an untrained ear to understand all those accents. The first time I sat down to eat with the Steiners, I had to ask Jess, the elevator girl from South Africa, to repeat herself two or three times on nearly everything she said. I just couldn't make out her words. At the same table were a couple of girls from England and one from Romania. It was an exhausting meal because it took constant effort to understand what was being said.

But I loved being surrounded by all the foreigners. They were so different. I didn't notice it much during my two-week vacation in Europe. I was busy with museums and bus tours and didn't have many long conversations with the locals and so I didn't notice any differences beyond the accent.

On the ship, after I saw them every day and as the novelty of the accents wore off, I noticed other differences. The facial structures like the nose and the cheekbones and the eye spacing all came together for a different look. Mannerisms and speech patterns differed at a cultural level. Clothing and hairstyles were different, and some of the skin tones were striking. They moved their lips and tongue differently when they talked. This was especially true for the non-native English-speakers. So not only could you hear the accent, but you could see it. And to top it off, these differences often came packaged in a beautiful female body.

That beautiful Bulgarian staff waitress brought my food one day in the staff mess.

"Thank you," I said.

"My pleasure," was her response.

The phrase struck me as the most polite and professional response possible, and her adorable Bulgarian accent elevated it even higher. I believed her. I mean, I really believed that she enjoyed bringing my lunch, but that evening a male waiter said the same thing after he brought my dinner. Suddenly the phrase wasn't so special.

Carnival had determined that "You're welcome" wasn't good enough and so the phrase "My pleasure" was mandated across the fleet. It was something the department heads were required to enforce. After hearing it constantly and learning that it was a mandate, it lost its allure, even when the Bulgarian said it, and it became a running joke as we all said it to one another in the crew bar.

I was on the ship for about two weeks and sitting with the Steiners for lunch when Jess asked me how old I was.

"Today is my birthday," I said. "I'm twenty-eight."

"*Really?*" Jess said. "It's your *BURRTH*-day? I didn't know it was *BURRTH*-day. We'll have to do something special since it's your *BURRTH*-day."

That night in the crew bar, the girls presented me with a birthday cake that had my name on it. All night long I just couldn't stop smiling.

I was about 5' 9" and 140 pounds, and in the same way that tall girls often preferred tall guys, I generally preferred girls who had a small frame. Jess was very pretty and little shorter than me, but she probably weighed more than I did.

What she did have—and what I was really attracted to—was that intangible asset of influence over others. She carried even more confidence than the sloppy-eating Slovak girl, and the other Steiners looked up to her and to some extent even followed her. If there was a leader among them, it was Jess. When she spoke, the others stopped and listened, even if they were interrupted. She was always assertive and her attitude gave her power. That power made me crave her.

I was fascinated by my attraction to her power, and I better understood, if only slightly, how the Bulgarian waitress could be attracted to that old F&B manager. I may be in the minority here because I think a lot of guys are turned off by powerful women.

Jess didn't have the status that came with being an officer or a manager, but I'd say she was more powerful than many female officers or managers. Her power was in her demeanor. She portrayed total confidence in everything she did and said. There were other Steiners who were better looking, but none I desired more. So, one night I found myself lying in her bed.

I had gone to her cabin to hang out. Her roommate put a CD in the boom box, and started dancing and singing as we all laughed and joked. Then the music was turned down and her roommate climbed to the top bunk to sleep. Jess and I lay down on the bottom bunk together. We hugged—there was no other choice on those little beds. We kissed a little and said goodnight, and I left to sleep in my cabin. The next morning, every other Steiner gave me playful smiles and said things like, "I hear you had fun last night."

This was a lesson on how fast news spread. A ship was the ultimate small town, and there were few secrets. More than ever, I was glad I had said no to the lady from Trinidad.

✡ ✡ ✡

Psychologists have described an infant's life as quintessential novelty. After nine months of solitary confinement, a newborn enters a world in which everything they see, hear, smell, taste, or touch is a first-time experience. The ability to even perceive these senses, at least the way they exist outside the womb, is new. When babies go to Wal-Mart, it's like walking into a football stadium for the first time where the enormity of it all can make you dizzy. Going outside is like traveling to a different planet. This is how I felt during my first weeks onboard.

Everything was new and nothing was familiar. It was things like the low ceiling, the accents, the way people looked, the contrast between passenger areas and crew areas, and the constant smell of sea air. There were so many new sensory experiences. First time passengers feel the same way when they embark, but to a lesser degree, I think. Passengers only see half the ship. Also, passengers mostly interact with other passengers who are like them and speak the same language and are sharing in the same new experience. I didn't have much in common with anyone. Only a handful of crewmembers were like me and had just started their first contract, but I had no contact with them. Even if I had, they were from a foreign country, and they were not I/S managers. I was on my own, and it was a bit overwhelming.

It took three weeks, which was six cruises, to get comfortable with the ship. By then, I wasn't getting lost, and was used to the three- and four-day embarkation cycle. I had plenty of friends. I was drinking more than I had on land, but only slightly. Since I had to work at 9:00 every morning, the few nights that I did drink a lot left me so miserable that I wasn't quick to repeat it. Jess was about to become my girlfriend. The day after we kissed, just when the ship started to feel like home, I received an email informing me that in two days I would fly to Miami for my next ship assignment.

CHAPTER 4

THE CONSEQUENCES OF LOSING YOUR VIRGINITY AT SEA

For some reason, I didn't hang out with Jess the next night. And because I had to be up early for immigration, a ritual all crewmembers went through when they signed off a ship, I didn't stay out late on my last night. Nothing else happened with Jess and I never saw her again.

I left the ship having earned $2,300. Most deck and engine officers were paid with direct deposit, but everyone else, including me, was paid in cash. Western Union had a $500 limit on money orders, and I paid $12.50 to buy five of them. Then I paid another couple of dollars to mail them home via certified mail. Being totally helpful and supportive, mom offered to deposit them in my bank account.

The inconvenience of getting money orders was notable. Time in port was precious, and I didn't want to waste it blowing fifteen bucks just to deposit a few weeks worth of wages. I decided to never do that again. Instead, I just used my desk drawer. At one point I had $5,000 in cash in my drawer, and my roommate had $3,000 in his. There were no locks on these drawers, and neither of us thought twice about it. Since I never knew when my homeport would change, I never got a bank account in port.

On land, I was making $55,000 a year as an IT Manager, but on the ship, I made only $30,000 doing essentially the same type of work. On land, I had to pay for rent, food, and utilities. On the ship, I only had to buy beer and toiletries. Cabins were free, food was free, electricity was free, water was free, and I didn't have a vehicle. With essentially no living expenses, I had roughly the same disposable income on the ship as I had had with my higher-paying land job.

That wasn't true for all crewmembers. Many of the tipping positions, including the crew-ranked positions, earned more than I did. Some earned twice as much. If they were from a third-world nation, the money they earned from a contract converted to a small fortune in their home country. Most would never be able to earn that much at home, where salaries could equate to pennies a day and where the unemployment rate could be as high as 30%. It worked out great for the crew from those countries.

Many of them took home enough money to support entire extended families. If just for themselves, they could work on ships for 5-10 years and retire in their home country as wealthy citizens. This was usually not the case for an American or a Brit or anyone from a relatively wealthy nation, and that was why there weren't many wealthy nationalities slaving as cabin stewards or waiters. Also, crewmembers from poorer countries were more motivated to work at sea, and they typically provided better service than, say, an American who could earn similar money on land without having to work as hard. Even so, the lure of living on a ship was enticing enough that people from over sixty countries made up Carnival's crew.

It worked out great for the cruise line, too. It was the ultimate in cheap labor. When I was a waiter in Texas, the restaurant paid $2.13 an hour. Cruise lines paid their waiters $0.15 an hour. That's not a typo and I'll say it again. Cruise lines paid their waiters *15 cents an hour*. About 95% of a waiter's total income was from tips. Although with tips a good waiter could make over $4,000 a month, the cruise line only paid about $50 a month to that waiter who worked eleven hours a day, seven days a week. To get away with this, cruise lines registered their ships in countries like Liberia or Panama so they wouldn't have to pay federal taxes or deal with the labor restrictions they would face if they registered their ships in the United States.

It worked out great for the passengers because it kept the cruises so affordable. The cruise industry might barely exist if it weren't for the cheap labor. Critics argue that the cruise lines exploit workers from the third-world nations. Maybe. But I think it's a global problem spanning all industries.

Many factories operate in third-world countries to take advantage of the cheap labor. Tech support and telemarketing calls are often with someone in India. It's basic outsourcing, and it's no different than what the cruise lines do. In some ways, it's better. Working up to fourteen hours every day on a cruise ship is pretty rough, but it's still better than working in a third-world factory, where child labor and mangled body parts are not uncommon.

The crew had free medical coverage during a contract, but passengers paid on a per incident basis. The ship's physician was a general practitioner and could administer antibiotics and other basic medication from an onboard pharmacy. The infirmary had an X-ray machine and a few hospital beds. Minor surgery was even possible, although it was avoided whenever possible. The most common onboard operation was an appendectomy, but even that was rare and used only as a last resort. Instead, the infirmary tried to stabilize patients until the next port, where they could be transported to a hospital. In extreme cases, the Coast Guard could land a helicopter on deck to pick up a patient and fly them to a hospital.

☆ ☆ ☆

After leaving the *Fantasy* and while still in Miami, I learned that my new ship would be the *Carnival Triumph*. The first thing I did was to go to Carnival's website to check the ship's itinerary. The *Triumph* was sailing out of New York City and up the east coast into Canada. Perfect. I'd only been to New York once, and I'd never been to Canada.

The first day any crewmember signed onto a ship, he was required to attend a safety class. Not all ships were configured the same, which is why the Italian safety officer led the new sign-ons around the ship to learn the location of things like muster stations and lifeboats. The day I joined the *Triumph,* there were fifteen other new sign-ons. As the safety officer led us to an elevator, the door opened to reveal a beer-gut-toting guy, about six foot two, dressed in baggy black pants, a black T-shirt, and black Converse cross-trainers. He wore a necklace made from black electric wire that had alligator clips on each end and a broken piece of computer RAM that hung down about chest high. He had shoulder length hair that was scraggly and bleached, but his dark brown roots had grown out so his hair was really two tones. He was going bald, so his scalp was visible through the long strands. His gait was characteristic of many guys who have long hair in that he swayed and bounced to the natural rhythm of the way his hair bounced. He walked toward our group with easygoing, down-to-earth confidence.

"Hey, dudes," he said as he addressed us and kept walking.

I was the only one who laughed. I met him later that evening and found out he was a DJ from Canada who used the call sign "Johnny Vancouver." I told him where I was from.

"Dude! You're from a place that has two asses in its name," Johnny said.

"What?"

"Yeah. Dall-ASS Tex-ASS."

From the elevator, the safety officer continued to lead us around the ship before taking us to the crew bar, which was otherwise empty and closed, for a two-hour training class that consisted mostly of a succession of videos. They covered some survival skills at sea, including demonstrations of how to deploy the life rafts and what equipment was included in them. There were tips on handling a crowd during an emergency, and throughout the videos the Italian safety officer interjected snippets of wisdom with his heavy accent.

Most of the crew got off the ship whenever they could, but for safety reasons, there had to be enough crew onboard at all times in case of a shipboard emergency. Carnival's policy was that a third of the crew had to stay onboard. Some people were scheduled to work anyway, but to maintain a third of the crew onboard, some had to stay even if they weren't working. This was called port manning.

Boat drill was initiated at the beginning of every cruise with seven short blasts over the ship's speakers and horn, followed by one long blast. These blasts were to be used in the event of an actual ship-wide emergency, but I never thought this was the best way to alert people.

What if you lost count and thought only six short blasts had happened? What if you were sailing through fog, when the ship constantly blasts the horn anyway, and simply ignored the seven blasts like you ignore someone who cries wolf? A better solution, I thought, would be for the captain to just get on the PA system and say, "Red alert. All hands to your muster stations!" and then blast that *Star Trek* red alert siren seven times. No one would mistake that.

My new ship was much larger with 45% more interior space. That was a staggering number considering how big the *Fantasy*-class ships already were. The layout was completely different, and every passenger lounge and dining room had a different name. Some of the deck names were the same, but their numeric value was different. What used to be Empress Deck 4 on the *Fantasy* was now Empress Deck 7 on the *Triumph*, and I was lost all over again for the next two weeks.

I had a roommate this time and it was JB, the guy that I had beers with in Miami. He was pure American, complete with Old Navy style button-up plaid shirts that clashed with the solid-colored shirts of the European-dressed majority that we hung out with. I hadn't packed any plaid shirts, hoping to fit in better. But JB had a confidence that made his plaid shirts just another reason people liked him. He was probably the most sociable crewmember onboard. It was his first contract, too, and although he had been onboard for only two weeks, he had a girlfriend and knew almost everyone.

My new cabin had a good three feet of space between the bed and the dressers. It was huge compared to most crew cabins and much bigger than the one on the *Fantasy*.

Crewmembers, of course, couldn't upgrade their cabins the way passengers could. Crew cabins were assigned based on rank, and higher-ranking positions generally had bigger cabins. The captain, chief engineer, and hotel director had the largest cabins onboard which measured about 600 square feet and were the size of a small apartment, with a separate bedroom and a living area that was large enough for a couch, love seat, and desk. They were never assigned a roommate.

Cabin size dwindled quickly down the ranks, and most crew cabins were 1/2 to 1/3 the size of passenger cabins. Even so, a lot of stuff was crammed into that space, including the bunk beds, a desk, two small closets, two dresser drawers underneath the bottom bunk, and a small television. The smallest crew cabins had so little floor space that roommates couldn't pass each other at the same time. One person had to climb into bed so the other person could get by.

My new bathroom was smaller than I ever thought possible. I could sit on the pot, wash my hands in the sink, and have my feet in the shower all at the same time. When on the toilet, I couldn't lean forward to rest my arms on my thighs because the sink was in the way. I had to angle myself away from the sink and sit off-center to lean forward and get comfy. Later, when I was transferred to another ship called the *Holiday*, the wall in front of the toilet was only three inches away from my knees.

The showers on both ships were so tiny that the wet shower curtain clung to my body the whole time and my elbows hit the wall when I washed my hair. But at least JB and I had our own bathroom. Crew-ranked employees on the *Triumph* had a suitemate configuration with four people sharing the same type of small bathroom set between two cabins, and crew-ranked employees on the *Holiday* had community showers.

Most crew cabins, including my cabin on the *Triumph*, did not have an ocean view and if they did, it was likely through a porthole the size of a dinner plate. The window in a passenger cabin and in the handful of high-ranking crew cabins was twenty times bigger. Passenger cabins with balconies had even more glass.

An ocean-view cabin was a seven-day cherry-on-top for passengers, but for the crew, many of whom were assigned to the same ship for their whole contract, it was an eight-month saving grace. Imagine living in a house that had no windows and no natural light of any kind. This was what most of the crew cabins were like, so even a small porthole, for the few who had one, was a big deal.

Some of the crew didn't see much daylight at all, namely those in the engine room or in the laundry department. And there was one guy, the refrigeration engineer, who essentially worked in a cave. He beeped me for computer help one day.

"Okay, I'll be right up," I said. "Where is your office?"

"It's next to the galley near the forward dining room," he said.

I hiked over there, but after roaming throughout both sides of the galley and dining rooms I couldn't find his office so I called him back.

"Meet me at the galley entrance," he said, "and I'll lead you in from there."

From there he led me to an unmarked silver door that was tucked around a corner and blended well with the stainless steel walls of the galley. When he opened the door we were greeted with a whoosh of air that ushered us into complete darkness. He had a holster for his flashlight that reminded me of the utility knife I always wore on my belt.

He clicked it on and guided me through a maze of air ducts that I had to crouch under and turn sideways to fit through. My uniform flapped as we walked past a dusty, two-foot-square wire net that covered a high-powered air intake fan. This was where all that whooshing air was going. Finally, we turned a corner and I saw his desk under the light of a single lamp. It was the only light source in the enclosure and I just couldn't believe that this was his office and that he was still sane.

Compared to the crew cabins, passenger cabins looked nice. The color scheme was consistent among the carpet, the walls, the bedspread, the furniture, and the piece of art over the bed. Most crew cabins didn't have drapes or colored walls and felt more like a hospital room. I had a linoleum floor that was cleaned once a day, but I still had to brush dirt off my feet before getting into bed. This was an especially annoying task while done in that semi-conscious haze after using the bathroom in the middle of the night. Passenger cabins had 25-inch TVs that dwarfed the 13-inch TVs in crew cabins. The crew's bedding consisted of sheets and a thin blanket that was tucked under the mattress. The blanket was a shade of navy blue that didn't match anything and was made of a coarse fabric. A few of the crew brought their own blankets from home or picked one up from Wal-Mart.

Officers and staff had a cabin steward who cleaned the floor, cleaned the bathroom, and made the bed every day. We had a mandatory tip of twenty dollars a week for the service. I always requested that my sheets not be tucked under the mattress because I hated having to undo them each night.

As an officer, I had full pick-up and delivery service for my uniforms. I left my dirty ones on the bed and my cabin steward would bring them back a couple days later, cleaned and pressed. Staff members had to take their uniforms to the crew laundry center, but the cabin steward delivered them after they were cleaned. Crew-ranked employees had to wash and iron everything themselves.

Most crewmembers had to do their regular laundry, like socks, underwear, jeans, and anything that wasn't a work uniform. We could pay to have them laundered on a per-item basis and I did that on occasion, but most of the time I used one of the self-service Laundromats.

There was one crew Laundromat. It was free, but it had only four washers and five dryers for a thousand crewmembers. Those machines ran twenty-four hours a day. 4:00 a.m. was one of the best times to find an empty machine, but even then I'd often have to wait or come back. I learned to do one load at a time because finding two available machines was nearly impossible. I also learned to use the passenger Laundromats. They weren't free, but they usually had available machines.

✳ ✳ ✳

To fully appreciate the impact that the ship environment had on me, I feel the need to explain my background as it relates to sex. The first time I witnessed desire was at a gas station. I was probably nine or ten years old and waiting in the car while my mom went inside to pay. On the way back to the car she passed a scruffy-looking guy who turned around to check her out. He looked right at her butt, squinted his eyes, scowled with approval, and shook his head as he whistled to himself. Then he looked through the windshield and realized I had just witnessed what he'd done. He snapped his head forward and kept walking.

"Why did he do that?" I asked my mom after telling her what happened. "What's so special about someone's butt?"

"I don't know why men do that," she answered.

I was old enough to be attracted to pretty faces, but too young to understand the appeal of other body parts. Being attracted to someone's butt made about as much sense as being attracted to two side-by-side bowling balls. They were just round.

Instead, I was more interested in playing with my Hot Wheels. I had one toy car that let you air up the tires with a toy air pump. The air pump had a small rubber air hose, and one day I lined up the holes to see what would happen. I pulled up on the handle and held it in anticipation, as if it was a dynamite detonator, and with a quick motion, I pushed the handle down to blow air into my urethra and... *Holy crap*! I had the instant sensation of needing to pee worse than I ever have in my life. I almost didn't make it to the bathroom in time. Urine came out first. Then a solid stream of air. Then a mixture of urine and air that gurgled out with the sound of a garden hose that had just been turned on.

At fifteen I was ready to lose the stigma of being a virgin so I went on the hunt, armed with an irresistible prop.

I'd received a plasma ball for Christmas that year. When plugged in and turned on, the glass sphere had beams of lightning inside that reacted when you touched it.

"What do you think?" I asked as I showed it to one of my sixteen-year-old buddies who was no longer a virgin and therefore an expert on the subject. "This would be a great way to *set the mood*, don't you think?"

That year my parents wanted to take a vacation and asked for my opinion one day.

"Which would you prefer," mom asked, "Disney World or a cruise?"

"A cruise," I said.

"How come?"

"Because that way the girls can't get away from you."

We went to Disney World.

No sex. But then I didn't bring the plasma ball.

Then one day it just happened. I was sixteen, and it was with a girl I had been dating for a couple of weeks. I told a buddy of mine, and it felt good when he bragged about it to the other guys at the lunch table. She broke up with me shortly afterward. Then I had a one-night stand later that year. The plasma ball played no role in either one. And if there is one thing that I've learned about women since then, it is that owning a plasma ball does not make them want to have sex with you.

At the end of the year, my high school held a blood drive and I wanted to do my part in helping the cause. I also wanted to know if I had contracted AIDS. The more I thought about it, the more worried I became and when the test results finally arrived by mail, I took a deep breath before opening the envelope. I was clean. No AIDS. Just type B positive blood.

The fact that AIDS and herpes have no cure terrified me so much that I quit looking for sex. After a year of intentional abstinence, I found another reason to abstain: I wanted to actually like the girl. I wanted my next encounter to be meaningful. No more one-night stands. I would wait until I had a girlfriend. I would wait until she agreed to get tested.

Time passed as I continued to abstain. And in the same way that a blind person hears things that others don't, abstinence made me notice things that others didn't.

Like the variation in the way girls kissed. Hardware was a factor. Thin lips felt different than full lips. Ethnicity mattered. Asian lips felt different than Caucasian lips. The way a girl country danced correlated to the way she kissed. If her arms were stiff and rigid, then her kissing would be rigid and forceful. If her arms were loose and flowing and her feet moved with a smooth, natural grace, then her kissing would be slow and sensual.

My abstinence made me think about things like sleeping with the midget that worked at Burger King. Or offering a homeless lady in New Orleans a steak dinner and a spot next to me in a soft warm bed. She was, after all, in my opinion, genetically attractive. Give her a haircut, some designer clothes, and some makeup and she would have been beautiful, had it not been for all those missing teeth. I used to play dominoes with the older crowd at a VFW hall, and one night an elderly woman hit on me. She had been eyeing me for a while before approaching.

"Your dark hair and light eyes look marvelous," she said in a hushed tone. "You really do look nice, and if I were a few years younger, mmmm, we would have us some fun."

I blushed. At the time I owned a red Ford Mustang Cobra that rumbled with 305 horsepower. I wanted to sit grandma down on the black leather seats and drive fast with the windows down while blasting Metallica to make her feel young again. Nothing happened, but I had thought about saying, "Let's have us some fun anyway." I was twenty-five. She was in her late sixties. She might have been seventy. *Seventy.* It was clear that this prolonged abstinence was having an effect.

The years passed without me having a long-term girlfriend. I wanted one. I wanted one all along. But every time I dated somebody, it always ended after a few weeks and I never made it past the two-month mark.

Looking back, I think my problem was that I didn't have a casual attitude. I was always looking for the right person, and

I was always looking for the long-term relationship. I was sure that the first person I loved would be the person I married. When I found someone I thought could be the one, I tried so hard to make it perfect and to get to the I-love-you stage that there was no way it was going to happen. Sometimes the only way to achieve something is to not care about it, and courting women is the quintessential example of this idea. If you care too much and try too hard, you'll never get the girl.

After foreplay one night, one girl I had just started seeing was ready.

"Nah," I told her, "we won't do that tonight."

"Can I ask why?" she asked after a moment of silence.

"Because I'd have to love you first," I said.

"That's a good answer. That's a damn good answer," she said and then stopped returning my calls a few days later.

What often happened whenever I said no, was that the girl liked me more, whereas I liked her less. She wanted to date because she had found a guy who was interested in more than just one thing. But I liked her less because I didn't want a girl who was ready to sleep with someone so soon.

I was content with this attitude toward sex. I liked that I was in control of myself, and for some reason it felt good to know that I declined when most others accepted.

✲ ✲ ✲

JB wasn't in the room when I first came in, but he had clearly claimed the bottom bunk by throwing his shirts on it and closing the bunk's privacy curtain. I'm no expert on bunk-bed protocol, but this struck me as presumptuous and I thought that a good game of paper-rock-scissors would have been better. I never brought it up and actually enjoyed the top bunk better since it had more light to read by. I also got to step on his bunk every time I climbed into bed, and it bothered him less than it would have bothered me.

Our cabin was at the front of the ship on Deck 1, directly above the thrusters. Every cruise ship had two sets of thrusters, one at the bow and one at the stern. They were fixed propellers that could push water sideways, and they enabled the ship to rotate and move side to side. They were used during docking maneuvers and when the ship pushed away from the pier. They also helped navigate through rivers and to keep the ship in one place when tendering in port.

To power the thrusters, and everything else onboard, the *Triumph* had six diesel electric engines that were each three decks tall and as long as a bus. The engines did nothing but generate electricity. There was no mechanical link from the engines to the propellers. Instead, the propellers were powered by massive electric motors, and 80% of the electricity consumed onboard was for propulsion. When the ship was docked, only two idling engines kept the lights on, but at sea, five engines ran at full speed with the sixth used as a rotating spare.

On the morning of my first port on the *Triumph*, I was violently awakened by the sound of a jackhammer that rattled everything in my cabin, including the metal ceiling panels that were two feet in front of my face. With no window, the cabin was dark except for a sliver of corridor light that ran underneath the door. Had I not experienced a much milder version of thruster vibration on the *Fantasy*, I likely would have headed straight for the lifeboats thinking that the ship was coming apart.

The thrusters were roaring monsters that infected everything around them with rage, and the closer you were, the worse it was. Most passenger cabins were peaceful enough because they weren't too close, but most of the crew cabins were located in all the worst areas of the ship. One deck higher, or even being a few steps farther away from the thrusters, made a huge difference. We lived on Deck 1, but there were crew-ranked cabins one and two decks below us and down there the noise and vibration from the thrusters were so bad that you literally had to yell to communicate. The ship usually arrived in the wee hours of the morning, and it just wasn't possible to sleep through intermittent earthquakes during the twenty-minute docking maneuver.

I walked into the crew bar at the end of my first week on the *Triumph*, and after taking everyone's order and buying a round of drinks, I sat down with JB and a couple of pursers.

The chief purser was there. She was an Indian girl who had been eyeing me all week.

"So you're the new I/S manager, eh?"

"That's me."

"And this is your first contract?"

"Yeah, but this is my second ship. I was on the *Fantasy* for three weeks."

"How do you like it so far?"

"I'm having a great time, but I've had a lot of hangovers in the last month."

"Well, you're only twenty-eight, so you can handle it."

"How did you know how old I was?"

"I'm the chief purser. I have access to a database that has every crewmember in it."

"I'm the I/S manager. And you must be talking about the A-Pass system. The server that runs that database is in my office." I had access to that database as well. In fact, I had administrative rights, which the chief purser did not have. "Why were you looking at my file?"

She looked away. "Well, it's part of my job to go through the files of all new sign-ons."

Wrong.

I knew she was lying because I combed through the A-Pass system to look at the file of every cute girl on the ship. It also came in handy to remember the names of the dozens of people I met those first couple of weeks. There wasn't much detail in the file. It was just a picture, a name, their home country, their age, and their start date with Carnival. But that was everything you needed when you were hunting. I pressed the issue.

"Were you checking me out?"

She said no.

I let it drop and sat quiet for a bit. Then, I said, "You're thirty-four, right?"

She nodded. Then her posture straightened and she perked up. "And how did you know that?"

"Because I was checking you out."

We laughed and then she finally admitted, "Yeah, I was checking you out, too."

We talked about how great it was to have access to that database, and then the conversation turned to sex.

"You know, of course, that as a new hire, you are more desirable."

"Really?"

"Yep."

"Why is that?"

"Because you are fresh meat."

"Uh, okay. But why does that make me more desirable than guys who've worked on ships longer?"

"It just does." She acted a little shy, a little embarrassed even.

"Is it because new hires are easier to get into bed?"

"No."

"Is it because new hires don't know the other crewmembers you may have slept with?"

"No."

I sat and tried to think of another possible reason when she finally gave me the answer.

"It's because new hires haven't slept around as much."

This girl had a seductive quality to her. She looked at me with lust in her eyes. Her teeth were pretty jacked up, but I could get past that. She was an officer and the head of her department, and once again I found myself attracted to power. I had never experienced the kiss of an Indian, which made me want to try it all the more.

A couple of days later, she sat down next to me during a crew party on Lido Deck. Ship-wide crew parties happened every couple months. There was a group of us at the table, and after a few minutes of chatting, the other people left and it was just the two of us. She rubbed my leg under the table. She actually slipped her pantyhose-covered foot out of her shoe and rubbed the skin above my ankle. I thought that only happened in movies.

I didn't know what to do so I ignored it. Maybe it was an accident. Then she did it again and went higher up on my leg. It was clear that this was no accident and I had to respond with something. So I looked at her.

"Hey, how's it going?" I asked lamely.

"You want to go back to my cabin? I have my own cabin, you know."

You're goddamn right I wanted to go back to her cabin. But there were two problems with this. First, I was self-conscious about my inexperience. She obviously was a very experienced lover, and I would have been embarrassed to reveal my lack of skills. Second—and the only reason really—was that her boyfriend was a staff captain, and he was *on the ship*. He had the power to fire anyone. As the official disciplinarian, it was part of his job. He probably had a wife back in Italy, but he could still fire my butt for being with his mistress. Even if he didn't fire me, he could make my life very unpleasant.

"I'm sorry, but I have to say no. I don't want to cause any problems with the staff captain."

She looked disappointed. A couple of moments later she stood up. "I'm going to the restroom. I'll be right back."

And then she didn't come back.

☆ ☆ ☆

I was in the crew bar the next night, talking to JB and a British guy from the gift shop, and we got on the topic of who had gone the longest without sex. JB said that before his girlfriend on the ship, it had been five months.

"I guarantee I'll win this contest," I said.

"I don't think so," the Brit said. "It's been, like, eight months for me. And you?"

"Twelve years."

It was such a ridiculous number that neither one of them came close to believing me.

"Don't be a wanker. How long has it really been?"

"It's really been twelve years. I was sixteen the last time I had sex."

"All right, whatever," the Brit said. It annoyed them both that I held to this story.

So I changed the subject. "What does wanker mean?"

"Well, it comes from 'wanking,' which means 'masturbating,'" the Brit explained, "but we don't say 'wanker' to mean 'one who wanks.' Calling someone a wanker is like you Americans calling someone a jackass."

☆ ☆ ☆

With all the people I was meeting and all the places I was visiting, it was high time I invested in a good digital camera. Our home port was in New York City so I took a taxi to the nearest Best Buy. That $50 round-trip cab fare stung. The camera turned out to be defective so I had to wait a week until we were back in home port and pay another $50 in cab fare to exchange it. Simple tasks like going to the store weren't as simple when you lived on a ship.

JB and I each had two dresser drawers in our cabin, and my drawers were full of junk left by the previous occupant. There was nothing I wanted to keep, but I didn't want to throw it all away. I had an idea.

It came from a running joke I had with a roommate from college that started when he came home from class one day.

"Hey, do you have any scissors?" I asked him.

"Yeah, they're in my bag," he said.

"Dude, these are brand new scissors. Did you just buy them?"

"Nah, I took them from Kinko's."

"What, you stole them?"

"They had a ton of them just lying around."

"Yeah, but you stole them."

"Uh . . . well . . . there was a sign next to a pile of them that said, 'Free. Please take one.'"

From then on, anytime we wanted to take salt and pepper shakers, or a beer glass from the bar, we could always justify it by saying that there was a "Free. Please take one" sign.

So, I gathered all the crap from my drawer and set it up in the crew Laundromat. I wrote signs that said things like, "Free Shoes! Please take a pair," and "Free Plastic Plant! Please take it." Ten minutes later I saw a guy from Indonesia making off with the entire lot, including the broken watch and partially used disposable camera.

✷ ✷ ✷

I got my epaulettes a few days after transferring to the *Triumph*, but JB didn't have his yet. We had the same job, and since we started at the same time, I wasn't going to wear mine until he had his. We both went without epaulettes for another three weeks until his came in, and when I finally put mine on, it felt good. Halloween was over baby, and I liked the distinction of being an officer.

There were three I/S managers on the *Triumph*. JB and I reported to an onboard senior I/S manager named Tom whose style was very different from what I was used to on the *Fantasy*. There was no rigorous 9:00 to 6:00 schedule. Except for embarkation day, and the one day per cruise that we had to print the onboard charge cards, we didn't have a schedule at all. We always got our work done, but we didn't go around looking for things to do. When we weren't busy, Tom was happy with sleeping in and doing nothing. We all spent more time together in the crew bar than we did in the computer room.

The computer systems on the ship were so diverse and specialized that no land-based computer guy could walk on knowing them all. There was a program that printed out which cabins had paid for a fruit basket to be delivered to their room on the first day of the cruise. It was written by Carnival programmers specifically for Carnival ships. The software that controlled the magnetic room keys was so specialized that unless you worked in a hotel, you had never seen it. Most of these programs and processes had serious usability issues. Each system by itself wasn't all that difficult to learn, but there were so many of them that remembering the ins and out of each user-unfriendly interface was daunting, especially when I used some of them only twice a month.

The systems even differed between ships. Newer ships had more technology and newer versions of existing technology. The older ships constantly played catch-up, and because of the cost and effort required to update the systems of an entire ship, it often took years, maybe even a decade, before they received the new stuff. I would later work on a ship that ran Windows 95 until it was finally upgraded to Windows XP in 2004.

Though I didn't have a schedule, I did have a pager. There were three of us, so we took turns carrying it. Lots of crewmembers had pagers. If there was a leaky toilet, then the plumber was paged. The plumber responded by going to the nearest ship phone and calling the number on his pager. If the chief engineer wanted his head electrician, then he paged him. And if anyone had a computer problem, they paged the I/S manager.

When I first carried the pager back on the *Fantasy*, it felt like a time bomb. Even though I could always call Dipsu for assistance, I was terrified and just prayed that the damn thing wouldn't go off. When it did and I called the person back, I fumbled over my words and said that I would check with my manager and get back to them. It's a horrible feeling to be ignorant of answers you're responsible for knowing. I had just started getting comfortable with the pager on the *Fantasy* when I was transferred, and since the *Triumph* was a newer ship with more systems to learn, I went through another couple of weeks of that awful feeling.

✲ ✲ ✲

There was a beautiful Romanian waitress who signed on to the *Triumph* the same day as me. It was also her first contract and I took every opportunity to strike up conversation with her. One night in the crew bar we spent some time talking and she told me about her boyfriend from back home and how much she loved him and how loyal she was to him.

Both DJ Johnny Vancouver and a social host named Dana saw me talking to her.

"Dude, so are you after her?" Johnny asked.

"Well, I was after her, but she has a boyfriend."

"That sucks," Johnny said.

"Is her boyfriend on the ship?" Dana asked.

"No, he's back in Romania."

"Well, then, don't give up," Dana said.

"What do you mean?" I asked.

"He lives halfway around the world," she said.

"She's crazy about this guy and told me she was going to stay faithful."

"Whatever." Dana laughed, having worked on ships for a couple of years. "She'll be dating somebody within a month, if not sooner."

There was a British maître d' on the ship who was 6'3", well built, with jet black hair and dark skin. The women found him very attractive. He was also a natural salesman who was passionate and convincing about any opinion he had on any subject. One day I went to his office and found him jamming to the album *Smokin'* by the American blues guitarist and singer Jonny Lang. He spent five minutes talking about how the singer was only fourteen when he released his first album and how his vocals and guitar playing were the best ever. I was sold. I borrowed his CD, but when I played it in my cabin, alone and away from him, it just didn't sound as good. There was something about the Brit's energy and passion that brought the music alive.

So we jammed to Jonny Lang while I worked on the computer in his office. In between his head bobbing to the songs, he started telling me about his interest in the Romanian waitress. Through him sharing his personal feelings and vulnerabilities, I came to like him more.

"I told her," he said, with the same passion and sincerity he had for the music, "I just *feel* something when I'm with you."

It wasn't just a cheap pickup line. It was a cheap pickup line that was true. He really meant it.

After a couple of weeks, he wore her down and they started pseudo-dating, but she wouldn't sleep with him. I'd stop by his office for updates.

"Have you slept with her yet?" I asked as I sat in his office one day.

"No, not yet," he said, as we sat in the privacy of his office. "I told her that I've never waited this long for anybody and that I wouldn't wait this long for anybody else."

"How long has it been?" I asked.

"Nearly three weeks. Can you believe it?"

Though a bit sleazy, he really did mean it. And the following week, the Romanian girl caved and slept with him.

I couldn't believe it. Dana was right all along. The Romanian dated the maître d' for three months before he broke it off because they were arguing so much.

He had a new girlfriend within a week. He told me about it when I went to see him in his office.

"Ah, Jay, I tell you. I am so happy right now. I didn't realize how miserable I became with that Romanian. This new girl is amazing." He was animated and full of energy like before. "She's got long blond hair, and she's an animal."

"An animal? What do you mean?"

"In bed, Jay. She's an animal in bed."

"Oh."

There was one girl on the ship that was dating the golf trainer and had made a point of telling everyone how well endowed he was. Then one week before she signed off the ship, she told everyone how she stopped having sex with the golf trainer so that she could be ready to see her boyfriend back home.

Her body was very tight and athletic. She had beautiful muscular legs, blond hair, a pretty face, a toned upper body, and six-pack abs. She was a party girl and constantly getting in trouble with ship's security.

"I don't take shit from anyone," she told me one night.

"I can tell. What do you do when security gives you a hard time?"

"Well, those security bastards sent me to the staff captain a few weeks back."

"Why?" I asked.

"Because I told the chief security officer to piss off. He was such a bastard," she said, getting all riled up.

"What did the staff captain say?"

"He spent five minutes telling me that I needed to calm down and stop talking back to everyone. And then I looked him straight in the eye and said, 'You know what? You're a dick and I don't agree with a damn word you said' and just let him have it."

"I can't believe he didn't fire you on the spot. Did you even get written up?"

"Yeah, I got written up, but I don't care. You get three warnings before they fire you, and that was only my first. Besides, I'm going home in five days."

It amazes me how much certain personalities can get away with. Her outburst probably turned the staff captain on. It would have turned me on.

She was one of the most candid people I've ever met. "I can't wait to go home and see my boyfriend," she said one night in the crew bar. Then she held out one arm in front of her and bent her knees and started grinding the air, saying, "I'm going to be riding him like there's no tomorrow."

"Can you imagine how awful that would be?" a friend of mine back home said after I told him the story. "You haven't seen your girlfriend in six months, and you don't even know that she's been cheating on you the whole time."

After the Romanian first told me that she had a boyfriend back home, I gave up on her and started exchanging stares with a Polish girl who was the piano player in the ship's classical trio. Her name was Paulina. That's right: a Polish piano player named Paulina.

She had an unbelievable figure, and like the other girls from the trio, every outfit she wore included a snug-fitting blouse and dress pants that stretched over and clung to every curve of her perfect butt and upper thighs. She was classy and beautiful.

I started pursuing her, but then a youth counselor from South Africa interrupted me.

I was dressed up in my Carnival-issued evening uniform—a suit and tie—for formal night. Johnny Vancouver was spinning the tunes in the disco as I danced with a handful of crewmembers, including that maître d', on a mostly empty dance floor. Officers and staff were allowed to dance in the passenger disco, but crew-ranked crewmembers were not. We were taking turns doing our personal jigs when a youth counselor, a girl decked out in a gray formal dress full of sequins, sidled up in front of me and started shaking her butt. She backed up to get closer and I put my hands on her hips, and then she backed up more until we were touching.

A couple of hours later we were kissing in her bed. All the while, her roommate, above us on the top bunk, rustled her blankets to get comfortable.

"Let's do it," she whispered in my ear as she arched her back.

"Do you have protection?" I asked.

"It's okay, I'm on the pill."

"Yeah, but I still want to use protection."

"But I don't have any."

"That's fine, we'll just wait 'til tomorrow."

"No, it's okay. I really am on the pill."

"I believe you, but I don't want to do this without a condom. Let's just wait until tomorrow."

The passion immediately died, and she exhaled with the frustration. We lay there for another couple of minutes before I kissed her goodbye and said goodnight.

The next night JB said he would be gone for a while so she came to my cabin and we climbed up to the top bunk. We started kissing. There was an endless supply of free condoms from the ship's infirmary, but I preferred to buy mine from a store. It was less embarrassing to buy them anonymously from a Wal-Mart teller than to get them from the infirmary where the ship's nurses would see you.

Ninety-one seconds passed, and it was over.

We lay on our sides facing the TV, but I was staring at the ground and said nothing.

"What's wrong?" she asked.

"Nothing, why?" I snapped out of it and tried to act normal.

"You got quiet all the sudden."

"I'm just watching the TV."

"Okay," she said.

We lay there for another five minutes until she had to leave for her evening shift with the kids. As soon as I closed the door behind her, I sat down and typed out what was racing in my mind. It was like those stream-of-consciousness exercises they made us do in grade school. Here's what I wrote, verbatim:

Week/Weak

Wish she was leaving in a week. A week is enough time to get stronger/better. A month is too much of a burden. Too long to be fake, and yet necessary practice.

74

Terrified. Dangerous. Want to talk, want to be understood . . . by myself. Do I regret it? Have I been poisoned?

What have I thrown away. The trash, the nonsense. I was ready to throw it away. It didn't serve me while I had it or did it. I suppose it defined me and the problem is that now that it's gone, I have to find a new definition. I think I am placing too much importance on this event but then I can't help the way I feel. I made the choice. I was ready. I knew it was a one way road. Hard to describe how I feel. I feel changed. Different. Not sad, not angry, not regretful, not happy, just different. It was no big deal and yet it was.

A few days later, when I had cell phone access while the ship was in Boston, I called a buddy of mine from back home named Ryan.

"Have you been dating anyone?" he asked after we chatted for a bit.

"Yeah, I've been seeing a girl for a few days now."

"Have you slept with her?"

"Yep."

"Yeah, whatever," he said, but I stayed silent. "Really?"

"Yep."

"Whatever, dude." Again I was silent. "Wait a minute! So you actually had sexual intercourse?

"Yep."

Pause.

"With a girl?"

"Of course with a girl!"

He kept asking in every way possible to make sure I wasn't deceiving him through some kind of conversational loophole.

"Dude, I can't believe it. How long has it been?"

"Twelve years, man. Twelve years."

"Did you use protection?"

"Absolutely."

"Well, how was it?"

"I don't know. A bit anti-climatic, I guess. I mean, we started, and it was over."

A week later I called a female friend of mine from back home. "So I had sex for the first time in twelve years."

"Okay." She chuckled. "That's wonderful. Who is this girl?"

"She's a youth counselor from South Africa."

"That's dangerous," she said.

"What do you mean?"

"Well, the HIV rate there is pretty high. Something like one in ten adults is HIV positive."

"Holy crap! Well, I'm using protection so it should be okay."

It was unsettling nonetheless. And she was right. AIDS was a big problem in South Africa. I didn't know it at the time, but the disease was more prevalent in the black population. And even though my new girlfriend was white and would have been screened for HIV before boarding the ship, there was no denying the risk I was taking.

"So how did it go?" my friend asked.

"Let me tell you, I suck. I was so uncoordinated and I had no rhythm. I was probably the worst she's ever had."

It was one of the worst for me as well. Of course, it was only the third time I'd had sex so I didn't have much to compare it to. I'd been imagining for the past twelve years that it would be phenomenal. I had placed so much significance on the event that it was impossible for it to be as good as I had imagined, especially when it lasted only ninety-one seconds.

The youth counselor had one month left in her contract. But that was too much time. A week would have been better. That would have been enough time to learn some coordination, but brief enough to keep from growing annoyed with her. She had a nice figure, but I wasn't all that attracted to her. I think a big reason for that was that she was my first. She destroyed something I'd spent twelve years building, and she didn't even know it. It wasn't fair, but I resented her for it.

Nonetheless, we continued our romance. One night we stood on the floor of my cabin. It was my idea and it was the first time I had done that position. Of course almost every position was new for me. Not long after we started, I heard a muffled snap.

"Hold on," I said, realizing what had happened.

I knew that breakage was possible, but I didn't understand how or why. I replaced it and pretended it was no big deal, but I thought about nothing but HIV afterwards. A couple of days later I went to the computer room late at night, when I was sure neither JB nor Tom would be there, and got online to research the symptoms of herpes. My heart sank when I read that lesions occur at the base of the penis and are often itchy. That was exactly what I had.

No.

Please no.

I looked away from the screen and stared at the wall with my mouth open. I had abstained for all that time only to contract herpes with the first girl?

Please don't let this be true.

I took a deep breath and kept reading. It said that the lesions of herpes resembled cold sores. That is not what mine looked like, and as the uncertainty returned, I began to feel better. But there was no question about it. I had to get tested.

Going to the onboard doctor was not an option. I didn't want that on my employee file, and I didn't want the staff in the infirmary to know. The nurses and doctors were people I drank with in the crew bar. I fixed their computers. The normal boundaries between the medical staff and the patient were not present. Our homeport was New York City so I looked online and found a free STD clinic. I had to stay on the ship at the next embarkation day so I had to wait an extra week before taking a cab to the clinic.

Now, I grew up in a middle-class suburb of Dallas. Every clinic or doctor's office I'd ever been to was clean and nicely decorated and furnished. The patients in the waiting rooms were middle-class or higher with clean clothes. This upbringing left me completely unprepared for one of New York City's free STD clinics.

The waiting room was unlike any I had ever seen. It had scuffed up linoleum instead of carpet. It had rows of mismatched cafeteria-style chairs with metal legs and stains on the worn-out fabric seats. There were no issues of *Home and Garden* or *Good Housekeeping* to flip through.

And then there was the clientele. There were about fifteen other people in the waiting room, none of whom could be remotely described as white-collar. They all wore scruffy clothes, and most of the guys hadn't shaved in days. The ladies wore facial expressions that indicated they were more embarrassed to be there than the guys were. This place was outright nasty. You could taste the disease. People go to their family doctor because they have the sniffles or because they want their cholesterol checked. People go to an STD clinic because their nether regions are infected.

I walked up to a woman sitting behind the window.

"Can I help you?" she asked with disinterest.

"Um, yeah," I whispered hoping the others wouldn't hear. "I'd like to get tested for STDs."

"Do you want an HIV test?" she asked, louder than I would have preferred.

"Uh, yeah. That would be great," I continued in my quiet voice.

"If you want to get tested for HIV, then you have to come back on a different day to have your results given to you in front of a counselor. This is mandatory whether you test positive or not."

"What about the results for the other STDs?"

"You'll get those before you leave today. What day would you like to schedule your visit with the HIV counselor?"

"Actually, let's skip the HIV test today."

A second visit would be inconvenient. I was already paying fifty dollars in roundtrip cab fare for this visit. I figured it was also too soon for an HIV test to detect anything anyway.

"Fill out these forms and bring them back," she said as she handed me a grubby clipboard.

I didn't want to touch that clipboard. I didn't want to sit on those chairs. But I did. As I sat there, immersed in filth, I understood why people don't go to free clinics if they can afford a doctor's office. When my name was called, I stood up and did my walk of shame over to the nurse.

The doctor was professional and competent. He had a polite, condescending tone, like that of someone talking to a child.

"Okay, so why are you here today?" he asked.

I told him about the breakage and about the blisters.

"Okay, and when did you last have sex?"

"Well, the condom broke about ten days ago."

"Okay, but when was the last time you had sex?"

"Yesterday." And I was reminded that the risk is there any time you have sex, not just when it breaks.

"Have you ever engaged in gay intercourse?" From this point on, he kept his head down as he went through his list of questions, and the absence of eye contact somehow made it less embarrassing.

"No, no gay sex."

"Have you ever engaged in anal sex with a homosexual male?"

"No, no gay sex."

"Have you ever engaged in anal sex with a female?"

"No."

"How many partners have you had in the last two years?"

"One."

He paused at that answer. "How long have you been with this partner?"

"Two weeks."

It was clear that he didn't believe me, but he marked it down on his questionnaire anyway. Then he was ready to see.

With his hands in latex gloves, he performed the examination.

"Well, that's definitely not herpes or any other type of STD. It was probably caused by the friction of a dry condom. The main reason they break is a lack of lubrication, so in the future, you should use lubrication if it starts to feel dry."

"Okay."

"Have you heard of K-Y Jelly?"

"Um, yeah. I'll make sure to get some."

"Okay, so now we'll do a swab test that will check for common bacterial infections like gonorrhea."

I nodded.

He grabbed a swab. It was a specialized Q-tip made of a long, thin wooden stick with a puff of cotton at one end. He squeezed gently with his thumb and index finger.

"Now just look straight ahead," he said, not looking up, "and take a deep breath."

I started to inhale and then gasped. He did a quick in and out motion, but it felt like liquid fire had been poured in. It hurt way more than playing with that toy air pump. I was tender, and it burned when I went to the bathroom for the next couple of days.

With half my urethra stuck to it, he took the swab to have it tested. As I waited, alone in the room, I heard a male voice from across the hall.

"NOOOO!"

It was a yell of pure agony and I turned my head to listen even though it was unsettling. I heard some sobbing, and then, "Nooo, nooo, nooo . . ." Someone had just been given their test results – HIV positive – and that reaction was why counselors were mandatory. I don't know how I could ever handle news like that.

About five minutes later the doctor came back and said I was clear. No STDs. No herpes. I had never received better news.

I couldn't wait to get out of there. This was a place where souls were tortured and genitals burned. It was hell on Earth, and I had taken a tour. I was lucky, though. The devil dismissed me and let me walk out with my life intact.

So they usually break because it's too dry. After leaving the clinic, I and went straight to Wal-Mart and bought the biggest package of lube they sold. It even had spermicide. K-Y spermicidal, baby. Never again would it break because it was too dry.

We continued to sleep together even though I had zero interest and zero attraction to her. I held on until she signed off because it was the easiest way to end it. This was a common practice on ships. Instead of dealing with a breakup and then continuing to see the same person every day, people just waited until the signoff date.

☆ ☆ ☆

The food was one of the most talked about amenities among the passengers.

"Where's the food?"

Or even better: "Where da food at!"

This was often the first thing out of their mouths when they boarded.

Well, the food was everywhere. Room service, the pizza bar, and the ice cream machines were open 24 hours a day. The massive buffet on Lido Deck was open for most of the morning and afternoon. Then there was the midnight buffet and the midnight dessert buffet that happened once a cruise. And of course the formal dining rooms served three squares a day.

Running the dining rooms on a cruise ship was a bit of a challenge. Within fifteen minutes, the restaurant went from empty to packed as 750 seats were filled. Thirty minutes later, the same thing happened again as the ship's second restaurant opened. The process repeated three hours later for the late seating. One galley, serving both dining rooms, served 3,500 people from a menu in a span of five hours, a claim that no restaurant on land can match.

The galley, or kitchen, was located in between the two restaurants. Ten thousand fresh rolls were baked each day. A row of thirty-gallon vats cooked everything from pasta to soups. Thousands of plates were filled with salad and pre-chilled by stacking them on trolleys that rolled into giant refrigerators.

No place on the ship was ever more alive than the galley during dinner on a sea day. It took 20% of the ship's crew to handle the dinner rush. Cooks sweated over grills and ovens. The waiters queued in line to pick up the entrees and then ran around like worker ants to serve each passenger a five-course meal. Meat sizzled and dishes clanked through the conveyor belt dishwasher. Voices yelled over all of it. The air was hot and humid from the steam, and the smell was a combination of food and disinfectant soap as the cleaning process tried to keep pace with the constant flow of dirty dishes.

As a general rule, crewmembers could not eat in the formal passenger dining rooms. Exceptions were made if a crewmember's family were sailing, but otherwise the crew ate in their own mess halls. They were divided by rank: the officer mess, the staff mess, and the crew mess for the crew-ranked crewmembers. Each progressively higher-ranked mess hall served fewer people and thus was smaller with a quieter atmosphere. Most people ate in their own mess hall, but depending on rank, some crewmembers could choose. Officers could eat in any of the mess halls. Staff could eat in their mess hall, the staff mess, or in the lesser-ranked crew mess, but they could not eat in the higher-ranked officer mess. Crew-ranked folks had no choice and could eat only in the crew mess hall. The freedom to choose the mess hall enabled friends or couples of different ranks to eat together.

The food in each mess hall was the same except that the officers' mess had an additional variety of bread and a few extra selections at the salad bar. The crew-ranked mess hall held about 200 people, who carried trays and self-served 100% of their food from a buffet line that was part of the crew galley, and thus full of cooked humidity and rowdy with the sights and sounds of a restaurant kitchen. The plates, bowls, and cups were plastic, and the napkins were paper. The tables were uncovered and pushed together to form long rows that could seat up to thirty. Crew-ranked crewmembers bussed their own trays at the washing area in the back of the mess hall. As part of the ship's garbage separation and recycling, they put paper waste in one bin and scraped off uneaten food into another. They stacked their trays and put dirty utensils into bins of soapy water.

Going up one rank, the staff mess was about 75% self-serve from a well-presented buffet line in the mess hall instead of the galley. The room was smaller and quieter, with room for about seventy-five people. Each table had a menu to help identify the buffet items and to order the entrees that weren't in the buffet. There were about four waitresses who brought out the entrees and bussed the tables. Some tables were round and some were rectangular. Some were intimate and sat only four people, and the largest tables sat no more than ten. The dining tables were covered in starched tablecloths, and each seat was set with utensils rolled in a cloth napkin and stylish glass instead of a plastic cup. The plates and bowls were ceramic.

The officers' mess was 10% self-serve with the buffet lines holding only soup and salad. Everything else was ordered from the menu and delivered. Two waitresses worked the officers' mess, and with room for only twenty-five people, service was faster and more personalized because the waitresses didn't have as many people to serve. Each table sat only four to six people, and though the same glassware and tablecloths were used, each seat had a full place setting. Instead of utensils being rolled up in the cloth napkin, the utensils were placed around a clean plate and the napkin was neatly folded and perched atop the plate. If the waitress was nearby when you sat down, she would pull the napkin off the plate and hand it to you. The waitresses also bussed the tables, but unlike the staff mess that had a tub for dirty dishes, the officers' mess waitresses always took the dishes straight to the galley and out of sight.

The officers' mess and staff mess halls were open three times a day, with a two to three-hour window for each meal. The crew mess was open a couple of hours longer for lunch and dinner to accommodate the crew-ranked employees who worked during normal mealtime. The crew mess also had a "no frills" midnight buffet every night.

The food in the mess halls was not passenger food. The menus were different, and the food was prepared in separate galleys. The crew never ate as well as the passengers. No lobster. Steak showed up only about once a month. Accustomed to quality steaks on land, the steak onboard, even in the passenger areas, never much impressed me and wasn't my favorite menu item. Rather, I went for the fish sticks. In fact, fish sticks were one of the favorites among all of the crew. If I was walking to the mess hall and passed someone who had just eaten, they would be all like,

"Dude! Fish stick night!"

I also looked forward to broccoli and cheese soup night. I would fill up on soup and bread and skip the entrée completely. Hamburgers and French fries were always available, but they became a last resort when there was nothing else edible on the menu. The fries were good when fresh, but the hamburgers always tasted like reheated leftovers. Watermelon, apples, and oranges were usually available, but the watermelon was usually under-ripe.

Crew-ranked employees could eat only from the crew mess, but officers and staff could sit down and eat the passenger food on Lido Deck. This privilege broke the monotony of the mess hall menus, but even pizza got old. Same with the Lido Deck buffet. After a few months, food from any buffet tasted the same and it became increasingly difficult to find something appealing.

So when one of the youth counselors invited us over to her house for some homemade lasagna, we all jumped on it. Her parents lived about twenty minutes from where the ship docked and when we got back and told people where we had gone, everyone wanted to go with us the next week.

✢ ✢ ✢

After my first ship girlfriend signed off, I started chasing piano player Paulina again. But less than a week after my first girlfriend left, I had slept with her roommate, another youth counselor named Lucy, and thus we were officially dating. We had a great time together and always made each other laugh, but she and I were never interested in a long-term relationship. We got along so well and it was perfect. This was the kind of dating I should have done sooner. It was a casual, non-committal type of dating, and it was the practice I needed if I was ever going to get serious about someone later.

Of course I hadn't even come close to finishing that giant tube of lube with the first girl so I continued to use it with Lucy. That was weird. It was obvious that a crinkled metal tube had been used before, and she knew who it had been used with.

But it worked like magic, and I never had one break again. But that wasn't the end of my problems.

"Oh no," I said with a worried look on my face.

"What's wrong?" she asked.

"Well, it came off and I didn't realize it." I was freaking out.

Lucy was also from South Africa. She was not on the pill.

Crap.

"You have to go to the infirmary and ask for the morning after pill," I said.

"It's okay, I'm not pregnant," Lucy said with the utmost confidence.

"Yeah, well, maybe not this instant, but there's a good chance you could be tomorrow."

"Don't worry, I'm not going to get pregnant."

"What do you mean? Are you unable to have children?"

"No, it's not that. It's just that I know I won't be pregnant."

"How do you know?"

"I just have this feeling. If I was going to be pregnant, then I'd feel it, and I don't feel it now. I'm always right about these things."

"Have you been pregnant before?"

"No."

"Then how can you just feel it?"

"I just can. Don't worry about it."

"Look, this would be a life-changing event, and I'd prefer to not gamble just because you have a feeling," I said as I thought about how many blackjack hands I had lost based on a feeling. "Do you have something against taking the pill?"

"No, but it would be embarrassing to go the infirmary and ask for one."

"I totally agree. But besides that, is there anything else?"

"Not really, but it's just not necessary because I know I'm not pregnant."

"So if I go to the infirmary and get the pill, would you take it?"

She paused for a second and looked at me. "Yes, yes, okay, I'll take it."

"Excellent. I'll be right back," I said as I started putting on my white pants.

"Are you going now?"

"You're goddamn right I'm going now. Stay here. I'll be right back."

"But I have to work in the kids' playroom in ten minutes."

"Okay, I'll just bring it up to you. Do you guys have water or sodas up there? If not, I'll stop at a bar and pick something up."

"Of course we have drinks up there. What's wrong with you?"

"Okay, cool. I'll see you in a bit."

I was out the door and left her in my cabin to finish getting dressed.

Even I was embarrassed to go to the infirmary for this, especially since I knew all the nurses.

I motioned to one.

"Do you guys have the morning-after pill?" I asked as I leaned in close in the hopes of obtaining some privacy. The other nurse sat only a few feet away and was talking to a couple of other crewmembers.

"What do you mean, to prevent pregnancy?" the nurse asked.

"Yeah."

"Well, those are for the girl."

"Of course they're for the girl. Can you give one to me so that I can take it to my girl?"

"Actually, no. She must come here herself so that we can explain how to use it and what to expect."

"Well, she's at work now. How long do we have before it's too late?"

"When did this happen?"

"Four minutes and thirty-two seconds ago."

"Oh, then you're fine. It is effective up to seventy-two hours later."

I went straight to the playroom to find Lucy.

"The nurse said that you have to be there yourself to get the pill."

"Well, I can't leave because I have to work until 10:00 tonight."

"The infirmary will be closed by then, but you have seventy-two hours to take the pill. Can you go in the morning at 9:00, when the infirmary opens?"

She said she would, and she did. They gave her two pills and told her to take them twelve hours apart. They said that she might get nauseous. She did. She actually felt awful all day. But she didn't get pregnant. Whew.

CHAPTER 5

HOW MUCH CAN YOU
DRINK WITHOUT DYING?

As the weeks turned into months on the *Triumph*, I drank more and more. Alcohol was omnipresent. It wasn't just in the crew bar, or in the piano bar, or the karaoke bar, or in any of the other bars around the ship. In port, we'd go to the beach and drink. If the ship was staying late, then we'd dance and drink at a bar or club. We were in Boston one night when I flirted with the owner of a bar called the Squealing Pig.

"Yeah, yeah," she said. "You got to have a girl in every port."

"Why would the crew need any girls in port when we have fifteen hundred on the ship?" I protested.

One day I got paged by an Italian bridge officer to fix the computer in his cabin. After I finished he gave me a shot of Sambuca from his private stash. He poured one for himself and we sat and talked, and after I finished my shot he poured another. So I drank it. Then he went to pour another and I had to talk him out of it because I was already buzzing and it was only 2:00 p.m. I was getting drunk more often in the crew bar, and because my senior I/S manager was so laid back, I could sleep off the hangovers by waking up late or taking naps during the day. I relearned the fact that liquor is less likely to give you a hangover than beer.

It was easy to blow $100 a week in the crew bar. It's a ridiculous amount considering that Coronas were only a dollar and cans of Bud Light were seventy-five cents. Mixed drinks were only a buck seventy-five. Some of the cost came from buying drinks for everyone else. It was customary for crew members to take turns buying a round of drinks, and after tip, it was easy to spend fifteen dollars for a round. Doing that twice a night, three times a week in addition to buying my own singles added up quickly. After a few weeks I tried to avoid the rotation of receiving and buying drinks because I always seemed to buy more than I ever received.

Sometimes I went to the crew bar intending to have only one drink and wound up sitting there getting completely hammered until it closed. It was impossible to go for just one drink, and you always drank more than you intended. It was the social pressure. As soon as you walked in you got sucked into laughing and having fun. Everybody had a drink in hand, and it was hard to leave because just as I was about to finish my last drink, somebody inevitably would buy me another. When I did manage to escape and return my cabin, I'd be bored because there was nothing to do there.

The crew bar had a stack of board games that few people ever used. But at 8:00 p.m., on the first sea day of every cruise, I played Monopoly with Johnny Vancouver, our friend Dana, and another girl named Sara who was the paymaster. I had not played Monopoly in fifteen years and never had any desire to play it. But on the ship I looked forward to it every week. Just about anything can be fun when you're with the right people, especially if everyone is drinking.

But somehow our Monopoly games were more than that. I mean I really enjoyed the game in the same way I enjoyed it as a kid. Whenever someone landed on Baltic Avenue or Mediterranean Avenue, the two cheapest properties, we'd all break into the voice of Eric Cartman from *South Park* and sing, "In the ghettoooo!"

We played and drank and munched on snacks that we bought from the crew bar. Johnny always opened his chips— those small bags that you get from the vending machines—by squeezing the bag until it popped and spewed greasy crumbs all over his black T-shirt. Then he'd drop his chin to look down at the crumbs and with one motion brush off the crumbs, stick a chip in his mouth, and look up at me with a blank expression as he chewed. It still makes me laugh to think of him doing that.

When the crew bar got busy, we had to wait in line to get our drinks, and this slowed our game playing. So we'd stack up and buy multiple drinks at a time. Johnny drank Godfathers, which is a mixture of scotch and amaretto. He usually ordered doubles because a single went down too fast. When even the doubles began going down pretty fast he started ordering quadruple Godfathers that filled an entire pint glass.

After having a few, I got hooked on those Godfathers and bought some scotch and amaretto to keep in my cabin. One night Johnny and I made Godfathers as we played *Star Wars, Jedi Knight II* on his Xbox. Johnny was a huge *Star Wars* fan and even had a tattoo of a storm trooper's mask on his forearm. I matched him drink for drink until I started vomiting in the sink.

"Sorry, dude," I said in between heaves. "I'm done for the night, and I can't play anymore."

"You Americans are so weak."

"Yeah, but I still kicked your ass all night with a light saber."

"Whatever."

Johnny headed back to the crew bar and kept on drinking for another few hours.

I tried to keep my drinking under control by not getting sloppy drunk every night. Sometimes I'd have only a few drinks and then firmly decline whenever someone offered to buy me one. They always looked at me funny when I did this. Heavy drinking was so commonplace that saying no, even for one night, seemed like strange behavior.

"Did you know," Johnny slurred one night as we listened to his music collection, "that antidisestablishmentarianism is like, the longest word in the English language?"

"What?" I said.

"Antidisestablishmentarianism."

"What does that mean?"

"It means people who are against those who are against establishments."

"What establishments?"

"You know, like powerful people that're in control of society and stuff. I think it has something to do with the Church of England. Dude, check out this song from Portishead."

I've only known a couple of people who were intimately passionate about music. Johnny was one of them. I used to think that people like him were snobs. They were too cool for "top 40" music and instead devoted themselves to learning the name of every obscure band that ever existed. But Johnny changed that perception. He wasn't a music snob, he was a connoisseur of sound. Music wasn't just background noise to him. It wasn't just something you sang along with. It was something to be savored, and for him, it was simply, truly art. Some songs had changed his life, and he described how there were a few songs that could actually make him cry.

He brought his portfolio of music onboard, and we used to listen to it in my cabin. He turned me onto countless bands that I would never have found on my own. Sometimes he'd take a CD up to the crew bar so we could listen to it on Monopoly night. Any time he ejected a CD, he lowered the volume before pressing the stop button in beat with the song. It was sacrilege to interrupt a song any other way.

One day while we were in port he bought a DVD by a band called The Prodigy. The disc had just one music video on it that was five minutes long.

"You paid ten dollars for one video?" I asked.

"Shut up, man," he said in a tone that told me I should never bring it up again. "The Prodigy is my favorite band."

That day he put the new video from The Prodigy in his Xbox and hit play.

"You have the DVD Playback Kit for your Xbox?" I asked.

"Yeah, of course," he said.

This meant we could watch my season three DVDs of *The Sopranos*. It was the first time he'd seen the series, and he was totally hooked.

We did a lot of talking, too. We talked about girls and about how beautiful Paulina was. We talked about our hometowns and growing up. We talked about our dads. And every guy knows that a milestone in a friendship has been reached when you talk about your dads.

The crew bar was always loud with music and voices, but most nights were uneventful. There was, however, an Italian engineering officer on the *Triumph* who was known for drinking any beer left unattended. If your beer went missing, it was likely that he drank it. Another Italian, fed up with the beer-snatcher, peed in a half-empty Corona bottle and left it out. Sure enough, the beer-snatcher grabbed it and drank the whole thing. Another bottle of "Corona" was left out, and he drank that one, too. After the third one, someone told him what he'd been drinking, and he went to his cabin and was sick for the rest of the night. The beer-snatcher, though, was in good with the captain, and so the guy who peed in the bottles ended up getting fired.

✳ ✳ ✳

Lots of people partied in the crew bar, but one man stood out above the rest: my roommate, JB. For five months we lived, worked, and partied together so I knew his ship personality well. JB was probably the most sociable and likable person onboard. Most crewmembers were pretty sociable, mostly because the closed environment forced you into constant interaction with others. I think I'm pretty good with people when I try, but I'm not always in the mood. Sometimes I just prefer to be alone. But even at my best, when I am both in the mood and trying, I was never as good with people as JB.

He made friends with all types of personalities. I always had trouble attracting the dancers. I never had that rock star aura that I think the dancers were especially attracted to. I wouldn't say that JB had rock star social status, but he was so likable that everyone, including the dancers, enjoyed being with him. He had the perfect combination of masculinity and vulnerability. He'd share his insecurities and personal thoughts with others, who naturally felt flattered when he asked for advice. Like the time his girlfriend left for vacation and he wasn't sure if he wanted to be with her when she got back.

"What am I going to do?" he'd say to whomever might be standing next to him.

Whenever a well-respected person shares something personal with you, it makes you feel good. It means that you are trusted and respected enough to hear their secrets, and somehow it doesn't matter that the feeling diminishes when you learn that he has shared the same secrets with others.

It was just one way that JB made others feel good. I don't know if he had read Dale Carnegie's *How To Win Friends And Influence People*, but I doubt it. He'd view it as a self-help book that some lame manager would want to push on him as corporate propaganda, but many of the things suggested in that book came naturally to JB. He took a genuine interest in people. It wasn't fake or labored. He just really liked people, and everyone who met him looked forward to hanging out with him.

We had three computer technicians visit the ship to work on the system that ran the in-cabin movies. JB worked with them all day, and when work time was over we all went out to a restaurant for dinner. Drinking and talking in a bar was something I constantly did on the ship and so doing it again, even on land, didn't interest me much. But JB was right at home. The technicians had a great time, and we went to the same bar for dinner and drinks again the next night. By then the technicians seemed to worship JB. They hung on his every word, and I'd become a wallflower. I wanted to be the person the technicians were excited to talk to, but I didn't want to be at the bar anyway so I privately admitted defeat and left early. I didn't join them on the third night.

JB, however, wasn't without his enemies, and he didn't like everyone. There was a sound technician who was in charge of the audio during the shows in the main lounge. He asked for a lot of IT favors, and we always helped him out. We'd give him a network cable, help with his personal laptop, and answer any general questions he had. He partially returned the favor when he gave us some gaff tape from his supply drawer.

Gaff tape is similar to duct tape except that it pulls up easily without leaving any sticky residue. It worked better than any tape we had access to, and after we used up the first roll, we asked the technician for another. Even though we constantly did IT favors for him, he said no to giving us more gaff tape. One night in the crew bar, he and JB got into an argument that lasted for a good five minutes.

"And I want my goddamn gaff tape," JB said as he ended the argument and walked away.

We had a new roll of tape the next day, but that didn't make up for it and JB never much liked the technician after that.

The biggest enemy I saw him make was an overweight housekeeping manager named Alan. It started when Alan paged JB with a condescending tone to ask for computer help, and culminated when Alan said something unpleasant about JB's girlfriend and then called JB a worthless I/S manager. When JB heard that, he went into an unbelievable rage, and he nearly lost control when he saw Alan a few minutes later in the crew bar. JB's face grew hostile as he stared at Alan. When Alan finally looked from across the room, JB gave him the bird with such force that JB's face started shaking as it turned a deep shade of red. I'd never seen anything like it.

I'd never seen somebody so visibly angry. Alan left the crew bar, and after that, inspired by a quote from the movie *Full Metal Jacket*, JB always referred to him as a "horrible disgusting fat body." Alan never paged JB again. JB talked about how much he hated that horrible disgusting fat body, and because JB was one of the most popular people on the ship, the housekeeping manager became somewhat of an outcast. But luckily, the *Triumph* was a temporary assignment and Alan was transferred a couple of weeks later.

JB was always good with words, and with non-enemies he had an unbelievable natural tact. One day he got an early morning page that woke us both up. We both had a hangover. JB had morning frog voice so it was obvious that he had been sleeping, but the crewmember on the phone was demanding and a little rude.

"I love it when you blow sunshine my way," JB said into the phone while half-asleep and still drunk from the night before. I liked that response so much I still use it.

JB told me that while having dinner with a female Carnival executive one night they got into a discussion about the scarcity of female executives. She had a reputation for a stern management style that could be abrasive at times.

"You know," she said to JB, "I intentionally manage that way because it's a man's world and I have to compensate for being a woman."

"But you don't have to be a bitch all the time," JB said.

"Wait a minute," I interrupted him as he told me the story. "You said those exact words to her?"

"Yeah, that's what I said."

"Was she offended?" I asked.

"No, she wasn't offended. She practically thanked me as she considered the advice."

I don't know how he got away with these comments. If I'd said, "And I want my goddamn gaff tape," I would have never gotten it.

If I had said, "But you don't have to be a bitch all the time," I would have been fired.

When I look back at pictures of him, he always has a facial expression and a relaxed posture that exuded confidence, even with his big ears. I never noticed he had big ears until the time he told me how a crewmember gave him a hard time about it.

"The other kids made fun of me all the time when I was little," JB said to the crewmember who joked about it, "and I don't want to fucking hear it from you right now."

It was the perfect retort. With one sentence he acknowledged a lifelong vulnerability, asserted himself with aggression, and dissuaded that crewmember from ever mentioning it again. He told me about it, entrusting me with this vulnerability. And I knew that I would never, ever make fun of his ears.

JB also knew how to make his girlfriend feel like the most important person in the room. She'd often walk up and interrupt me in mid-sentence to say something to JB. He never hesitated and always turned and listened to her as if I had simply vanished. I think she did it because it felt good to always be number one. It annoyed me, but it was also a lesson on how to treat a woman.

JB would sooner die than to be a rat. He said that he'd never told on the other kids in school. I don't know if he learned this from his brothers or his parents or on his own, but it's another example of why he was so likable.

Some argue that parents should encourage their children to report to authorities those who break the rules. "It's the moral thing to do," they say. It's a nice principle that will earn the respect of some, but it's a great way to lose the favor of many.

I can only imagine what he thought of me when I called ship's security because I smelled pot in the passenger corridor one day. I'm not a rat by nature, but it seemed like the right thing to do at the time. Security never found out who it was.

Two months later I saw a couple leaning over the rail, smoking a joint. They looked at me with guilty expressions as the husband moved to conceal it. I pretended not to notice and walked inside the ship without reporting them. It's different, I think, to rat out somebody after you've looked them in the eye. And maybe JB's strict no-ratting policy had rubbed off on me.

JB had a lot of favorite sayings. Here are some of them:

"Same same, but different." A friend from his hometown came up with that one to describe something that was similar to something else but with differences.

"He's blacklisted." This was for people he didn't like, and it only took one wrong action or comment to land you on JB's blacklist. The sound technician and Alan were on his blacklist.

"We're professionals." We used this phrase to describe drinking, sexual prowess, IT abilities, or anything we did.

"If there was a problem, yo, I'll solve it." He used this Vanilla Ice quote anytime we fixed a computer. Later, after I quit Carnival, I used it as a quote in my email signature for work.

"You're goddamn right." This was inspired by a line in the song *Mr. E's Beautiful Blues* by *The Eels*. We had that song in the computer room and in our cabin, and played it over and over. We even took it to the crew bar and listened to it there. He used that phrase any time he wanted to say "yes" with emphasis.

"Is it time to go to the crew bar?" I'd ask.

"You're goddamn right it is," he'd say.

"Dude, did you see that new cabin stewardess?" I'd ask.

"You're goddamn right I did," he'd say.

And he was extremely intelligent. He was a big fan of Carl Sagan and could match wits in any conversation on philosophy or science.

"Man cannot live freely without embracing suicide and crime." This quote, from the movie *Murder By Numbers,* was his favorite line in the movie. He told me that he'd often considered a life of crime because he knew he was smarter than the average crook and he thought he'd stand a good chance of not getting caught. I think he'd make a very successful criminal, though I know he's too smart to risk getting caught.

One day I walked in and the cabin smelled like a dumpster. JB's white shoes had been in the cabin for a few hours. I have a particularly keen sense of smell, more on that later, but his feet stunk so bad that I forbade him from ever leaving his shoes out in the open. They were to stay in the bathroom with the door closed. His feet were to be washed after taking off his shoes. The stench was too strong and the cabin too small to have it any other way. He was a bit annoyed with these requests, but he was cool enough to go along with it.

"So what do you think about sharing our first impressions of each other?" JB asked me one day.

"You mean back when we met in Miami?" I asked.

"Yeah, like when we hung out at the restaurant that night," he said.

"Okay I'll go first," I said. "I thought you nodded your head too much. I thought you agreed too much when Fonzo was telling us about ship life. I thought you just asked questions to look intelligent and to keep the conversation going. But otherwise I thought you were cool."

"Hmmm," he said as one corner of his mouth dropped down into a frown.

I was beginning to regret what I said. "So what was your first impression of me?" I asked.

"I thought you were a smart guy and a hard worker."

He had nothing but nice things to say, and I felt like a jackass.

I envied him. I looked up to him in nearly every way—every way except for his foot odor, and the way he disregarded his health. He smoked about a pack and a half a day, and when he ran out and couldn't buy any because the crew bar was closed, he rolled filter-less cigarettes from his private stash of loose-leaf tobacco. But smoking by itself wasn't a big deal. Lots of people smoked on the ship. Many smoked more than JB. But nobody—and I mean nobody—drank more than JB.

Any crewmember who knew him—and that was just about everyone—would agree that he was an alcoholic. And like Johnny Vancouver once said, "If the crew considers you an alcoholic, you're in trouble."

A few days after I joined the *Triumph*, he showed me pictures of his ankle after he'd twisted it during his first week onboard. It had a rainbow of color from the arch of his foot to the bottom of his calf, and he told me that he could barely walk for three days. He said that he was drunk and slipped at the bottom of a stairwell.

The crew bar opened at 6:00 p.m., and stopped serving drinks at 2:00 a.m. JB's normal routine was to have one or two beers when the crew bar first opened, then leave for dinner, and then go back to the crew bar and stay until it closed. If he could still physically drink, then he'd get some beer or liquor from our cabin and keep going until he'd had enough. Then he'd chug water before passing out. A couple of nights I watched him open a brand new 1.5 liter bottle of Evian and finish the whole thing with the bottle only touching his mouth twice. He was a professional and knew that the key to minimizing a hangover was to hydrate before going to bed.

I don't know how, but JB could be totally bombed out of his mind when he went to sleep at 3:00 a.m. and yet wake up at 8:00 a.m., still legally intoxicated, and work if he had to. But he didn't always have to. Much of JB's job could be accomplished any time during the day. Most days he was awake by noon, in time for lunch, but there was a span of a couple of weeks when he slept past 2:00 in the afternoon and a couple of days when he even slept until 4:00 p.m. Tom, our senior I/S manager was so laid back that he didn't care. It also helped that Tom and JB had become good friends.

"Did you know you slept on the floor last night, fully dressed?" I asked him one time.

"What are you talking about?"

"Well, after I left the crew bar, I walked in and you were passed out on the linoleum. You had your uniform on and hadn't even taken your shoes off."

"What, just lying on my back?" he asked.

"No, you were on your stomach with your neck twisted so that the side of your face was stuck to the floor."

"Were my shoes at least close enough to the bathroom to reduce smell?"

"They were still on your feet, so it didn't stink. But you took them off at some point in the middle of the night, and I kindly put them in the bathroom for you."

"Hmm, I do have a vague memory of getting back to the cabin," he said as we laughed. "But I don't remember crawling into bed and I don't remember getting undressed."

"Yeah, it's probably a good thing you have the bottom bunk."

101

Every day, at some point in the afternoon, his body would finish metabolizing most of the alcohol in his blood. And then he'd start to shake. The shake was uncontrollable, and it was physical evidence of his alcohol dependency. He'd put his hand out in front of his body with his palm facing the floor and spread his fingers and watch to see how bad the shakes were that day. If they were especially bad, he'd open our fridge and pop open a beer. Sometimes he'd have two beers before the crew bar even opened. Even today, I sometimes wake up with a tingling sensation after a night of drinking. I feel it throughout my body, but it's more intense in my hands and feet. I'm guessing this is the precursor to the shakes I observed in JB.

Symptoms of alcohol dependency manifest within six to forty-eight hours of being without alcohol. The shakes are considered a relatively mild symptom of withdrawal. Moderate symptoms include hallucinations and confusion, and the severe symptoms can progress to what is called "delirium tremens," and can include such potentially fatal symptoms as grand mal seizure, stroke, or heart attack. I would have put JB at risk for these severe symptoms, but he drank every day so he was safe.

JB told me that he was a heavy drinker before working on ships and that at one point he quit because it was getting out of control. He had trouble sleeping for three months until the alcohol dependency wore off, and then he didn't drink heavily again until he worked on ships. He said he drank more on ships than he ever had before. I'd say that Ozzy Osbourne was the only person who drank more than JB and lived to tell about it.

"When I'm sober," JB once told me, "I think too much."

"What do you think about?" I asked.

"Everything I don't want to think about."

"Like what?"

"Like what happened that day and what I said to others and what they said to me. I get stuck thinking about what I notice in others. I think about where I am in my life and what I want to accomplish."

"Why don't you like thinking about these things?"

"Because it's distracting. My mind mulls over them so much that it's just annoying. Sometimes it keeps me up at night. But if I'm hammered, then I don't think, and I'm happier."

I disagreed with him at the time and didn't understand why thinking was a problem until I started writing this book.

Thoughts can be like that annoying person who doesn't know when to shut up. They've often pestered me, but the constant chatter wasn't really the problem. The real problem, I think, is that when you're swamped with internal thoughts, it's harder to interact with the external world. Social skills falter. And I realized that I've been like that for most of my life.

I did lots of thinking back in grade school and high school. My low grades didn't reflect it, but my lack of friends did. In college I realized that my constant thinking was affecting my ability to socialize and so I made a conscious decision to do less thinking and more socializing. I wanted to live more in the moment, and with some effort, I became more of the social person that I wished I had been in high school. And it was always easier to be social with a good buzz.

After college I reverted back to thinking. I have always thought I would be a scientist who invented something humanity would benefit from. During my post-college thinking period, I decided that commercially viable nuclear fusion would be a good first invention. I hadn't quite figured that out when I went to work on ships, so I put nuclear fusion on hold and went back to being more social. When I left ships I went back to thinking again, and while writing this book, I really started to think too much.

The project consumed me as I racked my brain trying to remember everything. Then I labored over exactly how to say it. The book was all I thought about. When someone told a story, I would analyze their style and make note of what worked and what didn't in hopes that it would help me on the page. Movies, books, and magazines triggered thoughts that I would later write about. Ideas interrupted me all day long. I'd have to stop the car to scribble something down or pause a movie when it sparked an idea. I learned that you must write down these ideas immediately or risk losing them forever. This constant thinking helped me write, but I couldn't turn it off. And just like JB had described, it kept me up at night. I'd get out of bed three or four times to jot down ideas before I finally fell asleep.

As I crossed back and forth between these two worlds, thinking versus living in the moment, and as I observed people who were in one of these two worlds, I noticed that people who live in the moment seem to have more fun than those who think. A person in the moment is full of smiles and laughter and energy. A person who is in the middle of thinking is not. It's just like if you're holding a camera, then you're not having as much fun as the group of people in the picture, because the instant you start concentrating on what's in the viewfinder, you become detached from the event you're shooting.

Video games are fun because you're living in the moment when you play them. Playing sports is all about living in the moment. Of course, strategy and planning are involved, but the act of swinging a bat or catching a football is done entirely in the moment. Maybe high school popularity has something to do with thinking versus living in the moment. Kids who play sports are generally more popular, and I think one reason is because playing sports trains your mind to live in the moment. The geeks spend their time thinking and so they aren't as good at socializing. Those who think may accomplish more, but those who live in the moment may have a greater level of happiness. I would even venture to say that some of the people who commit suicide do so when and because they are trapped in thinking mode.

So, that is why JB drank. It kept him from thinking, which made him happy. And maybe that was the best part of ship life. You could get away with not thinking. Besides work, there were no responsibilities because everything else was taken care of. All the meals were cooked and all the cleaning was done. There were no bills to pay and very few errands to run. There was no need to plan for the future, and the crew could live in the moment each day.

CHAPTER 6

WHAT SAILING THROUGH A HURRICANE WILL DO TO YOUR CRUISE SHIP

Seasickness was the most common onboard passenger ailment. Dramamine and scopolamine were a couple of medications typically used to combat seasickness, and they were available in pill form or as a patch to be worn behind the ear. The crew built somewhat of a tolerance and didn't get seasick as easily. I never took any of the seasickness medications and was only seasick a few times and only when the seas were very rough.

Stabilizers are fins that extend from the sides of the ship below the water line to reduce the ship rocking from side to side, at the expense of using more fuel. Their angle of attack is computer-controlled on the newer ships, and they cancel out nearly all of the side-to-side rocking. Passengers, thinking they were so smart, often complained that the ship was moving too much and that the captain needed to put the stabilizers out. Of course, these recommendations were never passed along because the captain knows what he's doing. The stabilizers reduce the side-to-side rocking, but they don't keep the ship from pitching up and down. It is not a building and because it's on water, a ship will move even when the stabilizers are out. Especially in a hurricane.

I was on the *Triumph* when it sailed into a hurricane that ran up the east coast of the United States into Canada. During hurricane season, ships do their best to steer clear of the rough seas. Sometimes they'll park behind an island where the water is calmer and wait it out. And with good reason. Rogue waves, listing, sinking, collisions, grounding, flooding, and mechanical problems were all possible and more likely in a hurricane.

Because they're so dangerous, Carnival has a command center at their corporate office in Miami to deal with the challenges hurricanes present. Multiple big screen monitors display all kinds of weather-related feeds and satellite imagery along with the positions of each ship. The command center coordinates with the captain of each affected vessel to plan alternate routes and port changes if needed.

After I sailed through the hurricane, in between work and partying, I spent a few days writing an email for everyone back home. Using the time stamps from the pictures I took, I pieced together a timeline, and with some light revisions from the original, here's that email:

We are currently in Sydney, Nova Scotia off the east coast of Canada, and there is a little cloud called Hurricane Gustav in our path. We were supposed to go to Halifax tomorrow. Instead, we are going to skip that port to try to go around the hurricane and maybe even get back to our home port of New York on schedule.

My cabin is at the front of the ship and there is a lot of commotion going on. Since we have an extra sea day, the shoppies and the casino folks have to work instead of having the afternoon off and they're not too happy about an extra ten-hour shift. There is a storage area nearby and some crewmembers are securing the shelves with rope. They are also bringing the metal window protectors out of storage and putting them up in all guest cabins up to Deck 2. These are used to help keep the windows from breaking and if the windows do break, the protectors will hopefully keep the water from flooding in. I'm looking forward to the rough seas. I don't know if I will be seasick or not, but it should be a fun ride.

✻ ✻ ✻

It is now a week since the hurricane. We didn't sail right through the eye, but we still hit some tremendous weather. Here we go:

11 pm. We started the night in the crew bar as usual. Every once in a while a big wave would hit with a loud bang and shake the ship. A handful of people would cheer the wave while holding up their drink. Yeah, I cheered every wave. We left the crew bar early to walk around. And like watching footage of the Tacoma Narrows bridge, where you just can't believe that steel and concrete can flap that much without breaking, I was standing at one end of the I-95 and could see the ship bend and ripple as it snaked through the waves causing crewmembers to stumble in unison. I go to my cabin to put the TV on the floor just in case.

3 am. Time to go outside. Nearly all of the outside doors were marked off with a "Do Not Enter Due to Strong Winds" sign. We wanted to obey all written signs so we went to an exit with no sign. There were seven of us, and one of the girls was a youth counselor and had a key to the children's playroom. From the playroom, there is a stairway that leads up to the outside of Deck 12, where there is a small playground for kids of all ages. We were attacked with some serious wind on the playground. I just bought a digital camera that is able to take movies and I have a great clip of everyone playing in the wind.

This is when I noticed the first signs of damage. A handrail was supported by inch-thick glass panes. There were eight pieces of glass that were each three square feet and the wind was slamming the length of the handrail against the ship and all but two of the glass panes were cracked and one of them was knocked off completely. Even in my drunken state, it didn't seem very safe to be near such volatile glass especially when we stood downwind of it. But it held while we were there.

3:45 am. Everyone left except Johnny Vancouver and me. We decided to go up to the highest point of the ship - Deck 14. The wind was even stronger up there. We took pictures of each other as we tried to balance while leaning into to the wind. To take these pictures, I had to sit down on the deck because I couldn't stand up and hold the camera straight in the wind.

Then Johnny convinced me to jump up into the wind. I had watched him do it multiple times, but again even in my drunken state, it didn't seem very safe. Johnny is a good 80 pounds heavier than me and not only does this help keep him anchored, but it probably means he doesn't jump as high. But I couldn't let a Canadian show me up. I did a few baby jumps. Then I jumped higher and the wind carried me back a few inches before I landed, stumbling to gain my footing. The wind was too loud in our ears to talk and even when we yelled in each other's faces it was hard to communicate. So later when we were inside, Johnny told me that while I was jumping, he saw something. Something like a high velocity blur. Yeah that was my hat. It was tucked into the seat of my jeans until it came loose and blew out into the ocean.

We walked down some stairs and the ocean spray misted all over us even though we were on Deck 10. I guess thirty-foot swells will do that. We came in from the storm and chatted with a couple security guys we know and showed them some of the pictures we took.

As the seawater evaporated, our faces became gritty with salt.

4:45 am. Time for a BLT. I have worked hard at forging good relationships with the right departments, and room service is a strategic department to be friendly with. Most crewmembers are not able to order room service, but I can. I usually have them deliver it to my cabin, but we decided to pick it up this time. The chef had a horrible case of seasickness and that was the worst BLT I've ever had. The bacon wasn't crunchy, the bread wasn't toasted, and it was all slopped together and falling apart on the plate. I still tipped the chef $10 though. Poor guy. After he slid the plate across the counter, he just buried his head in his hands and went back to his misery.

We were hanging out in the room service area for about ten minutes and laughing with the girl who was taking phone orders while rolling around in her chair because the ship was moving so much. The whole time we were there, random cups or plates crashed down from the back. Three separate times while we were there, a huge stack of dishes crashed down. Fortunately they were plastic dishes and didn't break. The girl working there said that it had been happening all night. I got a great photo of the mess.

5 am. We head back to my cabin on Deck 1 and notice that I am locked out, which makes no sense because I have my key. The latch opens but the door only opens a couple inches. It's jammed. The movement of the ship caused my closet drawers to swing open, thereby preventing the cabin door from opening.

My neighbor couldn't sleep because the phone in my cabin had been ringing every two minutes for the last two hours. Her bed is on the same wall as my phone and she heard every ring and wasn't too happy. I borrowed various objects from her so that I could reach around my door and push the closet drawers shut. First I tried a CD case. Not long enough. Then I tried an empty Pringles can. Not long enough, but luckily the lid came off and spilled BBQ Pringle crumbs all over my floor. Then I grabbed a large Evian bottle and that did the trick. Once in the cabin, I notice that one of my desk drawers has flown out from the desk and dumped papers and pens and my stack of cash all over the floor. No big deal. Johnny and I were eating the crappy BLTs when we heard concerned voices in the corridor.

5:20 am. One of the guys down the hall had woken up to a sloshing sound. He stepped down off of his bed and into water. His cabin and the cabins around him are completely flooded and water is running up and down the corridor obeying the motion of the ship. We didn't know where the water was coming from. We tasted it. It was salt water. The ship is going down!

I seriously thought it was a hull breach, but it was just a fire water supply line that broke. The TV is still on my floor but there isn't enough water to reach my cabin, so I leave it there. I put the cash and everything else back in my drawer and leave it on the floor so it won't fall out again.

5:45 am. We hear that the front of the ship on Deck 4 is flooded so off we go. Sure enough those corridors and cabins are flooded even worse than my corridor. This water came from the waves that splashed up onto the deck and leaked in through the doors to the inside. As we are walking around, I run into Tom who tells me that he just emptied the contents of his stomach. The seasickness got him.

"I'm feeling much better now," he says with watery eyes.

Then JB's girlfriend slips and lands with a splash on the flooded floor. As she goes to change out of her wet clothes, we notice the benches that store extra life jackets. These things are ten feet long and bolted to the deck but they have been completely ripped off, flipped upside down, and slammed into the bulkhead. There is one on each side of the ship, and they're both cracked open with neon orange life jackets spilling out. The emergency lights on the life jackets are water activated and they're all illuminated. A couple days later, I hear that quite a few life jackets had been blown out and were floating in the ocean.

The sun is coming up now and we try to get outside to see the rest of the damage, but the life jackets are blocking the door. We could force our way out, but instead we decide to check out the waves from Deck 6 at the front of the ship. That was probably a good idea. I didn't realize it at the time, but it wasn't wind that blew those benches off. It was the waves that engulfed the bow of the ship and if one hit while we were out there, it could have slammed us into the metal bulkhead or against the corners of the splintered life jacket benches or just swept our monkey asses out to sea.

6 am. Now we have lots of daylight. Outside we can see the ship smack the waves. What a sight. I have a great one-minute video of the spray from these waves going over our heads—remember we're on Deck 6 or about 60 feet above the water—as it completely whites out our field of vision.

6:10 am. Time to see the damage that our friendly neighborhood crew bar sustained. It's at the front of the ship on Deck 4 and completely flooded. I unplug the computers used for crew Internet access to keep the water from shorting them out. About ten of the 25-foot metal ceiling strips have either fallen or partially fallen to the floor. Fluorescent ceiling lights are dangling by their power cords but still working and turned on. I walked around in ankle deep water and took some video of the sloshing and the sound of the waves crashing against the ship. Sea water is an excellent conductor of electricity so it's a good thing I'm wearing sandals.

6:20 am. I decide to check on my cabin. For the last hour, that water pipe continued to leak and the flooding did reach my cabin. Water was everywhere but there was no trace of the Pringle crumbs. They had been washed out into the corridor along with trash from everyone's cabin and it's floating up and down the corridor. My girlfriend Lucy, who kept my neighbor from sleeping while calling every two minutes on the phone, finally came to my corridor to look for me. She had a key to my cabin and, being much smarter than me, had put my TV on JB's bed along with my drawer and anything else that was on the floor. That was awesome of her. She kept everything from getting ruined.

The electricians cut power and evacuated all the crew from the flooded cabins of Deck 1 and Deck 4. We all stood around on the I-95 and watched the electricians, safety officers, and joiners run past us with water pumps and hoses and trash cans to handle the water. I went back to the corridor to watch them vacuum it up and saw one of the electricians vomit in the corridor. A little later, I watched him vomit again. He just hunched over and puked right on the floor, not in a trash can, just right on the floor of the corridor. But the water was sloshing back and forth and so the vomit quickly dilutes and disappears from sight. The rough seas have not subsided and with all the upset stomachs the ship has turned into a vessel of vomit. There are piles of puke everywhere. Especially in the passenger areas.

6:40 am. I walk by the laundry room on Deck 0 and hear water hitting the floor. Time to inspect. The crew laundry room has four washers and five dryers and they are always in use. But now the power to that room had been cut so it is dark and strangely quiet except for that heavy dripping sound. I have just enough light from the hallway to see what's making the noise, so I point my camera at the ceiling and the flash lights it up. It was a great picture of water gushing out of the A/C vent in the ceiling. The laundry room is directly below my cabin and the flooding from my corridor leaked in and ruined the electrical motor that runs the A/C for the Deck 1 cabins. My corridor was without A/C for about a day.

8 am. They tell you that alcohol can make you more seasick but I swear that's what kept me feeling okay. Now that my buzz has worn off, I'm seasick in addition to having a hangover. I just feel awful. As I walk through the ship, especially at the front, I feel the cycle of the waves. The floor gives a slow, strong push that makes me walk with shorter and faster steps as the bow climbs a swell. Then my feet take slower steps and my stomach fills with butterflies as the bow descends down the back side of the swell. Then a boom that rattles

everything as the bow pierces the next wave to repeat the cycle.

I finally decide that I should get some sleep. I lie down on my left side and feel horrible. I lie down on my back and feel a little better. I lie down on my right side and feel the best that I can at the moment. The human stomach empties to the right so this must be why it feels better on that side.

1 pm. I wake up and take a shower in the dark and go do a little work although I am nauseous. I check on my cabin a little later and most of the water in the corridor and my cabin has been mopped up. I grab some towels to soak up the rest from my cabin. The diluted vomit sloshed all over the corridor and into everyone's room and left an awful rancid meat stench for days. I never did vomit myself.

The stage where all the shows take place was damaged pretty badly and they cancelled the shows for the rest of the cruise. The storm is over and we are now docked and all set to continue our regular schedule. I stand on the pier to look at the front of the ship. The paint has flaked off in various parts and the area around the anchor has rusted. Later, when I'm back on the ship, I notice at the very front of the ship on Deck 4, some stress bending and some places where welded joints have failed and broken apart and already rusted.

It lasted about 24 hours and was the best roller coaster I've ever been on. Most of the crew hated the rough seas, but I had a blast. Tom has been on ships for three years and has been through a number of hurricanes but said this was by far the roughest one he's been through.

I had a number of responses to that email. Here's what my mother replied with, and these are her exact words:

> I told you not to go down with the ship but I suppose I forgot to say 'Stay inside during a hurricane!' It was one of those 'duh, I thought you already knew that!' Haven't you ever heard of being swept overboard? You would have been a goner! Glad you enjoyed it but mostly I'm glad you survived it in spite of your ignorance.

Yes, mom.

Many passengers complained or were disappointed with that cruise, and I think Carnival gave everyone a partial refund. But if I were a passenger I'd actually pay extra for a hurricane cruise, and if Carnival could guarantee thirty-foot swells, I'd pay double.

☆ ☆ ☆

See pictures from my time at sea, and watch video of what happened inside the ship during the hurricane. Just go to Facebook and search for "The Truth About Cruise Ships."

☆ ☆ ☆

As luck would have it, the hurricane hit just a few weeks before the ship's biannual dry dock. Dry dock is where the ship sails into a basin that is drained, leaving the ship resting on supports and completely out of the water so that the underside can be serviced. Ships can also be wet docked if it doesn't need any work below the water line. Depending on the work list, ships can stay docked from two weeks to six months, and in either case, no passengers are onboard so repairs or changes happen throughout the ship. I couldn't wait to see all of this go down.

The ship pulled into Virginia at what is now Northrop Grumman Shipbuilding (NGS). The complex is worth some four billion dollars and is the largest privately owned ship-building facility in the United States. I was on deck as the ship pulled into the dock, and I stared up at a structure that towered above our 14-story ship. NGS has one of the largest cranes in the world, and it's operated from a 23-story-tall control station. The crane has a lifting capacity of 1,100+ tons and could pick up stuff within a 22-acre range. We parked right under it.

The dock that serviced us was the same one that launched the *USS Ronald Regan* aircraft carrier. The *Ronald Regan* wasn't in active service yet but was wet-docked nearby. The carrier's flight deck was a little longer and about twice as wide as the Carnival *Triumph*, but the two ships weighed about the same. Although the carrier's control tower was taller than the *Triumph*, the *Triumph* actually looked larger.

Aside from seeing the *Ronald Regan* and the giant crane, pulling into dry dock was anticlimactic. Everything moved at a snail's pace. Once the ship was inside and moored, the entry gates closed. Slowly. The water was then pumped out at a rational rate, which meant it took over twelve hours to drain. It was like watching grass grow. The enormity of what took place was fantastic—and seeing a cruise ship out of water was amazing—but watching us get to that point was boring.

We were docked across from Naval Station Norfolk in Norfolk, Virginia. Covering 4,300 acres, the base is the world's largest naval station and is a homeport to 75 ships and 134 aircraft. Annual traffic includes 3,100 ship visits and 100,000 flight operations. And it has nukes. Most of the carriers and subs are powered by onboard nuclear reactors, and the subs carried ballistic missiles armed with nuclear warheads. This, along with the fighter jets buzzing overhead, made it a cool place to be.

The shipyard we docked at also had nukes. NGS can build and service every type of nuclear-powered and nuclear-armed submarine, and it's the only U.S. shipyard capable of building an aircraft carrier as big as the *Ronald Regan*. With all of that firepower, security was tight and the crew was instructed not to take any pictures of the shipyard.

With the exception of a few cooks, waiters, and cabin stewards that had to stay to serve the crew, many of the crewmembers had little to no work. Some of the crew left for a three-week vacation or transferred to another ship during dry dock. The rest stayed onboard. The crew from the engine department was required to stay and worked long hours on the repairs. At least one I/S manager had to stay onboard at all times, but with no passengers, we didn't have much to do and it felt like my first time off in months.

The crew could leave the ship on a shuttle bus that came by every few hours. I took my camera one day, determined to get a forbidden picture. It was cloudy and rainy and the bus windows were fogged up so I wiped a spot on my window. I played with the camera settings to try to compensate for the low lighting. I wanted to time my picture to look down a cross street, and when I pushed the button, my flash went off right in front a blue security truck that was at the front of the cross street. I had just enough time to see that my picture was out of focus, poorly lit, and full of smeared fog before our bus was pulled over. The guard from the blue security truck said something to the driver. Then he looked down the row of seats.

"Who has the camera?" the guard asked as he faced everyone on the bus.

"That was me." I half-raised my hand.

"Please step forward."

I walked to the front of the bus with the camera in my hand, but with the memory stick safely hidden in my pocket. He could have my brand new $600 camera, but I was keeping that blurry picture.

"What's the problem, officer?"

"You can't take pictures in this complex."

"I'm sorry."

"I'm going to have to ask you for the film."

"It's a digital camera. I don't have any film."

"All right, then show me as you delete the picture." He was actually really cool about it.

I reached into my pocket and put the memory stick in the camera. I started pushing buttons to delete the picture, but he was talking to the driver and wasn't really watching me.

"Okay, all gone," I told him.

"Thank you. You guys have a good day," he said and then turned to step off the bus.

I walked back to my seat with a bus load of crewmembers watching me.

"Did you really delete the picture?" Sara asked.

"Nope. It may be blurry, but it's a keeper."

There wasn't much to do that was close to the shipyard. There were only a couple of dive bars and a few diners, but there was a topless bar where we could really feel like sailors.

There wasn't much to do on the ship either. The crew bar was closed, and crewmembers were prohibited from stockpiling alcohol to consume during dry dock. But JB spent so much time in the crew bar and, having befriended the bartender, worked out a deal. And so one night I helped JB carry down four cases of beer to get him through eighteen days of a closed crew bar.

"I think that will be enough," he said as we beheld our cabin fridge, stuffed with nothing but beer.

But after the first week, it was gone. All gone. Now to be fair, he didn't drink it entirely himself. He gave some away— a case at most. But he did drink the remaining three cases in seven days. When you do the math, it's only ten to twelve beers a day.

Completely out of alcohol and with eleven days left in dry dock, he called on his likeability factor once again and got the gift shop manager to loan him a couple of bottles of scotch. They were loaners because the gift shop wouldn't be able to enter the transaction until the shop registers opened at the end of dry dock.

The best part about dry dock was having the stage technician, Bud, take a small group of us to his parents' house about forty-five minutes away. We got to cook our own steaks on a patio, which just like the homemade lasagna in Canada, was a very big deal.

It always amazes me how people change in front of someone's mother. On the ship, we were drunken slobs who cursed liked sailors and lusted after anything that moved, but we all transformed into polite and considerate beings around Bud's mother. It was the same thing we did, I suppose, around any of the passengers. At Bud's house, everyone cleaned up after themselves, and we were all over-eager to help with the dishes.

I learned that Bud, who was about 5' 6" and 130 pounds, could kick all of our asses. He was a black belt in karate, and his mother had framed a picture of him doing an impressive flying side kick. You'd never guess it from the little guy that staggered through the crew bar and always carried two stacked Budweiser cans in one hand and a smoke in the other.

Bud used his mom's car to drive us to the club scene in Virginia Beach, and we met a larger group of crew that had to pay cab fare to get there. It was a 70-mile round trip, and even after splitting the cab fare four ways, it was still expensive for them; on top of that, we all bought drinks that were four times the price we paid in the crew bar. The local American girls were dying over the British and Australian accents and paid no attention to me. But it didn't matter because I got to cook steaks on a grill.

After clubbing, the five of us stayed at a hotel. The room was a mansion compared to the itty-bitty ship cabins. There were only two beds, but we weren't ready to sleep so we kept drinking. Then Dana got into a WWF wrestling match with one of the guys. It went on for fifteen minutes while the rest of us cheered them on. They were both exhausted, and when it stopped, the guy started coughing. It was a hard and painful-looking cough that went on for a full five minutes and left him red in the face with watery eyes. Like many of the crew, he was a heavy smoker. He was only twenty-five.

I was sitting on the bed, and despite all the noise and commotion, Bud had passed out next to me. I took some video of him snoring through the commotion of the wrestling match. We started winding down when I noticed that I was sitting in Bud's spilled beer. He fell asleep and we had to shake him awake. He grunted and slowly gained consciousness.

"Who the hell poured beer on me?" he demanded as he looked at his soaking wet boxers.

"Dude! That wasn't us. I think you pissed yourself!" I belted out, and we all broke into laughter.

The bed was soaked. It was going to sleep three of us, but he had peed right in the middle and it had spread too much for us to sleep on the edges. He lit a cigarette and tolerated me taking some pictures. Then he put on something dry, crawled back into his wet spot, and was snoring again in sixty-one seconds flat.

Dana and her wrestling opponent took the dry bed. Sara, the paymaster and fellow Monopoly player, gathered some dry blankets and I helped her spread them on the floor in between the wet bed and the wall. We had to share the covers because there weren't enough dry sheets for us to sleep apart. The space was narrow, but we were thin and our bodies fit just right. If the space had been any smaller we would have been uncomfortable, but if it had been any bigger we would have tacitly wished it were smaller. She and I were good friends with the just the right amount of sexual tension. We had never acted on it. We had never talked about it. But it was there, and it was why we didn't feel awkward lying so close to each other.

There was a pleasant anxiety as we each waited to see if the other would initiate something. Maybe fingers would brush the skin of a shoulder. Maybe a foot would creep. I was wearing boxers without a shirt. She had on black bottoms and a snug fitting black tank top.

"I'm taking my shirt off," Sara said after a few minutes of silence, "I can't sleep if I have clothes on. But I'll keep the bottoms on just to keep it decent."

Lucy was still my girlfriend, but she wasn't with us, and though I really enjoyed dating her, I wasn't emotionally attached. Lying next to Sara, I realized that this was the first time I'd ever been in a situation in which infidelity was a real possibility. Everyone else was in a deep, alcohol-induced coma. We had sufficient privacy between the bed and the wall. But in the end I stayed faithful out of principle. Sara and I fell asleep, and the night was over.

I was back on the ship the next day and slept there for the rest of dry dock. The ship was in shambles, with repairs and updates happening everywhere. Pallets of supplies were hoisted and crowded onto the open decks or fork-lifted through the hull doors, before being transported and dumped in a work area.

Thick, brown paper was rolled out from giant spools to protect every inch of carpet from spills and from the dirty shoes of contractors. Every section of tile was covered with plywood to shield it from the forklifts and from dropped tools. We stepped over 200-foot extension cords and all kinds of temporary tubing as we navigated around pallets and other crewmembers on the I-95.

Fumes dominated the ship's interior: paint fumes, carpet glue fumes, the smoke of welded steel, dust from steel grinding, and every other toxic byproduct of the restoration. And I don't deal well with fumes.

A few years after I left ships, Mirka painted our master bedroom, and I made us sleep in the guestroom for three months until there was no trace of paint in the air. I despise candles. Fragrance-free laundry detergent and fragrance-free bar soap are mandatory and I prefer that those around me don't wear cologne.

Oh yes. I'm that guy.

I inherited a keen sense of smell from my grandmother, who, like me, could smell the rain before it arrived. But my issues run deeper than the sense of smell because I'm more allergic to fumes than anyone I know. To put gas in the car, I start the flow, lock the handle, and walk upwind. Otherwise the gas fumes irritate my throat.

I am the canary in a coalmine.

Luckily, there were no fumes in my cabin during dry dock, and I tried to hold my breath in all the other polluted areas. I propped open every exterior door to bring in fresh air. It helped with the areas near the doors, but did nothing for the rest of the ship.

A year later my hiring manager asked me to join a team of ten other I/S managers at a shipyard in Italy to install the computer systems on a new ship. The ship wasn't complete, and I asked him if there were a lot of fumes like in dry dock. He said yes, and I said no. I would never be able to do that.

Dry dock was also noisy. Sound travels exceptionally well through steel, so one person armed with a steel grinder could wake up everyone, and there were hundreds of contractors all over the ship that were hammering, grinding, and sand-blasting.

The water supply was contaminated with rusty sediment that got stirred up from draining and cleaning the freshwater tanks. The first time I flushed with the rusty water, the toilet bowl filled up with orange that looked more soiled than before I had flushed. The water heaters were off so we had to take cold showers with that orange water, and sometimes we couldn't even do that because the water was turned off completely.

You can do anything to a ship during dry dock. In the '70s a vessel would go in as a rusty cargo ferry and come out as a shiny cruise ship. Some cruise ships have literally been cut in half to pop in an extra section that, like a stretch Hummer, extended the overall length and carrying capacity.

The biggest structural change to the *Triumph* during that dry dock was taking out two staircases in the disco and replacing them with a solid floor to help cut down on noise complaints from the nearby passenger cabins.

The entire hull below the water line was sandblasted and repainted. Much of the carpet was replaced, and some passenger cabins were refurbished. The engines were overhauled. The bow of the ship had been dented during the hurricane and a giant dent popper straightened it out.

The air vents went silent when the ventilation system was turned off. It got stuffy, especially in our cabins, where breath and wet shower stalls made it humid. Some ships went into dry dock in the Bahamas, where the sun and the heat made the interior so unbearable that the crew took their blankets and pillows and slept outside on deck. We were in Virginia in October, and though the air inside was unpleasant, it wasn't that bad.

✵ ✵ ✵

A couple of weeks after dry dock, Dana was sitting on a flight of metal crew stairs and chatting with some friends. She talked about her wrestling match back in the hotel and how good a wrestler she was.

"I could take you out," she said to one of the male crew-members.

"I'd like to see you try," he said while standing a few feet from her.

In a fit of drunken prowess, she lunged from the bottom stair but misjudged the distance and instead of a wrestling tackle, she landed in front of him with her face hitting the steel floor. Then she scrambled forward and wrapped herself around his ankles.

"See, I got you!" she said.

The next day she had a black eye from landing on the floor. It was two days before her parents were scheduled to cruise. When they arrived, she invited me to eat with them at their table in the passenger dining room, but I had strict instructions to go along with the story that she had merely bumped into a wall.

There was a Canadian casino girl who was constantly hammered, and one night we were hanging out backstage and walked past where the parrots were kept. These were highly trained parrots that belonged to cruise director Corey Schmidt, who performed an excellent show with them. When they weren't performing, the birds were kept in cages in a small room offstage. Corey told me that one of his birds was so highly trained that it was worth about $30,000.

The door was open so the Canadian girl walked in to look at the birds and tried to get them to talk.

"Polly want a cracker?" she asked.

The bird ignored her.

"What is your name?" she asked.

The bird still ignored her, so she poked it with the eraser end of a pencil to make it squawk, and it was at that moment Corey walked in. He yelled at her and she went running off.

On another day, Dana found the same Canadian girl passed out in a crew elevator. She was lying on her back with her feet poking out, causing the elevator to buzz because the doors couldn't close. They kept bumping into her legs and then opening back up.

JB came back to the cabin after the crew bar closed and opened the refrigerator to find it once again out of beer. He'd been drinking all night, but wanted more. I had an open bottle of Johnnie Walker Scotch Blue Label. On land it would cost $300, but the ship's duty-free gift shop sold it for $100, so I bought a bottle and shared it with Johnny Vancouver, JB, Dana, and anyone else that walked by my cabin that day. There was about a third of the bottle left that night and it was the only alcohol JB had access to at 2:30 in the morning. I told him he could have a little bit, but he didn't want just a little bit. I told him he could buy the rest of the bottle for $30.

Sold.

An intoxicated tongue cannot appreciate the taste of expensive alcohol, but there he was, drinking deep and straight from a bottle of Johnnie Blue. It's why I call him JB. He'd nearly finished the rest of the scotch before chugging a liter of water and passing out for the night.

CHAPTER 7

MY BIGGEST MISTAKE FROM WORKING AT SEA

The itinerary of some ships is scheduled to change throughout the year. Often when a ship changed its itinerary it also changed its homeport, and this was called repositioning. To maximize revenue, the cruise line sometimes booked passengers on these repositioning cruises. This meant that passengers would embark at one port and disembark at a different port, but often the ship sailed without passengers while repositioning.

The *Triumph*'s home port changed from New York City to Charleston, South Carolina after our time in dry dock. Then it changed again a couple of weeks later from Charleston to Miami. It only took a day to reposition the ship each time, so instead of booking passengers for a one-day cruise, the ship sailed empty.

I'd never heard the ship so quiet. I'd never seen it so empty. Even on embarkation day, during that three-hour window when no passengers were onboard, the passenger corridors were alive with cabin stewards and their cleaning supplies. But not during those repositioning cruises. There were no vacuum cleaners. No stomping kids. No trays of consumed food from room service. It was uncanny how barren the entire ship became with 3,000 fewer people onboard.

With little work to do, and finally well rested, the crew had the run of the ship. We took beers up to Lido Deck and relaxed like passengers. The passenger disco, normally off limits to the crew-ranked folks, opened up for a ship-wide crew party. It was standing-room-only at its peak, and I'd never seen it so busy.

During the first repositioning cruise, my manager's girlfriend walked up as I was watching everyone on the dance floor.

"Hey, what's up?" I asked, turning to face her.

"Nothing much," she replied.

"Where's your boyfriend?" I asked, as I hadn't seen Tom that night.

"I don't know," she said, scowling. "And who cares."

"What?"

"He doesn't treat me right."

"What do you mean?"

"He never asks me to spend time with him." She flicked her wrists, adding emphasis. "All he wants to do is get drunk with that roommate of yours."

"What else is there to do?" I asked, defending them both.

"We could spend time in port!" she fired back. "He can schedule his time off in port whenever he wants, but I can't and he never asks me when I'm off in port."

She was crew-ranked, and so her schedule was far less flexible than ours.

"Have you ever spent time in port together?" I asked.

"No. I had a free day in Halifax last week, but he said he had port-manning. He doesn't even try. I cannot believe what I put up with."

Her ten-minute rant was somewhat entertaining, so I just nodded and listened, knowing I'd tell Tom all about it the next day. She finally calmed down a little.

"So you want to get together?" she asked as she raised her brow and looked me up and down with those let's-get-it-on eyes.

"Um, I don't think so," I said chuckling. "Thanks, though."

And with that, she said goodbye and left for the night. I told Tom the next day.

"That's funny," he said. "But whatever. Go for it if you want."

"Nah, man, I wouldn't do that to a friend."

I was in the crew bar one night talking to a cabin stewardess who in the past month had given me the let's-get-it-on eyes herself a couple of times. She was telling me about how she had started seeing someone, but she didn't want to tell me who it was. It was supposed to be a big secret.

"Oh, you mean the staff captain?" I commented.

"How did you know?" she asked as she slapped her hands on the bar.

"Actually, I didn't. I was just joking. But now I guess I do know."

The secret was out, and she looked embarrassed. Then she gave me the let's-get-it-on eyes again, but I wasn't attracted to her and didn't want any problems with the staff captain so I passed.

There was a lot of casual sex among crewmembers. JB slept with a beautiful girl from Thailand who worked in the staff mess. At eighty pounds, she was so petite that it was practically illegal.

"Dude," he said to me after the first time "she is so small that her whole butt could fit in just one of my hands."

The stories were endless. I knew an American youth counselor who was dating one of the Italian engineers, and they snuck onto one of the suspended lifeboats one night to have sex. And I once stood at the front of the ship in a public area late at night with my arms spread out like in the movie *Titanic* while things happened. I even answered my pager while making love in my cabin once.

"Okay, did you reboot yet?" I asked the security officer over the phone while continuing my movements. "Did you check the network cable?"

Our itinerary changed to include an overnight stay in the Bahamas. Overnight stays were coveted because it gave the crew the rare chance to enjoy the island's nightlife without a curfew. Then our itinerary changed again to alternating seven-day Eastern and seven-day Western Caribbean runs. This diverse itinerary was ideal because we got to see more ports.

The first time we docked in St. Thomas, JB, having been out on deck already, came to the cabin to tell me about it. "This is what cruising is all about."

"What do you mean?"

"Get dressed. You got to see this."

I followed him out on deck and was met by a view unlike anything I had ever seen. I never knew that mountains could be covered in green vegetation while floating in crystal clear, teal-colored water.

Later than night, Johnny Vancouver was telling JB and me about Cozumel. We were to dock there for the first time on our next cruise. Neither JB nor I had been there before.

"Dude, Cozumel is crazy," Johnny Vancouver said. "There's so much drinking there that JB may die."

✵ ✵ ✵

It was time for my girlfriend Lucy to sign off. I had mixed feelings about this. We had a lot of fun together, and I was sad to see her leave. But at the same time, I was ready to go back on the hunt. I immediately started chasing Paulina again. One night after we had both been drinking, we kissed a little. Then I had to put her on hold once again.

I'd talked to a Lithuanian girl a little bit on the ship before we happened to be at the same beach in St. Thomas one day. We spent the day tanning and wrestling in the water. Few things are more fun than playing flirtatious water games with beautiful girls in the ocean. Salt water makes their skin shiny and slippery. She was in a bikini and I was in my bathing suit so there was a lot of skin-to-skin contact. I saw her in the crew bar a couple of days later, and after talking for a little while, we went back to my cabin. I lasted about two minutes and three seconds.

She came to the crew bar the next night around midnight when she finished her shift. We talked briefly and then went to her cabin this time.

She stopped before opening her cabin door. "I have something to tell you."

"What?" I asked.

"You have to promise not to get mad."

"Uh, well, I don't know if I can promise that because I don't know what you're going to say," I said, worried that this could really spoil our plans for the night.

"I won't tell you until you promise not to get mad." She looked at the linoleum and scraped off a scuff mark with her foot.

"It all depends on what you're about to say." I was going postal if she had herpes.

"It's nothing too bad." She looked up at me with innocent eyes. "Just promise to *try* not to get mad."

"All right. I promise to try not to get mad about whatever it is you want to tell me."

"Okay, I show you," she said and opened the door.

I quickly scanned the cabin. If it was something dangerous, I needed to be ready to react. But it was just a normal, cramped cabin. She grabbed something and handed it to me. They were 5x7 pictures. I flipped through all four of them and stopped when I was back at the first one.

"This is my daughter," she said as she pointed.

"So you have a kid, big deal." I said.

"And this my husband," she said, pointing again.

"You mean your ex-husband?"

"No, we're still married."

I flipped through the pictures again. This time looking more closely at the people in them. I didn't know what to do or how to respond. There was a guy and a child in one picture. Then the Lithuanian girl and the same child. Then all three of them in the last two pictures.

"This is my family. Does that bother you?" she asked.

"No," I lied, continuing to stare at the pictures.

"Are you sure? You not angry?" she asked, genuinely concerned.

"Yeah, I'm sure. Where is your daughter now?"

"She's in Lithuania with my parents."

Then she handed me more pictures and I flipped through more images of her family. I had my fill and handed them back. Then we climbed up to her top bunk.

She got completely naked. The lights were on this time, and I stared for a second. She was beautiful. Her skin was tanned and soft. She was nicely proportioned. She had imperfections, but she was confident in the light and that, of course, made her even more attractive to me. At the time I was reading a book about World War II and for some reason her figure and facial structures reminded me of the pictures I had seen of the European nurses from my book. I felt like I had been transported to the 1940s. That was pretty cool. And then we had sex, inches away from a wall covered with more pictures of her husband and her seven-year-old child.

That was pretty messed up.

I was trying to last longer because she seemed a little disappointed when it ended so soon the first time. I was doing okay but then she started moving too much, and thus it was over. Two minutes and seventeen seconds this time. She dropped her arms on the bed and rolled her eyes with a sigh. There was no question that she was disappointed this time.

"So I don't think we should see each other anymore," I said after we got dressed.

"What?" She didn't like that.

"Yeah, I think maybe we should just be friends."

"Why?" she said, still not liking this.

"Well, it bothers me that you're married. I didn't think it would, but it does."

"Why didn't you say that when I told you?" she asked, getting madder by the second.

I should have asked her to promise not to get mad before I told her. "Well, I didn't think it would bother me, but now I realize that it does."

It was true that it bothered me. It bothered me the moment she said it. If she had told me before we had sex the first time, and I wish she would have, then I definitely would have said no. But this time my drunken mind was full of lust and justified that since we had already been together, one more time wouldn't change anything.

This was my biggest mistake from working at sea because it did change something. What it changed was that I was now someone who had knowingly slept with a married woman. I had consciously decided to be with her one more time before ending it. Though I didn't realize it back then, the abundance of sex in the ship's environment was clearly taking its toll on my character.

"You're making me feel bad. You're making me feel like a whore," she said, now visibly upset.

"No, no," I said, trying to do damage control. "This is about me, not you."

"But if what you did was wrong, then what I did was worse."

133

"No, no. This is just me and how I think and what I want to do." I wasn't making it any better.

We went back and forth for a few minutes and at the time, I couldn't understand how my reaction affected the way she felt. She could live however she wanted and I just didn't want to be a part of it. I was succeeding only in digging myself deeper, so I left.

I saw her a few days later in the crew bar. Because it was early in the night, the music wasn't very loud and we could have a conversation and still keep our distance.

"Hi," I said.

"Hi," she said back.

"So are you getting off in port tomorrow?" On land, you ask co-workers what they're doing over the weekend. On ships, you ask if they're getting off in port.

"Not tomorrow, but in a couple days I will." Though reserved, she was being very mature. "We'll be docking next to the *Fascination*, which is where my husband is. It's been a few months, and I'll finally get to see him."

"That's fantastic," I said and meant it.

She finished her drink and said goodbye.

About a week later I saw her in the crew bar again. We stood at the bar in the same places as last time and, like before, it was early in the night and we could comfortably talk at a distance.

"How was your visit with your husband?"

"It was nice."

"Did he last longer than me?" I chuckled as I said this. I thought that belittling myself would somehow atone for making her feel bad.

"That is private." She snapped with a scowl. "Don't ask questions like that. Just leave it alone."

I didn't understand how she could share the most private thing she owned, her body, and then get mad when I asked a question. Logically, that made no sense. Emotionally, it made perfect sense. But there is nothing logical about emotion. I understand that a little better now that I am married and have experienced romantic love, but back then I had no insight into what was making her so angry. I just can't imagine what a relationship with her would have been like. What would I have done and how would I have felt when she told me that we couldn't hang out in port together because she was going be with her husband?

✡ ✡ ✡

Every ship had an Internet café for the passengers and a separate one for the crew. It was how the crew kept in touch with their family back home and their friends and spouses who were on other ships. I was one of ten people on the ship that had free Internet access. It was great, but the speed of the satellite connection was as slow as a dial-up connection. Still, I was able to order some flowers online to be delivered to mom for Christmas.

The other way crew kept in touch was to go to the row of payphones at the embarkation terminal and use a phone card. They could even call from the ship phone, but at $3 a minute, most people didn't. Passengers could call land as well. I saw the revenue statement from one of my ships. It had earned $15,000 that month from ship-to-shore calls.

I was one of about twenty crewmembers who had a phone with free access. I had to be able to contact the shore-side I/S department for work purposes, but I also sneaked in some free calls to family on occasion. I called mom and dad to wish them Merry Christmas when the ship was at sea. My personal cell phone only worked in U.S. ports, and though I could only use it one day a week, I preferred this to using the ship phones. The ship phones went over the satellite and the connection wasn't that great and was prone to dropping calls.

The *Triumph* had an A/V system that let passengers order and watch movies from the TV menu in their cabins. The crew TVs couldn't do this but as I/S managers, we were in charge of that system. In the computer room we had a bank of over fifty VCRs with multiple tapes for each movie, which meant we could take a few to watch in our cabin.

JB loaned one of the tapes to a girl in the cabin next to us. A couple of days later, a different person asked to borrow one. Before we knew it, everyone was asking JB to borrow a tape. At one point we had about twenty tapes out on loan, and then JB put a stop to it. It was inconvenient to administer, and we'd have some explaining to do if one of the tapes went missing.

In addition to the workout facility the passengers used, there was a crew gym. Officers and staff could use either gym, but the crew-ranked folks were restricted to the crew gym. Since ships rocked back and forth during rough seas, I was surprised to see the gyms stocked with free weights. It didn't seem very safe, but I was glad to have them. The crew gym on the *Triumph* was small and had very little ventilation. It always smelled of sweat, but it was downright unbearable when Smelly Guy was there.

Smelly Guy was a crew-ranked chap from the Philippines and always came to the gym already in need of a shower. He'd get on the treadmill for twenty minutes and work up a nice sweat before lifting weights for another thirty minutes. The air would become so acrid that I could taste his stench. It hung in the air for a good twenty minutes after he left. One time after Smelly Guy left, the lingering stench sent a bridge officer into a raging fit of Italian expletives.

The crew had the opportunity for self-improvement in the crew training center. Most of the lessons were computer-based, but there were lesson books as well. There were tutorials for languages, math, and computer skills such as Microsoft Excel and Microsoft Word. The room only had about a dozen computers, but that was plenty because only about 10% of the crew ever went there.

The only people crewmembers could really get to know were other crewmembers. They could meet plenty of passengers, but every passenger was a short-timer who would be gone in a few days. Passengers were people we'd never see again, except in those rare instances in which a crewmember would stay in touch with one of his passengers. Otherwise, crewmembers were friends and coworkers and neighbors. The don't-date-coworkers rule didn't apply because there was no distinction between work friends and regular friends, and this was another major difference between land life and ship life.

Friendships developed at lighting speed because the crew spent so much time together. There was no getting away from one another. We worked, partied, and ate together every day, seven days a week.

Everyone, I think, has three personalities. There is a personality at work, a personality at play, and a personality around a love interest. When you know someone in all of these settings, you get a more complete picture of who they are. I only know a couple of land-based friends to such a degree, but I knew lots of crewmembers this way.

A work personality is reserved. People censor their actions and words to maintain that professional persona. Company-sponsored social events can give you a glimpse into someone's personality at play, especially if alcohol is involved, but even then most people hold back and you rarely get to know their personality at play.

A play personality is relaxed. If you haven't worked with any of your regular friends, then you won't know their work personality. Are they hard workers or lazy? What do their colleagues think of them? Do they brown-nose the managers?

A personality around a love interest can be many things. Guys can be tamer. They can be uncomfortable. Girls can soften. Some couples latch onto each other. Some guys bear hug their honey and focus solely on her. Some guys look at other girls. Comments and actions are often different when someone is with or away from a love interest, and this gives you extra insight into who they are.

I was with crewmembers in all three personalities multiple times a day. I saw couples both together and apart. I worked with people in the morning and then partied with them at night. Even the closest of friends on land rarely interact this way, and it might take years to know a few people on land the way you know dozens of people on the ship in a few months.

☼ ☼ ☼

People connect with their own kind. It's why passengers cheer when someone from their home state is introduced on stage. It's why a tourist will talk more with someone from their hometown than with someone from the country they paid to visit. Even though there were sixty nationalities on the ship, the crew got along very well and everyone had friends from many other countries. Nonetheless they always connected more strongly with their own nationality, and I think one of the main reasons for this was language.

Even though English was the universal language onboard, each nationality put its own accent on it, and unless you're used to it, differently stressed syllables can make a word incomprehensible. Understanding everyone took effort, especially if English wasn't their first language. After four months, I could understand most of the accents without making people repeat themselves. It was a skill that continued to improve the entire time I was on ships.

But even when I understood the words, I didn't always get the meaning. I often had to ask questions to clarify. It required patience because non-native speakers took longer to convey thoughts. They spoke with inefficient sentences and often struggled to remember a word.

For example, an Italian bridge officer beeped me one day, and when I was unable to understand him over the phone, I walked up to his office.

"So what's wrong?" I asked once I got there.

"He no checka my email," he said.

"Okay, so did *you* try to check your email?" I asked, wondering why I was talking to this guy, if it was someone else's problem.

"He should open dis program," he said with flailing arms, "and checka my email."

"Who else sits at your desk and checks your email?"

"He no checka my email," he said, ignoring my question.

"Who?"

"Zee computer," he said with one final swoop of his hands.

Finally it clicked. This Italian had a loose grasp of pronoun usage. So I replaced "he" with "it" and it made more sense.

"He no checka my email," converted to, "It isn't checking my email," or "The computer isn't checking my email," or simply, "My email doesn't work."

It also took time and patience to be understood. I learned to speak slowly with simple words. If I asked, "Was the transition to ship life easy?" and they responded with, "What?," I'd replace "transition" with "adjustment" or "get used to." Or I would restructure the entire question and ask, "When you first joined the ship, was it hard to be away from home?"

Once I learned to be understood, I realized that many passengers did not know how to be understood. They would just repeat the same wording two and three times, with that condescending tone that is loud and slow. "Was theeee transition toooo ship life eeeasy?"

No matter how much effort it took on my part, it always took more effort for the non-native speakers. It's harder to speak a foreign language than to be understood by someone who speaks your language. English was not the first language of many crewmembers, and after laboring to speak it all day, they craved their native tongue. It was the only time when conversation was easy.

And so I think that effortless conversation was why crewmembers from the same country bonded so strongly. Even though I spoke English all day, I still craved conversation with a native speaker whose accent matched mine. And after working on ships, it never offended me when foreigners spoke their language in front of me.

☆ ☆ ☆

As I/S managers, we were isolated from shore-side management. They never knew what happened unless we told them or someone complained. Ships that sailed from Miami received some scrutiny because shore-side management could board once a week. When the *Triumph* repositioned to Miami, we cleaned the computer room for the first time since I'd been there because our shore-side manager was coming to inspect.

His name was Brant Anderson, and he had a military background. When Colin Powel was the Chairman of the Joint Chiefs of Staff, Anderson was his communications aid. He was one of the most entertaining guys I'd ever worked for. His favorite movie was *Full Metal Jacket,* and he could quote it line for line. He included sound bytes of the movie in his emails, and JB, having just bought the movie himself, started replying with follow-up quotes and we had a good laugh with some of those exchanges. Anderson's email signature included quotes like, "We help you get your ship together," and "Like scrubbing bubbles, we work hard so you don't have to." It was true, he did work hard at taking care of all the I/S managers in the fleet.

I had been on the *Triumph* for five months when Anderson sent me an email one day.

"You'll be disembarking the *Triumph* at oh-eight-hundred hours in five days. I'm going to put you on a bird to Cozumel, where you'll take command of the *Holiday*'s computers."

He heard that I wasn't very busy on the *Triumph,* and since Dipsu had spoken so highly of me, Anderson didn't want to waste me on a ship that had little work to do. Thanks a lot Dipsu.

Johnny Vancouver's contract ended the same day as mine did.

"Hey, Sara," he said when she showed up for our Monopoly game that week. "I'm signing off at the next home port. So you want to kick it?" Then, "Hey, Dana," he said when she showed up a few minutes after Sara. "I'm signing off in Miami. So you want to kick it?"

It was a running joke he said to every girl he knew for the next five days.

It had only been two weeks since I'd broken it off with the married Lithuanian girl, and Paulina and I had kissed a couple more times. But despite my efforts, it wasn't going anywhere.

I took an interest in Sara one night in the crew bar. "Hey, I'm leaving in two days. So you want to kick it?"

Sara took a sip of her Corona.

Then she looked at me and said, "You mean like at the hotel when I was next to you half naked and you didn't make a move?"

"I was with Lucy! I didn't want to cheat on her," I said in my defense.

She shrugged, and our conversation got distracted as Dana walked over.

A few minutes later I was about to go up and flirt with Sara some more to let her know I was serious, but then Johnny Vancouver and I started talking to Heather, the production singer from Chicago.

Before I knew it, he and I were taking turns kissing Heather on the neck as we stood in the crew bar. It was a spur of the moment contest to see who the better neck kisser was, and she was the judge. Johnny Vancouver won. But then, sensing that Heather had taken an interest in me, he shuffled away into the crowd.

She was forty years old and looked fantastic. Forty. It's a magical age for women. It's when you can playfully make fun of their age and they don't get offended. And once they hit forty, they don't mess around. They play no games. It's been my experience that if they want to sleep with you, then they tell you right away. If they don't, they tell you right away. It's that simple. I was twenty-eight, and it was the perfect age. Not too old. Not too young. Available for all.

I was flirting. Heather allowed it. She didn't exactly flirt back, not in the way a twenty-year-old girl would giggle and feel flattered at the attention. Instead, she held my gaze with a suspicious eye as I talked her up for about five minutes. Then she lost her patience.

"So do you just want to have sex or what?" she asked with a slight frown, continuing to hold my gaze.

"Uh, that's not necessarily what I meant," I said with a nervous chuckle, not knowing how to respond. I couldn't tell if it was an invitation or if she was offended.

She said nothing and kept looking at me, her expression unchanged.

"You look fantastic, and I am attracted to you," I went on, trying to answer with a yes and a no at the same time. "But I don't want you to think that I'm just interested in one thing."

Heather crossed her arms without changing her expression.

"It does sound tempting and all," I continued, saying the same thing in a different way, "but that's not necessarily the type of person I am."

"All right, well, I'm going to my cabin," she said. "Do you want to have some fun or what."

I looked down and couldn't help but smile as the flush filled my cheeks. I contemplated for a second—exactly one second. I didn't want to seem too eager.

"Okay," I said, still smiling as I looked back at her and nodded.

"All right, give me about ten minutes and then come to my cabin," she said, waiting for a response.

"Okay."

I figured she wanted to hop in the shower for a quick rinse. Older girls are so smart. I decided that it was such a good idea that I went to my cabin and hopped in for a quick rinse of my own.

I grabbed some protection and the crinkled tube and then sat down. I watched the clock and waited for the ten-minute mark. I couldn't believe it was going to happen like this. I got up and walked to her cabin, still smiling. Production singers had their own cabins, so we wouldn't have to worry about a roommate. I knocked on the door.

She had a regular bed, not a bunk bed, and it was twice the size of mine. Her cabin even had a porthole. She was wearing thin jogging pants and a small T-shirt. Nothing fancy, but still fashionably feminine.

"Hi," I said.

"Hey, come in," she said.

She closed the door and I immediately put my hands on her waist and leaned in. We started kissing. We undressed and went right to it. There was none of that first date, first kiss awkwardness.

Three minutes and five seconds.

Heather wasn't as conspicuously disappointed as the Lithuanian, but I did sense an unspoken displeasure, and that was aggravating. She talked about getting ready to sleep and asked if I wanted to stay with her or sleep in my cabin.

But I had a better idea—a stroke of genius really.

"We're not going to bed," I proclaimed. "Just give me about twenty minutes and then we'll have Round Two."

"Oh," she said, a little surprised. "Well, okay."

And that is how I learned to last. Thirty minutes for Round Two. An hour and a half for Round Three. We went all night until dawn—*dawn*—and it was amazing. It was sex for the sake of sex. And she was talking dirty. Actually she was screaming it. She was dropping F-bombs all over the place. Repeatedly commanding me with her F-bombs. When she wasn't articulating dirty phrases, she was belting out moans in all directions. And as the production singer, she had some serious pipes. I was sure security was going to knock on the door at any minute.

We collapsed after Round Three and stared at the ceiling, exhausted.

"You're a nice surprise," she said catching her breath. "Where were you three weeks ago? I could have lost ten pounds."

I'm not sure what was better, the sex or hearing her say that. If there is one thing a man likes to hear, it's a compliment on his sexual prowess, whether it's true or not.

Then she got up and looked at her hair in the mirror. It had been an aerobic workout, which was awesome and new for me, and with all the sweat and heat she looked at me and said, "You did me so hard that you curled my hair."

I could have married her on the spot.

But she and I were both ready to be alone and simply sleep. I went back to my cabin and fell into a deep coma until noon. It was my last day on the ship, and I saw her in the crew bar early in the night.

"Hey, what's up?" I said, walking up to Heather.

"Hey, there," she said. "I'm a little surprised that you didn't ignore me."

"Why would I do that?"

"Some guys would."

I shrugged.

"So are you coming over again tonight?" she asked.

"You're goddamn right I am," I said. "But this is my last night on the ship. Would you mind if I partied with my friends for awhile first?"

"Not at all. Just come over when you're ready."

So I drank and partied for the next six hours and then knocked on her door at 1:00 AM.

It was a repeat of the night before. More phenomenal drunken monkey sex. It was good. It was shake your head good. There was more dirty talk, although not as loudly as before because I mentioned how surprised I was that none of her neighbors complained.

Idiot.

Three more rounds and once again the sun was up. We said our goodbyes and I got an hour of sleep in my cabin before I had to wake up and sign off the ship.

Anderson greeted me at the gangway and walked me to the shuttle bus.

"So how is that roommate of yours doing?" he asked.

"He's great. We got along really well, and I'll miss him."

"I hear he drinks a lot."

"He's not the only one." I was referring to me and trying to cover for him.

"Well, hell, ain't that the truth," he said. "I have a lot of alcoholics working for me."

"That doesn't bother you?"

"I don't care. As long as they get their job done and it doesn't affect the service the passengers receive, there isn't much else I can do."

"It's probably unavoidable."

"Yeah, I hear you."

The shuttle took me to my hotel, and after unpacking, I took a shower and walked over to corporate headquarters. There was a senior manager there, a couple of levels above Anderson, and I chatted with him as I sat in his office with red eyes and sheet burns on my ankles.

CHAPTER 8

SHIP SOCIOLOGY - HOW PEOPLE REALLY ACT WHEN NO ONE IS WATCHING

I spent a few days working at the corporate office, and it was a welcome reminder of normal land life. When 5:00 p.m. arrived, I got to physically leave without a pager. When I went to a bar, I saw people I didn't recognize and I didn't have to eat during a scheduled meal time. When the weekend arrived, I actually had two days of zero work.

I had lined up an interview for a friend from college named Brandon, and the timing was perfect. We hung out for the night and shared a hotel room. It was a connection to my previous life, and that in itself was a vacation. He nailed the interview and got the offer that day, and that gave me a land-based friend to share the ship experience with.

Like quitting a job or moving to a new city, I was sad to leave my friends on the *Triumph*. But at the same time, it was a nice change and I only wish it would have happened two weeks sooner so that I would have been on the *Holiday* when the thrusters malfunctioned and the ship drifted onto a sand bar in Playa del Carmen. The captain couldn't free the ship, so the remainder of the cruise was cancelled. All passengers were flown home except for a few who were afraid to fly and refused to board an airplane. Carnival put them up in a hotel until another Carnival ship was in the area that could float them back to the states. After three days, and with the help of the tide, the ship was finally freed. Maybe not quite as fun as the hurricane, but I wish I could have been there.

While I was at the Miami airport en route to the *Holiday*, I scanned the line at my terminal looking for fellow crewmembers.

They're easy to spot. Their clothes are non-American, they travel alone, and they carry multiple giant suitcases.

"You work for Carnival?" I asked as I walked up to a girl who fit the profile.

"Yes, I do," she said with a British accent.

"Are you going to the *Holiday*?"

"Yes. You, too?"

"Yep."

"Hey," someone else called out after overhearing us. "You guys going to the *Holiday*, too?"

Within ten minutes, there were five of us, and we were all headed to the *Holiday* except for one guy who was going to the *Victory*. We landed in Cozumel and the five of us piled into a shuttle.

The one guy slotted for the *Victory* was Italian. Carnival's bridge and engine officers were almost exclusively Italian. They were a proud group, and there were almost no Italians in any other department. But this guy was to be a waiter, and the *Victory* would be his first ship.

"I wish I was going to the *Holiday,* too," the Italian said, looking on as the rest of us laughed and got along so well.

"No, man," we replied. "The *Victory* is a much nicer ship. We all wish we were going there. Don't worry, you'll meet plenty of people."

His lack of confidence reminded me of how I felt on my first ship. I never saw him again, but with his low social confidence and crew-ranked status, I'd bet the Italian officers chewed him to pieces.

When I saw the *Holiday* for the first time, I couldn't believe how small it was. It was half the size of the *Triumph*. The *Holiday* maxed out at around 1,800 passengers whereas the *Triumph* could carry 3,600. A few months later, the two ships were parked next to each other in Cozumel, and again I was forced to refer to the *Holiday*, a 46,000-ton vessel, as really small.

I stepped on the ship and walked through a narrow crew corridor looking for the I-95. I was confused and I couldn't find it. Then I realized that I was on it. It was half the width of the *Triumph*'s I-95. I walked from the starboard hull to the port hull and couldn't believe how narrow the ship was.

As small as it was, I got lost all over again. The layout was different, and every bar and lounge had a different name. I had almost learned the deck names and numbers on the *Triumph,* but once again, they had all changed. What used to be Empress Deck 7 was back to Empress Deck 4, and after that, I gave up on trying to remember it all. I was thirty years old before I could tell you that September was month nine without counting it out on my fingers. So I stood no chance of learning these changing deck names every few months. I knew Lido was Deck 10, but that was it.

Because it was so small, the *Holiday* was normally staffed with only one I/S manager whereas almost all of the other ships had two or three. It meant that I wouldn't report to anyone, and I could do my job on this ship however I saw fit. On the other hand, it also meant that I wouldn't have a more experienced I/S manager who could split the workload and know all the answers to the things I was still learning.

But when I signed on the *Holiday*, there were two I/S managers. They had been sent to clean up the mess from Mr. Temper who was the previous I/S manager. Since the *Holiday* sailed out of New Orleans, our managers from Miami rarely saw the ship. With little supervision, Mr. Temper got away with being lazy and had left too much unfinished work for one person to do. One of the two I/S managers signed off at the next port, but the other one, a guy named Nolan, stayed on for another five-day cruise to help me transition.

Nolan was quintessentially Irish, complete with red hair, fair skin, and an accent that made comprehending him a struggle, at least for me. There weren't many Irish crewmembers so his accent was unfamiliar and he had to slow down and repeat sentences for me.

He'd been on ships for eight years and had worked in a couple of departments before becoming an I/S manager. He started off as a chef, and when we walked through the galley, he knew half of the chefs from having worked with them in the past.

He had been on ships for so long that he could walk onto any ship and know at least fifty crewmembers. He was liked and respected by everyone, including me, and very helpful in preparing me to take over the ship.

"Dude, you should have seen it when we got here," the two of them said when I stood in my new cabin for the first time with a disgusted look on my face.

"There is junk everywhere. It was worse?" I asked.

"Oh, yeah," they replied. "We already threw out two full bags of trash."

"Seriously?"

"Yeah, dude, we even picked up the dirty underwear for you. You should be thanking us."

"Well... thank you."

The mess in my cabin was reflective of everything Mr. Temper had touched. The computer room had boxes and broken hardware stacked to the ceiling. I'm not exaggerating. It was literally piled up to the ceiling, and I actually had to hop over a pile of junk to get to my office chair.

"You'll probably hear other crewmembers complain about him," my shore-side hiring manager said, referring to Mr. Temper. "I just ask that you try to ignore it and not ask for details."

But I didn't have to ask. Everyone volunteered the details. Almost every department I visited had issues that had been unresolved for weeks, and when I showed up they told me all about what a jackass Mr. Temper had been.

"Whenever we beeped him to fix the security machines," one security guard told me, "he just showed up and kicked the machine."

"You mean like lightly tapping in a joking way?" I asked.

"No, he yelled and really kicked it. Kicked it hard."

"Wow," I said as I began fixing his network cable.

The cable was similar to a phone cord, and whenever the release clip broke, the cable kept falling out of the wall jack.

"What are you doing to the cable?" the security guard asked. "It's broken."

"I'm replacing the connector," I said, handing the repaired cable to him. "See? All better."

"The other guy just threw the whole cable away," he said as he stared, dumbfounded, at the shiny new connector.

"You mean he'd throw away a hundred-foot cable every time?"

"Every time."

I had other people telling me how violently he kicked and cursed their PCs as part of his repair method. I also heard that after an argument between two crewmembers in the crew bar, he yelled at the top of his drunken lungs that he was the highest ranking officer in the bar and that he was ordering everyone to leave. But this wasn't the military and everyone just ignored him.

The main difference between Mr. Temper and me was that I had patience and was cordial to the crew when they asked for help. He was at the end of his contract and was burned out.

Back on the *Triumph,* I carried the pager with confidence partly because I had learned the systems, but mostly because I always had Tom, who knew how to do everything. Nolan also knew how to do everything and he was my safety net on the *Holiday*. It was okay if I didn't know the answer because he always did.

But Nolan's last day eventually arrived, and after shaking his hand and saying goodbye, I sat in the computer room and the magnitude of my responsibility set in: 2,500 passengers and crew depended on the computers and holy crap I was the only person onboard to keep them working.

It was pretty stressful to think about, especially since I still didn't know how to fix it all. There were systems that didn't break until Nolan left, and again I got that unpleasant feeling of not knowing the answers that my job title suggested I should know.

It took a month on the *Holiday*—a full seven months into my contract—to finally get comfortable admitting that I didn't know the answers to everything. One day it just clicked. I didn't have to know all the answers, at least not on the spot. I just had to know how to find the answers. Usually this meant looking something up online or talking to the right I/S person in Miami.

"I don't know, but I'll find out and get back to you," I'd say, armed with my new mindset. That one sentence released me from the new-hire stress I'd hauled around up to this point.

One of my other challenges was to quit emailing the *Triumph* pursers. I interacted with the pursers more than any other department and emailed them multiple times a day. After five months on the *Triumph*, I could type their email address faster than my own password. Muscle memory took over and for my first month on the *Holiday* I kept emailing the *Triumph* pursers when I meant to email the *Holiday* pursers. They'd reply, telling me that once again I'd emailed the wrong ship.

One of the cruise directors had a similar problem. He kept getting on the *Holiday*'s stage in front of thousands of passengers, saying, "Welcome to the *Carnival Destiny*."

The crewmembers on the small ships were less segregated than on the large ships. This is what everyone on the *Triumph* kept telling me when I first learned of my transfer. I didn't understand how it was possible to be less segregated because everyone on the *Triumph* already seemed very friendly. In my opinion, the different departments already mingled. As an I/S manager my department was very small, and I always spent time with the other departments.

But on larger ships like the *Triumph,* many departments had reached critical mass, and except for boyfriends and girlfriends and occasional conversations, crewmembers mostly socialized within their departments. Although I didn't notice it while I was there, dancers partied with dancers, shoppies partied with shoppies, and so on for the medium-sized departments like the casino, the spa, the youth staff, the photographers, and the pursers. Then I saw how different it was on the *Holiday.*

On the *Holiday*, the departments were half the size and lacked enough people to compose a self-socializing group. As a result, there was a lot more interdepartmental mingling. Steiners with shoppies, casino folks with dancers, and so on. Big departments, like the ones that included the waiters, the cabin stewards, and the Italian officers, still had enough people that they mostly kept to themselves.

The ship culture was a lesson in sociology. And because of the closed environment, these group tendencies were more easily observed. What really got me was that even after experiencing the more friendly nature of smaller ships, most crewmembers rejoined their respective cliques back on the larger ships.

✳ ✳ ✳

I was onboard when Bob Dickinson, then Carnival's president and CEO, came to visit the *Holiday*. He brought a posse of senior vice presidents from the corporate office, and after a cursory inspection of the ship, he held a group meeting with the ship's department heads and managers.

One of the lounges was roped off, and folding rectangular tables were set up to seat all fifty of us in a big square formation, with Bob at the front center. I took my seat and the meeting went something like this:

"Okay, thanks for coming, everyone," Bob said as he kicked off the meeting. "I try to visit each ship at least once a year to hold this meeting. It helps me stay connected to the fleet, and it gives the department heads a chance to make suggestions for improvement.

"After our meeting, I'll hold another one for the rest of the crew and give them a chance to speak up about any improvements they would like to suggest. I can't promise that every suggestion will be implemented, but we do make every effort to honor reasonable requests.

"For example, televisions were installed in every cabin as the result of a suggestion. We also did much to curb the onboard bribery because of a waiter who complained. For those who don't know, bribery used to be rampant on ships. Waiters, for example, would pay the maître d' to get assigned to the best-tipping tables. I'm sure it still happens to some extent, but by mandating that anyone getting caught would be fired, we were able to significantly reduce it."

That was the first I'd heard of the bribery, and I was impressed that the CEO would visit each ship and invite complaints, especially since there was probably so much redundancy from each ship. Bob went through his agenda for the meeting, and one by one, everyone in the room had their chance. One of the complaints involved the captain.

When this captain had joined the ship, he set two new rules. The first was that crewmembers had to wear their nametags anytime they left their cabins. All the other captains I had worked with required the crew to wear their nametags only in the passenger areas. We all grumbled over this rule because it

154

made our leisure time feel less like time off and reminded us of our inescapable servitude to the ship. But we did have a good laugh when one of the social hosts took off his shirt in the crew bar and stuck his nametag through the hole he normally used for his nipple ring.

The second rule from the new captain was that higher-ranked employees were not allowed to eat in a lower-ranked mess hall. This was a definite invasion of the crew's leisure time and did not go over well. A few weeks before Bob's meeting, I was alone with the captain in his cabin and had just finished working on his computer when I asked him about his eating rule. He told me that as someone with a military background he didn't think it was appropriate for employees of a different rank to eat together.

During Bob's meeting, a girl from the onboard crew training center complained about this rule. Bob shook his head, confused as to why this was being brought up.

"Well, the rule is that higher-ranked crew can eat in the lower-ranked mess halls, but not the other way around," Bob said.

"Yes, but that isn't the rule on this ship," the crew trainer insisted.

"Why isn't that the rule on the ship?" Bob said, turning his head to the captain.

"It is not so much a rule as it is my preference," the captain said.

"Why is this your preference?" Bob persisted.

"I just think that people of the same rank should eat together."

"Yes, well, I'd like to give the crew a chance to eat with whom they'd prefer. Will that be okay with you?" Bob asked.

"Yes, of course," the captain said, defeated.

That was the only time I ever saw someone tell the captain what to do.

It was freaking awesome.

☆ ☆ ☆

I would later read from Bob Dickinson's book, *Selling the Sea,* that ships staffed by sexy and socially competent captains sold more cabins. Even if it's not with the captain, and say, only between passengers, there is no question that sex is one of the main activities onboard. *Cosmopolitan* magazine conducted a survey and found that 80% of the passengers polled felt more sexually excited at sea than they did on land. If you've been a passenger, then maybe you know the feeling. I think most cruise passengers do, even if they aren't aware of it. If that's true, then why? What is so seductive about a cruise?

I think it's because the ship environment is so different than what people are used to on land. First-time passengers have it the best because everything is new, but almost every passenger reaps the benefits from leaving their land-based routine. Maybe it's their land-based stagnation. On a cruise you get to see, smell, taste, hear, and touch so many things that are unavailable or uncommon on land. The drastic change in the environment stimulates all five senses. With the brain so stimulated, dopamine levels rise. Dopamine makes you feel good. It stimulates the libido. And then it's time to get your sex on.

Carnival, as a corporation, did everything it could reasonably do to prevent the crew from sleeping with the passengers. According to policy, crewmembers who were caught were supposed to be fired. It made good business sense because it was a liability if passengers were ever sexually harassed.

Even though it was company policy to not sleep with the passengers, it happened so often that we had a nickname for it.

It was called "coning," from the infinitive "to cone." Passengers were referred to as "cones." Some say it's because during boat drill, the passengers look like the neon orange traffic cones, but others say it's from the 1993 movie *Coneheads* where, just like the aliens in the movie, passengers ate everything in sight.

Many passengers had nothing against a romantic encounter with a crewmember. Some preferred it. Some found it enhanced their vacation. Getting caught did not guarantee that a crewmember would get fired. There was a shade of gray, and politics governed such situations. A crew-ranked crewmember was more likely to get fired than an officer. A male crewmember might be more likely to get fired than a female crewmember. If a passenger filed an official complaint, then it usually didn't matter who it was because he or she would probably get fired, but otherwise it was at the discretion of those who enforced the rules. If you were caught by a security officer who liked you, there was a chance he wouldn't report it.

"I don't care if you cone," the chief of security once told me. "Just don't cause an incident."

I knew an onboard golf pro who managed to cone at least one passenger on every cruise. We were doing five-day cruises, and during his entire six-month contract, there were only three cruises that he failed to sleep with a girl.

"Have you ever been caught?" I asked him in the staff mess one night during dinner.

"Oh, yeah," he said. "Twice, in fact."

"Did you have to go see the staff captain?"

"Oh, absolutely."

"What happened?"

"I sat down across from his desk and he said, 'Now you understand the rules, right?' I said, 'Yes sir, I understand the rules.' Then he leaned forward on his desk and said, 'Now just don't get caught!'"

"Did you get written up for it?" I asked.

"He just told me not to get caught, and then he sent me on my way."

The Italians were usually hunting for girls in the disco on formal night. I also knew a DJ from Canada—not Johnny Vancouver but a different one—who told me about the time he coned a passenger in the sound booth. After they finished, she wanted to stay with him.

"No, girl, you got to go!" he said as he held out her clothes. "We can't hang out or else I'll get caught."

I knew a room stewardess—a beautiful Hungarian—who told me all about the passenger she had coned.

"Is the first time I done this," she told me.

"Oh, yeah? Were you worried about getting caught?"

"No, because he was in cabin I was assigned to clean. It was easy to get away with it."

"That's cool."

"Yeah, but listen," she went on. "This guy was total loser."

"Was he dorky looking?"

"What do think I am? Of course not. He was very cute."

"So why was he such a loser?"

"He stand like this," she said as she mimicked him by holding her hands in the air, "then he start moving like this," she said, her long, dark hair bouncing all around as she acted out the guy's movements. "Then he start saying, 'You like that? Does that feel good? Yeah, you like that?' Can you believe that? What total loser he was."

I talked to a Steiner who had a passenger ask for a happy ending, which is when a masseuse finishes the session sexually.

"It happened again," she vented to me in the crew bar one night. "I can't believe it. I can understand it happening on occasion to one of us up there. But this is the second guy in three weeks, and it hasn't happened to anyone but me. I mean, do I look like a whore or what?"

"No of course not. Was this guy young? Maybe he just liked you." I was trying to make her feel better.

"No. This guy is old and married. I saw him walking around with his wife and two kids. And besides, that's hardly how you would tell a girl that you fancy her. What's wrong with you?"

"Oh, yeah, I guess that's true. I can't believe he would do that with his wife onboard."

"You know there was a girl a few months back, before you were here, that got fired for actually giving happy endings. Now *she* was a whore."

"Really?" I said. "How did she get caught? Those massage rooms are private."

"She propositioned the wrong guy and he told on her," she said.

☼ ☼ ☼

I was on the *Holiday* for two and a half months, and thanks to Mr. Temper, had worked ten hours on average, every day. There was just so much to do, and I was playing catch-up the entire time. This is how a typical day went:

My beeper goes off at 4:00 a.m. I have been asleep for one hour, and though still drunk, my hangover is already creeping on me. I call the number back. It's room service, and their printer isn't working.

I don't want to get up. I put on jeans with holes in them, a T-shirt, sandals, and wear a baseball cap backward. It's too early for my uniform. I walk up to their office, and luckily it only takes two minutes to fix the printer. If they had tried, they would have fixed it themselves, but whatever. I go back to my cabin and crawl in bed.

It feels like I have just fallen asleep when the beeper goes off again, but it's actually 8:00 a.m. One of the bridge officers tells me that his user account is locked. I walk half a step to my desk and use the computer in my cabin to unlock his account. I answer a few emails while I'm there, and go back to bed.

The beeper goes off again thirty minutes later and it's one of the pursers. She tells me that a computer at the front desk isn't working. I ask if she's rebooted the computer yet. This is always the first question I ask because it fixes 85% of all computer problems. I've trained everyone on the ship to reboot before they call me. Sometimes they forget, and this is a new purser so I don't have her trained yet. She says she has not rebooted the computer. I tell her to do that and to let me know if the problem persists.

I lay back down in bed. Five minutes later, the beeper goes off again. It's the same purser and the computer still isn't working. I give up on sleep for now and take a shower before going up to the purser's desk.

While in the shower, the beeper goes off.

Once I dry off, I call the number and unlock the user account for the guy in the engine control room. I mean, how hard is it to type in a password? You get three attempts before it locks you out. Those damn Italians can be such a pain. I put on my uniform and go to the purser's desk. I find that the network cable is unplugged, and when I plug it back in, everything works fine. It annoys me that some people don't even try.

I have to print the Sail and Sign cards today. These are the charge cards that the passengers use to buy drinks, and on the newer ships—not this ship of course—the same card acts as a key to their cabin doors. The next cruise will have 1,700 passengers so I have to print 1,700 cards. It takes about four hours to print them on this special machine I have in the computer room.

But first, I have to get some cases of blank cards from the supply room. I push a trolley down to the other end of the ship and down an elevator, where I wait for the supply room manager. We load up boxes of blank cards. I get back to the computer room—about twenty minutes since I left—and start printing the cards.

The hopper on the card-printing machine only holds about seventy cards so I have to babysit for four hours. I keep pulling out the printed cards and loading in more blank cards. At least I'm not on the *Triumph* where it takes eight hours to print 3,500 cards.

While I'm doing this, I continue to get paged. The gift shop is having problems with their receipt printer. One of the bar terminals isn't working. The chief engineer's personal laptop won't connect to the ship's network. The chief security officer has run out of space on his email account. The spa manager doesn't know how to use a floppy disk.

I have to be patient. I try to teach my users how to do the easy things on their own. As I'm walking all over the ship to put out fires, I keep stopping by the computer room to refill the hopper on the card-printing machine.

I stop by my cabin because I need to use the restroom, and as I'm sitting there, my pager starts vibrating again. Crap. I came prepared, and so my cordless cabin phone is right there on the sink. I reach over and call the number back while still sitting. It's the maître d', and he's having problems with the program he uses to assign the dining room seating for the next cruise.

On the way to the maître d's office, I go to the computer room and refill the hopper. After helping the maître d', I go back to the computer room and again refill the hopper. While I'm there, a dining room waiter brings his personal desktop computer to me. He thinks it's not working right. I tell him that I'll look at it if he pays me and he agrees. I don't give him a price. I just want him to know how much I hate it when people ask me for help with their personal computers. I spend thirty minutes looking at it, and tell him that there's nothing wrong. He is very grateful and gives me twenty bucks. I shrug after he leaves and decide that it was worth my time. I refill the hopper.

I'm having problems with the system that manages the bar terminals. It's a problem that I can't fix and I have to call corporate for help. While waiting on hold with tech support, I get beeped. I have two phones in the computer room, so I grab the other phone and call the cruise director, who is having problems with her printer. I'm holding a phone receiver up to each ear.

While I'm talking to the cruise director on one phone, tech support in Miami comes back on the other line. I tell tech support to hold on. Then I tell the cruise director to hold a second while I talk to the guy in Miami. I answer the questions from tech support, and he puts me back on hold. Then I go back to the cruise director and start talking about her printer when a security officer comes into the computer room holding his digital camera and a blank CD. I motion for him to wait a second. I finish helping the cruise director and we hang up. I start talking to the security officer when tech support comes back on the line to say they have fixed my problem. I hang up the other phone. Back to the security officer. He wants me to offload his pictures onto the blank CD he's holding. I start burning the CD and then put more blank cards in the hopper.

Since the pager hasn't gone off in the last ten minutes, I start going through that pile of junk that Mr. Temper left for me. I throw away some broken CD-ROM drives and some random cables. I find a broken bar terminal and fill out the paperwork that's required to send it back to corporate.

I'm in the middle of boxing up the bar terminal when the beeper goes off. It's the purser's desk. Their fax machine isn't working. I refill the hopper and fix the fax machine. When I get back to the computer room, I finish boxing up the bar terminal and carry it to the I-95. I set it on top of a pallet so that it will get offloaded during embarkation day.

I get back to the computer room and finally finish printing the cards. I call room service and they come pick them up. Although printed alphabetically, the room service folks have to break all 1,700 of them into smaller groups by hand, so that the embarkation staff can find them quickly. I go eat dinner, and while I'm there, the beeper goes off. It's the bar manager. He can't copy any files to his network drive. I sit back down and take two more bites of food—it wasn't that good anyway—and go help the bar manager.

The beeper finally is quiet, and I go take that nap that I've been dreaming about all day. The beeper wakes me up at 10:00 p.m., and I unlock the housekeeping manager's user account. Now that I'm somewhat rested, I head up to the crew bar to start playing darts. By midnight, I'm hammered. I leave the crew bar at 2:30 a.m. and go up the passenger's pizza bar. I make it back to my cabin around 3:00 a.m. and pass out. I get paged at 5:00 a.m. because the security kiosk isn't working and they need it for embarkation day.

✵ ✵ ✵

It took six weeks to clean out Mr. Temper's seven-foot pile of junk. I worked on it every couple of days whenever I had the time and was in the mood. There was still a backlog of work around the ship, but at least the computer room was clean. Unrecognizable, really. You could actually see the floor. Then I got word that Mr. Temper had convinced the Miami managers that he should fly out to my ship for a day trip. He was back from vacation and was certain he could use his expertise to make the security machines connect over the wireless network. It was a problem I had never been able to fix.

I was looking forward to seeing his reaction to how different the computer room looked. I made sure I was with him when he walked into the computer room for the first time. He did a double take and paused to look at the absence of mess. Then he kept walking and didn't say a word.

"Yeah, I had fun cleaning up your goddamn mess," I wanted to say.

But he was there to help, so I bit my tongue. I might as well have said it because he wasn't able to fix a damn thing. After working on it all day, he left the ship and I sailed with the same problem. His trip had been a total waste.

✲ ✲ ✲

I had seen my parents when they happened to be in Portland, Maine the same day the *Triumph* docked there. We hung out for the afternoon, and mom did a huge favor by taking $5,000 worth of pay and depositing the cash back home. But now that a few months had passed, I had saved another stack of cash. I finally decided that my dresser drawer wasn't a good place for cash or a passport, so I signed up for an onboard safety deposit box. They were available only to the crew, and except for the $25 refundable deposit, they were free.

Shortly after Mr. Temper left, my parents came to cruise with me. As a crewmember, I was able to get my family a decent rate for the cruise: $24 per person. They only had to pay the port charges.

"Your mom," one of the gangway security guards said to me.

"This is no time for a 'your mom' joke," I snapped.

"What? No, no. It's just I can't believe how much she looks like you. I knew she was your mother the moment I saw her."

"Yeah, pretty cool, huh?" I said.

I took my parents to the staff mess for lunch one day and handed them the menu.

"That's nice," my mom said. "So where do you want to eat?"

"Well, let's eat here," I said.

"Why would I want to eat here when I can eat the good stuff upstairs?" mom asked.

"I have to eat this slop everyday for eight months. Don't you want to try it once?"

"No, thanks. We're going to the Lido buffet. You coming?"

"Fine."

Because I had family onboard, I got to eat in the formal dining room for dinner. It was a nice break from the staff mess. My parents fell in love with our bar waitress who was from Slovenia.

"Ah, Jay, she is beautiful. She's so nice and so friendly. What a sweetheart."

"Yeah, she has a boyfriend," I said, doing my best to pretend.

I didn't have the heart to tell them the truth. She was definitely beautiful and her boyfriend was the gift shop manager. But on the previous cruise they had to put their affair on hold because the gift shop manager's pregnant wife had come to cruise with him. Once his wife left to go back to London, he'd resumed his relationship with the bar waitress. The wife did not find out and there was no drama. I couldn't believe the amount of tacit trust there was among the crew.

I gave mom another $6,000 in cash to deposit, and after my parents left, I returned to my normal routine. After being on ships for seven months, I was drinking more than I ever had in my life. I drank almost every night and was getting smashed six nights a week. My tolerance grew, and I became accustomed to daily hangovers. In the same way that inactive people don't

165

realize how much better they would feel if they exercised, I didn't realize how rotten I felt until I'd wake up after one of those rare nights without alcohol. I'd feel so good and full of energy during the day that I'd head straight to the crew bar at night.

"Oh, hi, Jay," one of the casino dealers said one night. "You were a riot last night."

"What?"

"Yes, you kept talking in the third person."

I reached hard for the memory.

"I think I remember that. Yeah, it's all coming back to me. Yeah. Jay does that sometimes," I said.

"Yes! Just like that. You kept saying things like, 'Sometimes Jay has to go to the bathroom.' Or 'Sometimes Jay gets really drunk.' I had a good laugh."

✿ ✿ ✿

As hard as I tried, I went through my longest stretch of inactivity while on the *Holiday*. An entire month had passed since I last slept with someone. And believe it or not, a month is a very long time onboard, especially if you're trying. We called it dry dock.

"Hey, Jay, who you dating these days?" someone would ask.

"No one," I'd say with a frown. "I'm in dry dock."

"Ah, that sucks, man."

Maybe it was the ten-hour workdays. Maybe it was because the *Holiday* was a smaller ship with fewer girls. Maybe it was because I played chess in the crew bar. Yep, that was it, and thus I realized my mistake: you should never play chess in the crew bar if you want a girl to sleep with you.

One night I got invited to a party in the casino manager's cabin. Florina was a tall Romanian girl wearing an all-white

166

outfit that showed off her tan figure. Her hair was bleached almost completely white and she looked great. We started kissing at the party. We went to her cabin so she could freshen up—you know, a quick rinse—and then we went to my cabin. It was over pretty quick, but I knew what to do.

"Are you ready for Round Two?" I asked, touching her face.

"No," she said, pushing me away.

Then she got dressed and left. I didn't understand. I thought all girls wanted Round Two.

I went to bed, but a few hours later a purser woke me with a page and I had to put on my uniform to go fix a printer. Breakfast was a rare occasion for me, but since I was awake, I stopped by for bacon and eggs.

There she was, Florina, sitting with someone. Breakfast is always pretty empty in the staff mess, and they were the only two people at the table. I said good morning and sat across from her. She looked uncomfortable and was acting strange. She avoided eye contact, but tried not to be too rude about it. The guy next to her was also Romanian. After a couple of minutes, they finished their food and left.

I saw her later that day.

"What was that all about?" I asked.

"Our time together was just for one night. Sorry, but I do not want to date."

"Was that guy your boyfriend?"

"No," she said.

I didn't believe her, but I wasn't too upset. I went back on the hunt, but got stuck in dry dock for another three weeks.

CHAPTER 9

HOW SAFE ARE YOU
ON A CRUISE SHIP?

Much can go wrong on a hotel-size vehicle. Most maritime accidents happen in the fishing and shipping industries, where thousands of injuries and an average of seventy-five deaths occur each year. Fishing vessels are comparatively small and often sail in dangerous waters with the crew exposed on deck. In the shipping industry, safety standards are often ignored and aging ships continue to sail, whether or not they are seaworthy. These ships, weakened with rust and fit for a scrap yard, are the first to go down in a heavy storm.

In contrast, cruising is actually very safe. The industry, knowing it can't survive without a pristine safety image, holds itself to much higher standards than the shipping industry. According to the CLIA, a trade group that represents 97% of the North American cruise market, only one passenger—an elderly woman from the fire onboard the *Star Princess* in 2006—has died from a maritime accident in the last twenty years. It's a remarkable statistic, given that over 100 million passengers have cruised in the same time period.

That statistic does not include people who die from natural causes. On any given day, a quarter million people are taking a cruise, so death at sea has to be planned for. Each ship has a morgue to keep the bodies cold until they're transported off at the next homeport. But sometimes the number of bodies exceeds the morgue's capacity and the walk-in food freezers have to be used. One time a chef rolled some meat out of the freezer and unwrapped it to find a human foot poking out. A body had been stored there but no one had told him. He started screaming and ran out of the galley and was so terrified that the doctor had to tranquilize him.

The statistic also doesn't include those who die from jumping overboard. It only happens to about one in a million passengers, and inadequate railings are never the cause. The railings are tall and very sturdy. Suicide and foul play are sometimes to blame, but mostly it's because people get drunk and stupid.

"Man overboard" is a nightmare for the captain, whose biggest responsibility is the safety of everyone onboard. But it's also inconvenient for the rest of the passengers, who are likely to either miss a port or arrive late because the ship spent time looking for the person in the water. Sometimes nobody even knows that there is a man overboard until they turn up missing the next day.

The crew is trained on what to do if someone goes overboard. The procedure is to alert others around you by yelling, "Man overboard port!" or "Man overboard starboard!" while throwing a life ring in the water and immediately calling the bridge. The ship will then turn away from the person so as not to chop them up with the propellers.

Two passengers went overboard at the same time from the *Grand Princess* in 2007. Even during the daytime, victims are usually heard before they are seen, but only if they're still conscious and able to keep themselves afloat after hitting the water. These two passengers went overboard at night, which made locating them exceedingly difficult. The captain had the remaining passengers go to their cabins and asked them to be as quiet as possible. Then he turned off the engines and the ventilation system. The crew heard the cries for help and used the spotlights until they found them.

In another incident, a guy was drunk and started running toward his cabin window. He was probably hoping to bounce off, but the window gave way and off he went into the water. It took eight hours to find him, but he survived.

Sometimes the crew can't find the person before they drown. This was thought to have happened when a Navy SEAL fell off a cruise ship at night. Nobody could find him, but it turns out that he actually swam back to Miami. Even drunk, he was able to paddle several miles back to shore by using the glow of the city as a beacon.

But many people don't survive after going overboard. Just hitting the water can knock you unconscious. The impact force of smooth, calm water is worse than frothy seas, and unless you hit the water feet first, you're likely to have some sort of injury.

My college had an Olympic-size swimming pool complete with diving platforms, but the highest the general public was allowed to jump from was the five meter platform. It was only sixteen feet above the water and still, if you landed wrong, it could daze you.

Imagine doing a belly flop from Lido Deck which is eighty feet above the water or five times as high as the diving platform. A jump from that height could easily result in a dislocated shoulder, a broken back, or a broken neck. Try staying afloat with an injury like that. Only when your fear of staying on the ship is greater than your fear of hitting the water, should you jump.

There was one couple that argued a lot during their cruise, and the tensions escalated until the husband said he would jump if the wife didn't get off his case. She yelled that he wasn't man enough to do it. So off he went into the water and to his death.

The death statistic also doesn't include people who die because they are assaulted, which rarely happens, and it doesn't include crewmembers who die in the workplace, which also rarely happens. Of course, these types of deaths also happen on land. The fact is, there are so many ways to die, and being on a cruise ship doesn't make you invincible. Just like anywhere else, general caution and common sense will go far toward keeping you alive.

I was onboard when a crewmember from a different ship drowned from swimming too far away from the beach. The entire fleet mourned. I never met him, but he was one of our own, and it made me consider my own mortality. A collection can with his name and picture was set up on each ship, and the money was pooled together and given to his family.

There were a few other crewmembers who died while I was onboard. It was never anyone from my ship, and I never knew any of them. Repetition diminishes a tragedy's impact, and I hate to admit it, but each collection can and its picture affected me a little less than the one before.

One of the rarest occurrences on a cruise ship is a hijacking. Cruise ships usually avoid the pirate-infested waters, but there have been a couple of attempts over the years. Two speedboats full of pirates tried to hijack the *Seabourn Spirit* off the coast of Somalia in 2005, using machine guns and rocket-propelled grenades. The crew fought back with high pressure water hoses and a Long Range Acoustic Device (LRAD). An LRAD produces a high volume beam of sound that is painful to the ears and can even blur the vision of anyone within its usable range of 300 yards. The pirates weren't able to board and finally gave up after thirty minutes of trying. One crewmember took a bullet and another sustained hearing damage from the LRAD, but no one was killed and none of the passengers were injured.

Twenty years earlier, in 1985, the *Achille Lauro* was successfully hijacked off the coast of Egypt. The hijackers killed an American passenger and threw his body overboard, but gave up the ship a few days later.

The most dangerous and likely thing to go wrong is an onboard fire, but major incidents are extremely rare. Ships employ dedicated firemen, who, in the event of an onboard fire, don full protective clothing complete with masks and air tanks.

The firemen visited checkpoints throughout the ship during daily fire patrols. I was at a captain's safety meeting when the social host complained about the timing of one of the fire patrols. The firemen had figured out that the best time to visit the checkpoint behind the stage was during the Vegas-style shows. They were likely to see a lot of skin and maybe a boob as the dancers raced through costume changes.

"These firemen," the captain said, turning to his staff captain, "they are smart guys, no?"

Everyone chuckled, but the captain said he would take care of it.

Laundry areas were the only places where passenger clothing irons were permitted. With tile floors and metal walls, the laundry areas were less combustible than the cabins which had carpet, drapes, and bedding. Candles were strictly forbidden because an open flame was an active fire waiting to spread. If the ship listed, the candle could fall over or something could fall into it.

Even with all the restrictions and precautions, multiple fires of some sort broke out on cruise ships every year. Most were small and quickly contained without any injuries or major damage. An electrical panel might burn up or a fire may spread a little from the onboard incinerator. But when a fire got out of control, the consequences were disastrous.

In 1965, the *Yarmouth Castle* went up in flames in the Caribbean and about 90 people went down with the ship. The fire started because a mattress had been stored too close to a ceiling light. In 1980, an engine fire on the *Prinsendam* got out of control and the captain made the abandon ship call. There was no loss of life and all 520 passengers and crew escaped with no major injuries, but the ship later capsized and sank in the Gulf of Alaska.

In 2006, the *Star Princess* caught fire from what is thought to have been a cigarette that was left burning. It quickly spread and took seven hours to contain. The captain was minutes away from calling for all passengers to board the lifeboats. One elderly passenger died–the one from the statistic above–and another eleven passengers suffered from smoke inhalation. Seventy-nine cabins were destroyed and another 204 were damaged. Afterwards, the ship went straight to dry dock for repairs.

One fire that received a lot of media attention happened in 1998 on Carnival's *Ecstasy*. Because it happened only thirty minutes after sailing, the ship was within range of the Miami news helicopters. The fire started in the main laundry, where some crewmembers were welding, and ignited a large amount of lint that had accumulated in the laundry ducts.

One girl from the *Ecstasy* was later transferred to Mirka's ship. She told Mirka, my wife, that she didn't know her ship was on fire until her regularly scheduled program was interrupted with live footage of a plume of black smoke from her own ship.

There were reports of other passengers who learned of the fire this way, too. Dipsu, the guy that trained me on my first ship, was on the *Ecstasy* during the fire. He told me that the noise from the news helicopters added to the general chaos. Terrified, some passengers demanded that the lifeboats be launched before it was too late, but this never happened.

The fire knocked out the *Ecstasy's* propulsion systems and left it adrift. Being close to Miami proved a blessing because the Coast Guard was able to send a number of tugboats to douse the fire with their high-pressure fire hoses. The fire was at the stern and one tugboat tied up to the front of the ship to keep the bow upwind and away from the smoke. This helped keep the fire from spreading. It took about two and a half hours to put out the fire, and then six tugboats towed the crippled ship back to Miami. In the aftermath nine passengers and fourteen crewmembers were treated for minor injuries.

✵ ✵ ✵

Expert "pilots" board ships to help the captain navigate coastal waters whenever sailing in or out of port. Pilots generally work only one harbor, so they know the danger spots better than anyone else. Even with this precaution, ships still run aground just about every year.

In 1983, the *S.S. Universe* ran aground with students enrolled in the onboard "Semester at Sea" program. No one was hurt, and the students finished their semester in a nearby hotel.

One of the most famous groundings was the maiden voyage of the *Mardi Gras* in 1972. It was the very first cruise of a brand new company called Carnival Cruise Lines. The ship had just left Miami, and the pilot thought he would impress everyone by speaking Italian.

"Turn left," he said in Italian.

The person behind the wheel thought he clearly heard "Turn right." It all happened very fast, and within moments the ship was stuck and the passengers got to see the ship's propeller splashing sand and water fifteen feet high. No one was hurt, and the bartenders immediately started serving free drinks. The passengers loved it. One of the bartenders invented a new drink from rum and called it "Mardi Gras on the Rocks." Carnival continued to serve that drink for many years.

Whenever the *Holiday* sailed, the lower hull door stayed open. This hull door was where the passengers would enter and exit the ship when we were in port. The door stayed open for about fifteen minutes after sailing because it was where the pilot stepped off the cruise ship and onto his little pilot boat.

Anything with moving parts will eventually break, and cruise ship propulsion systems have lots of moving parts. Ships have at least two propellers and can usually limp along even if one breaks down. It just can't sail as fast or stay on a tight schedule.

I was on the *Holiday* when her forward thrusters went out. The ship was just as fast, but we weren't as maneuverable. Right after the thrusters were fixed, we had a period of about two months when the *Holiday* lost the engines about once a week. With no engines, the propellers and the thrusters stopped working and left us adrift. Most of the time the engines came back online pretty quickly, and the lights only went out for a few seconds. But a few seconds was enough to cause havoc in my computer room as half my servers–the ones that weren't on battery backup–went down. The ventilation system also went down and the computer room started getting warm. I had to open the doors in the computer room and grab any fan I could find to prevent the servers from overheating.

One afternoon we lost both the engines and the interior lights and just floated adrift in the Caribbean for an hour. The seas were calm so we weren't in any danger, but I needed to wait in the computer room for the power to come back before bringing all the servers online.

"Hey, when is the power coming back?" one passenger asked me on the way up there. Like I would know.

"Do you know when the lights will be back on?" another passenger asked me, just a few paces from the last one.

I tried to hide in the computer room, but had to keep the doors propped open to let the heat out.

"Excuse me," yet another freaking passenger said as she poked her head into my domain. "Do you know when the power is going to come back?"

Because losing power had become so commonplace on the *Holiday*, we grumbled that if we lost power at the wrong time, say in the Mississippi River, then it could be really bad. Our homeport was New Orleans, and from there it took about seven hours to sail down the river to get to the Gulf. There were multiple sharp turns, and we passed a lot of industry along the banks of the river, a number of barges, and occasionally another cruise ship.

Then it happened. There was the familiar thud of the engines dying once again. Everything went quiet. The air vents went silent. The lights flickered. I caught my balance as I felt the ship decelerate.

"It's only been a few hours since we left New Orleans," I said to myself. "We're still in the Mississippi."

I ran up on deck to see what was what. The engines had gone out just before a left bend in the river and, unable to maneuver, we kept going straight. We'd plowed head on into the riverbank and the current swung the tail end of the ship around so that we were facing the wrong direction at a 45-degree angle.

I looked out over the railing, and there was a guy on land who'd walked over and was gazing up at us. It was dark so I could just barely see him.

"Hey, are you guys okay?" he shouted up to us.

"I think so," I yelled back.

In 2007, a barge collided with Carnival's *Fantasy* and left a 30-foot gash in the hull. No one was hurt, but the next cruise was canceled while the ship was repaired. Also in 2007, the *Norwegian Dream* collided with a container ship and knocked some containers and a bunch of SUVs into the water. The *Norwegian Dream* had also collided with a container ship in 1999, and the impact had been strong enough to knock some passengers out of bed.

The *Holiday* was lucky that there wasn't a chemical plant or another ship in our path when the power went out. The cargo ship *Bright Field* ran into the pier in New Orleans in 1996. Engine failure was to blame in causing $17 million worth of damage and injuring 66 people.

The *Holiday*'s engines came back online after a few minutes and the ship unstuck itself and parked on the side of the river. We had to wait for the Coast Guard to board and give us permission to continue sailing. The riverbanks were soft and muddy so the ship didn't sustain any damage.

A couple of days later, the captain beeped me for help with his cabin computer. As usual, it was just the two of us in his cabin.

"This window, how do I make it bigger?" he asked, pointing at the window of his spider solitaire game.

"I can't make it any bigger," I said after playing with it for a few minutes. "It must be a limitation of Windows 95."

"A limitation of what?" he asked.

"The computer is old. That is the problem," I said, and he was okay with that.

He was my favorite captain despite his rules about nametags and mess halls. Whenever I helped him with his computer, we usually chatted for a couple of minutes before I left, and I was especially interested in talking to him that day.

"I'm sorry about what happened in the Mississippi," I said, bringing up the topic.

"You mean the grounding?" he said, averting his eyes.

"Yeah."

"Yes. You see, we were going with the current, and without power, I had no way to control the ship. If we had been going against the current, then even without power the rudder would have given me some control. Probably I would have been able to steer through the bend in the river and more gently park the ship next to the shoreline."

✲ ✲ ✲

Of course, a boat's worst-case scenario is sinking, and there are thousands of vessels at the bottom of the sea to attest to the very real possibility of this. Collisions took some of them down. Fires also played their part. But bad weather is to blame for most ships sinking. In fact, no ship has ever been built that is strong enough to survive the full wrath of what the sea can unleash. Ocean storms are just too powerful, and so avoiding bad weather is the key to staying afloat. Rough seas are more common in the shipping industry because they're forced to sail in rougher waters.

The captain typically does not go down with the ship, at least not intentionally. His job is to keep the vessel afloat as long as possible. This gives everyone onboard more time to escape. In an ideal situation he would make sure everyone is off the ship before boarding the last lifeboat.

But the 1991 sinking of the cruise ship *Oceanos* was anything but ideal. A leak in the engine room caused the ship to lose power, and the water continued to rise until it became unstoppable. Once the crew realized the ship could not be saved, they fled in panic. The captain was one of the first people to leave the ship, basically leaving the passengers to fend for themselves. A couple of onboard entertainers actually organized the rescue operation, which made them the last to leave the ship. The entertainers recorded video of it all, and there is a great clip of it on YouTube. You can find it by doing a search for "cruise ship sinking."

It took eighteen hours for the *Oceanos* to sink, and the last people onboard were lifted off by helicopter just minutes before it went down. That was not the case in 1987, when the ferry *Herald of Free Enterprise* set sail without closing the front or rear cargo doors. It took on water so fast that it capsized and sank in sixty seconds. Actually, it only partially sank because the water was so shallow. The ship ended up on its side half-submerged, and because it happened so fast, 193 people died.

I never got to experience a collision. I was never on a sinking ship either, but I'd volunteer for both. I would probably regret wishing for it if it ever came true, but I often visualized what it would be like to escape a sinking ship without the aid of a lifeboat. You know, like in *Titanic.*

I knew where I was at all times and could get to any spot on the ship while stepping in and out of crew and passenger areas just like Dipsu did when he gave me my first ship tour. I'd know the exits, and I'd be able to get to one faster than most passengers. I could save lives and be a hero. Then again, I lose my bearings after an elevator ride, so it's probably best that I don't get put to the test.

I wonder if I'd lose my bearings if the ship were to nose down. Would I still know which way was "up" on a staircase? And if the ship did nose down, what a sight it would be to watch those long passenger corridors convert into a scary plunge that was eighty stories tall.

Another danger at sea, albeit extremely rare, is rogue waves. They are loosely defined as open water waves that measure at least fifty feet from crest to trough. They're often encountered near storms or hurricanes but can even occur in calm water. The real monsters can be over 100 feet high and have been described as a "huge wall of water."

Rogue waves differ from tsunamis, which are mostly harmless in the open water because they are only a few feet high. Ships usually don't even notice a tsunami. It's not until a tsunami reaches the coast, where the rising seabed causes the wave to rise, that it becomes dangerous.

Tsunamis happen after earthquakes and other big releases of tectonic energy, but no one is quite sure what causes rogue waves. One theory holds that small waves merge to become a large wave. Other theories claim the shape of the seabed or ocean currents plays a part. It actually took a couple of thousand years before rogue waves were even a confirmed phenomena, when, in 1995, a wave sensor recorded an 85-footer that hit the Drauper oil platform near Norway. For thousands of years before that, anyone who witnessed a rogue either went down with the ship or was left to tell the tale to disbelieving listeners, none of whom could believe that open water waves could be that big.

When it comes to sailing, the danger of any wave depends not only on its size, but where it strikes the boat. The front of a ship is designed to cut through the water, and so a wave that hits the bow will do far less damage than a wave that hits broadside. The side of a ship is the weakest spot on any ship. The *Titanic* would likely have survived the iceberg if it had smashed into it head on. A T-bone collision between ships often results in the sinking of the side-impacted ship while the one with bow damage stays afloat. A wave that hits broadside can shatter windows and send torrents of water flooding in, but an even bigger danger is that it can capsize or completely roll a ship and send anything unsecured, like bodies and grand pianos, as seen in the movie *Poseidon,* bouncing off the walls. And that's assuming the ship's hull is still intact for things to bounce into.

It's estimated that at least one vessel is lost to a rogue wave every year. Rogue waves are thought to be the cause whenever a ship sinks mysteriously. A wave has more energy than you might imagine. When you're on the beach and a four-foot wave hits your body at twenty miles per hour, there is enough force to make the impact uncomfortable. That force grows exponentially with height, and a 100-foot wave could not only blow out windows, flood the ship, and capsize it, but it could dent, tear, and rip the hull apart as if it were paper. Instead of a wall of water, imagine a wall of wrecking balls swinging in unison at twenty miles per hour.

One morning about 9:00 on the *Holiday*, I woke up gripping my sheets to the sensation of being lifted out of my bed. My head was about two feet higher than my feet. I heard a scraping noise and opened my eyes to see the TV slide across my desk and bump into the wall. After a few seconds, the angle of my bed became mostly normal again. It was a pretty intense listing and I couldn't wait to see what happened, but I was hung over and just fell back asleep.

A few hours later I walked around the ship to hear the stories and to see the damage. Passengers had slid across Lido Deck while still in their chairs. Their plastic plates and bowls bounced on the floor and sent up a shower of scrambled eggs and soggy corn flakes. Sausage links tumbled through it all. Breakfast food made the tile floors greasy, which made it hard for anyone to keep their footing. Outside, a few deck chairs rolled and bounced overboard while the rest piled up against the railing. The six-foot floral cooler in the formalities shop toppled and broke the glass shelving and crystal vases filled with water and flowers. The shop also had glass shelving along the walls that either fell off or was taken out by the cooler. The gift shop was trashed, with all the carefully arranged trinkets and souvenirs scattered onto the floor. Surprisingly, only a few liquor bottles were lost, and I only had to replace one printer that cracked on the floor in the maître d's office. One of the hostesses had just bought a laptop, and it fell off her desk and broke the monitor. But luckily, no one was injured beyond a few bumps and bruises.

A freak wind was to blame for that listing. It was a clear day with normal seas, and out of nowhere a 50 mile per hour sustained wind hit us broadside. The ship listed about eighteen degrees. The captain changed course to reduce the effect, but the ship continued to list about ten degrees for the next four hours until the wind abated. It was disorienting to walk—and to see others walking—at an angle down the square corridors. During lunch in the staff mess, the chairs slid to one side because the floors were still greasy from the breakfast spill. A few of the crew pushed themselves up to one end of the staff mess to have sliding chair races.

Listing can be dangerous, and when a ship rolls back and forth, it can throw people out of their chairs and toss them side to side as violently as the camera gimmicks did in the original *Star Trek* series. Any item that's not secured, from a wine glass to a stage prop, can become a deadly projectile. The injuries can be severe, including broken legs, broken shoulders, broken ribs, cuts around the face, and even paralysis or death. Smaller boats get tossed way more and are more likely to capsize than the big cruise ships, but enough bad weather can cause injuries even on the monster ships.

In addition to excessive winds, a ship can list simply turning too sharp. Every new ship goes through a series of "sea trials" long before its maiden voyage. It's like a test drive to make sure the ship performs the way it should, and one of the tests is a sharp turn at high speed to intentionally list the ship. The *Holiday* initially failed this test and was deemed un-seaworthy because it failed to recover well. It was originally designed with a rounded underside at the back of the ship which made it unstable. So before it went into service, a couple of custom-made flare pieces were attached to its back section near the waterline. The design flaw was later corrected for the *Holiday*'s sister ships, the *Jubilee* and the *Celebration*, and if you compare pictures of the three ships, you can see the difference.

In 2006, the *Crown Princess* listed 24 degrees after the person steering the ship turned too sharply. It sent passengers and crew tumbling to the side of the ship, and emptied the water in swimming pools. It sent those grand pianos tumbling. Three hundred thirty-four people were injured, 94 of whom were hospitalized with broken bones and cuts from broken glass and flying objects.

✼ ✼ ✼

The *Holiday's* listing event happened at the end of my first contract. I'd been wrong to think a vacation was unnecessary. After eight months, I was completely exhausted and doing as little work as possible. My energy and motivation were utterly gone. If there were projects or requests that could wait, then they waited for my successor. Had I stayed for another six months, I would have created my own seven-foot pile of backlogged work. At last I understood why most contracts didn't exceed eight months.

I had come to hate my cabin, although there were lots of reasons to like it. I didn't have a roommate which was a huge privilege in itself. Roommates were inconvenient, although I never had any real issues. I knew an Internet café manager who had a gay roommate. The gay guy was liked by everyone and was fun to drink and party with, but one night the Internet café manager was asleep on the bottom bunk when his roommate came back from the crew bar with another gay crewmember. The two gays climbed up to the top bunk.

"All right, this is how it's going to work," one said to the other. "First I'll do you, and then you're going to do me."

After hearing that, the Internet café manager left the cabin for an hour before coming back to sleep.

Only 1% of the crew had their own cabin without a roommate. Instead of bunk beds, which were uncomfortable to sit on because of the limited head room, I had only one bed. The room was carpeted, and I even had a porthole, which was also rare.

But my cabin was very close to the engines. In fact, I was directly above them. And in the way that an old car shakes more than a new one, the *Holiday,* which was Carnival's oldest ship at the time, vibrated far more than the *Triumph.* With pistons the size of 55-gallon oil drums, my cabin shook with the anger of 31,540 horsepower. Unless we were in port, where the engines only idled to keep the lights on, my cabin was never a relaxing place to be. Sleep was never restful. Even though I was drunk almost every night, I still had trouble sleeping through the vibration.

The I/S manager who replaced me boarded the ship on my last cruise, and since there was only one bed in the I/S manager's cabin, I moved out and into a passenger cabin. It allowed him to unpack only once, but more importantly, it allowed me to live in a passenger cabin. I requested one of the cabins at the front of the ship around Deck 6 or 7. Although those cabins had a little vibration from the thrusters, they had zero vibration from the engines, and I found them to be the most peaceful location onboard.

Ryan, my friend from Dallas, stayed with me in the passenger cabin on that last cruise. I registered him as my stepbrother on the official paperwork and got him a four-day cruise for $24.

Greg was my replacement I/S manager. After telling him how exhausted I was, he took the pager and said he'd call me if he needed any help. He never called, and I only worked three hours on my last cruise and only because I insisted. This meant that I could drink and party even more than normal and sleep off the hangover without interruption. And that's exactly what I did.

Ryan and I spent most of our time with a couple of youth counselors, Melissa and Katie, who were roommates. They were both very pretty. Melissa tanned her skin to a dark, rich color which was beautiful. Katie had some of the softest lips I had ever touched. I noticed this earlier in the contract when I gave her a sip of my White Russian one night. I was holding the glass by the rim while Katie grabbed the straw and rested her bottom lip on my finger as she drank. I told her how soft her lips felt on my finger, and from then on she made a point to come over and take a sip of my drink to hear the compliment again.

At the end of the first night, I wound up in bed with Melissa and we kissed a little for the first time. At the end of the second night, I wound up in bed with Katie and we kissed a little for the first time. At the beginning of the third night, I saw the Bulgarian girl I shared an office with. She didn't normally go to the crew bar, but she was there that night.

This Bulgarian had an amazing body, with thin, well defined, muscular legs that were perfectly tanned and shiny and firm. She was an officer and wore the short officer skirts with no stockings. She had a habit of standing and bending at the waist while she worked on her computer, and I don't think she realized what this did to me. Maybe she did. Even though we shared an office, I never came on to her. She was very friendly, but made it clear that there would be nothing between us. But that changed when I saw her in the crew bar that night.

She was sitting with a friend in one of the booths, and I joined them.

"So this is your last cruise," the Bulgarian said.

"This *is* my last cruise. So, you want to kick it?" I asked.

She didn't say anything. She just looked me up and down as she raised her brow ever so slightly with the expression that says, "Yes." It was the let's-get-it-on eyes. I couldn't believe it, and I didn't know how to respond. I had been joking, but she was serious.

Once again I was about to sign off the ship and girls were interested in me. I now fully agreed with what everyone had been telling me all along: crewmembers were more sexually desirable when they were about to leave. It was true for both guys and girls. When you knew the expiration date of a ship relationship, then you could indulge without the risk of commitment. You wouldn't be stuck with someone who annoyed you, and you wouldn't have the discomfort of breaking up then continuing to see them every day.

"All right," I told the Bulgarian. "I may give you a call."

"Okay," she said with the invitation still in her eyes.

I got up and continued to party with the youth counselors. That night, the third night of my last cruise, I wound up in bed with Melissa. We kissed some more, but she didn't want to go any further. It was weird to go back and forth between the two roommates. I don't think Melissa knew, but Katie did and she was a little jealous and probably offended. But somehow Katie was with me on the fourth night and ended my dry dock when we slept together. She had a great personality, and I would have enjoyed dating her sooner. I would also have enjoyed being with the Bulgarian or Melissa for that matter, but that never happened.

Ryan and I drank past 4:00 a.m. every night and slept past 1:00 p.m. every day. The only exception was on the single port day. Ryan had never been to Cozumel so he forced me out of bed and off the ship before noon. The ship sailed at 4:00 p.m., so after getting back on the ship we both took naps, got up in time for dinner, and proceeded to get hammered again in the crew bar.

The last night of the cruise was a late one, and we didn't go to bed until about 6:30 in the morning. We got an hour and a half of sleep before we had to drag ourselves off the ship. We were both exhausted and hung over, and I was hauling three

186

big pieces of luggage. We had booked a hotel room for a night in New Orleans and after eating Popeye's chicken for breakfast, we slept until 7:00 p.m.

That night, we drank hard on Bourbon Street until 2:00 a.m. and then went to Harrah's Casino and gambled until we got sloppy drunk for the fifth night in a row. We left the casino at 8:00 a.m., and the bright morning sun made us squint with pain. The sidewalk was spinning. While stumbling forward, I suddenly needed to use the bathroom so I peed on a palm tree right in front of the casino. It would have been too difficult to go back inside to find a bathroom.

We got back to our hotel room, slept for two hours, and left for the airport. Ryan and I were on different flights and went our separate ways when we got to the airport. I wore sunglasses in the New Orleans airport, on the plane, and again in the Dallas airport. Anything brighter than starlight hurt. When I met Ryan again in the Dallas airport, I saw that he had been wearing sunglasses the whole time as well. Ryan describes those five days as being one of his most intense drinking binges ever. I concur, and it was the perfect way to end my first contract.

I had one day of rest before Ryan and I drove five hours to Hallettsville, Texas for the annual "42 Tournament." Forty-two is a game similar to spades except it's played with dominoes. I meet a group of ten friends there every year. After being at sea for eight months I was homesick. The tournament that year and all of the familiar faces that went with it meant a lot to me. To celebrate, I drank a lot.

Ryan and I drove back on Sunday and then went to the airport Monday morning to fly to Rome for a seven-week backpacking trip through Central and Eastern Europe.

Our schedule was intense. We visited twenty-nine cities across seven countries. We went to Egypt and saw the pyramids, which, in my opinion, are the number one most striking destination on the planet. We drank five nights a week and got drunk often. Just like on a ship, if you drink or smoke, then you'll probably do more of that on a backpacking trip.

My new ability to understand accents came in handy. There were multiple times when Ryan gave up on trying to order train tickets because he couldn't communicate with or understand the ticket clerk. It was just like my first month onboard ships.

"Jay, you translate," he'd say as he stormed away from the counter.

I'd use my trained ear and my slow, simple sentences to get what we needed.

Backpacking through Europe was a great environment to take advantage of my newfound hunger for sex. I was a boning machine. I slept with a French girl we met in Italy. Then we went to Poland to meet up with Paulina, the piano player from the ship. It was an awesome experience to be able to hang out with a friend who was a local. She took us to restaurants and bars that we would never have found on our own, and she ordered food from menus written only in Polish.

I was hoping to be with her, but it became clear that she was more interested in Ryan, so I backed off. The three of us were at a bar and Paulina left to go to the restroom. Ryan told me to stay gone for a while the next time I got up to use the restroom. So I did.

While I was gone, Ryan performed an unbelievable act of altruism. He tried to talk her into being more interested in me than him. And it worked. I don't know how he did it, but it worked. I have since referred to him as the ultimate wingman.

When we left the bar, Ryan took a taxi back to our hotel and I walked Paulina home. She had an extremely small, one-room apartment that she shared with a roommate. Her standard of living was much less than what I was used to. In fact,

I had seen that most of the people in those Eastern European countries had a standard of living that was much less than what I was used to. It was one reason why there were more European crewmembers than American crewmembers. The low standard of living on the ship wasn't as shocking to them.

We stood at the bottom of her stairwell and kissed.

"I want to be with you tonight," I said.

She stood and thought for moment. Ryan and I were catching a train the next day. It was like my last night on the ship, and I would never be more desirable to her than at this moment. It was now or never.

"My next ship is *Destiny*," she finally said. "You promise you won't come to *Destiny*."

Ships dictated the terms and conditions of romance even while we were on land.

"Okay, I promise to not go to the *Destiny*."

"All right. Wait here and I'll be right back," she said as she went up to her apartment for a few minutes.

I assumed she was hopping in the shower for a quick rinse.

She came back down and we took a taxi to my hotel. She talked to the woman at the front desk and ordered a room. It felt dirty. I mean, it was obvious that at 2:30 a.m., there was only one reason why a person who was already staying at the hotel would order another room with a girl.

Our time together was everything I thought it would be and more. We both enjoyed each other's body and presence. We stayed up all night and completed Round Three.

Paulina was a music teacher and had to leave straight from the hotel to get to her class on time. She got no sleep. She had no time to shower and just sprayed on some perfume.

"Now I teach my students and smell like perfume and sperm," she said just before leaving.

The circumstances meant that it would only be a one-night stand. But somehow it meant something. At least to me. We created a connection that night that would have otherwise been difficult because of the language barrier.

I spoke zero Polish, and her English was pretty broken. We could convey thoughts, but it took a lot of effort for us both. As I look back now, I realize that this would have made it difficult for us to date, and I don't think either one of us would have been happy in the long run. I think she knew that at the time, and it may be the reason why she didn't want me on the *Destiny*.

We said goodbye, and then six days later I slept with an American girl in Munich. It almost felt like I had cheated on Paulina. For some reason, it felt like I should have waited longer before being with someone else.

We got back from Europe and had one day to rest before my annual campout in East Texas. It's a guy's weekend where we sleep in tents, cook meat over the campfire, play dominoes, play poker, and drink. It ended on Sunday, and Anderson called me on Monday.

I said, "Dude, I'm exhausted. I need a couple weeks to detox before my second contract."

"No can do," he said. "I need you out there right away. Wednesday, in fact. I'm going to put you on a bird to Puerto Rico, where you'll join the *Carnival Destiny*."

CHAPTER 10

HOW *NOT* TO BREAK UP
WITH A ROMANIAN

In the early 1900s, a cruise was simply transportation. It was the only way for the masses to cross the ocean. Later, the affluent began taking cruises as a novel and elitist type of vacation in which the exotic ports were the selling point. Then in 1958, Pan American offered the first transatlantic jet service and ended the era of boats being the only way to cross the ocean. From there, cruising grew to become the vacation it is today, one in which the ship, instead of the ports, is the destination.

The industry started small with only 500,000 passengers cruising in 1970. Then a TV show called *The Love Boat* started airing in 1977. It ran for ten years and helped the industry grow to 14 million cruising passengers in 2010. New ships are constantly being built, and in 2010 there were about 200 cruise ships in the North American market.

Carnival is king, and they dominate the industry. Over half of all people in North America who go on a cruise do so on one of Carnival's lines. The Port of Miami serves more cruise ships than any other city and is rightly called the "Cruise Capital of the World." It has seven passenger terminals, and twenty-five percent of all North American passengers start their cruise in Miami.

Of the sixteen ships Carnival had in its fleet, I had been assigned to the only one I'd promised to avoid. I didn't know how Paulina would react, but I was looking forward to dating her if she would have me.

I told Anderson that I could leave on Wednesday. Then I hung up the phone and went straight to Carnival.com to see what ports the *Destiny* visited. It had one of the best itineraries because it sailed to the obscure ports that most ships didn't, like Barbados and Martinique and Aruba. Anderson told me that Dipsu was on the *Destiny,* and I was looking forward to working with him again.

☆ ☆ ☆

I was filled with energy and smiles when I boarded the *Destiny.* It had been two months since I had lived on a ship, and the time away had rejuvenated me. At the gangway, security put me in their log book and paged Dipsu just like when I'd first boarded the *Fantasy.*

"Hi, good to see you again," Dipsu said.

"Yeah, you, too. I'm glad to be here."

"Did you hear that you're getting transferred back to the *Holiday*?"

"Yeah, right," I said. "So how have you been?"

"I'm fine, but it's true—you really are going back to the *Holiday.*"

He was great at keeping a straight face and must have heard about how unhappy I was on the *Holiday.*

"Whatever, dude. So do I have my own cabin?"

"No, you're sharing with the Nicaraguan guy. He said you guys met back in Miami when you first started. But you really are going to the *Holiday.* I'll show you the email Anderson sent yesterday."

I didn't believe him until I saw Anderson's email, and then I didn't believe Anderson's email until I called Anderson.

"I'm sorry, man," Anderson said, "but the girl I sent to the *Holiday* refused to stay there."

"Why?"

"She said the ship was making her ill."

"Making her ill?"

"Something about the vibration from the cabin made her tongue go numb."

"All right, ha ha. This has been a very funny joke. You and Dipsu can stop this now."

"Jay, I'm not joking. She refused to stay."

"Well, I didn't enjoy that vibration, either, and I've done my time. Isn't there someone else you can send? I'm already on the *Destiny*."

"I could put someone else there, but it would mean relocating multiple I/S managers around the fleet to do it. You were just there, and you're the only person available who could take over the *Holiday* without needing a week to train on it."

"Did you try to talk Miss Numb out of it?"

"Not really."

"All right, I'll call her on the *Holiday,* and I'll call you back," I said.

"Okay."

I made a ship-to-ship phone call and was lucky to catch her in the computer room.

"Hi, this is Jay Herring, and Brant Anderson is sending me to the *Holiday* because you refused to stay there."

"Hi."

"I didn't like the vibration in the cabin either, but I stuck it out and I think it's only fair that you do the same."

"It's awful. It gives me headaches, and I couldn't sleep. Then my tongue went numb, and that's when I decided that I couldn't stay here. I mean, if my tongue goes numb after one week, what's next? My face? My whole body? I just can't stay here. I'd like to, but I can't. I told Anderson that I'd need to quit if he couldn't put me on another ship. My health is just too important to me."

"Don't you think *my* health is important to *me*?"

"Maybe it doesn't affect everyone the same. I don't know. All I know is that this is between me and Anderson, and this is what he decided. I'm sorry."

"All right. I have to go, see ya," I said, hanging up before I heard her say goodbye. I called Anderson back. "So when do I leave," I said, defeated.

"Couldn't talk her out of it, huh?"

"No."

"You'll fly out from Aruba five days from now. Miss Numb will join the *Destiny* tomorrow and take your spot."

"Who's going to be on the *Holiday* until I get there?"

"Greg will cover the *Holiday* until you arrive."

"Why can't he just stay there? You could put Miss Numb somewhere else."

"He's at the end of a contract, and I need to send him on vacation."

"All right, fine. Well, thanks for explaining it."

"Hey, thanks for doing this," he said.

I was crestfallen. There was nothing I hated more than that stupid, vibrating cabin on the *Holiday*. A roommate in a smaller cabin that didn't have carpet or a porthole would have been far superior.

I tried to make the most of my time on the *Destiny*: getting off in the new ports, socializing around the ship, and bragging about my recent European travel.

Paulina arrived a week after I left, so I didn't get to see her, but I did see people I knew from the *Triumph*. That was fun and just went to show how small the crew community was.

Miss Numb boarded the *Destiny* and stayed in a passenger's cabin for a couple of days until I left. I went to see her on my last day to make her tell that whiny story to my face.

"When I first boarded," she said, "I asked a guy in the cabin next to me why the thrusters were on when we were at sea. He said the thrusters weren't on. Then I asked why the cabin was shaking so much. He said it always shakes that much when the engines were running."

"Yeah, it does," I said, glaring at her and having every right to be angry.

"I just can't believe it's always like that." Her eyes looked everywhere but directly at me. "I just didn't want to be there."

"Yeah, me either," I said, continuing the stare.

She rambled on some more but I'd had enough and said goodbye. I believed her story about being uncomfortable in the cabin. I believed her story about having a numb tongue. I don't know how you could make that up. But I also believed that she embellished to get transferred away from that crappy cabin.

In high school, I wrote a research paper about animal testing, and during my research, I read about some horrific experiments. One of them involved monkeys. An apparatus had been designed to shake a monkey's head to see how it affected the monkey brain. The results showed that short bursts of shaking did not have long-term effects, but as the duration increased, the effects worsened until finally, after many minutes of violent jerking back and forth, the monkey's brain turned into a vegetable. I constantly thought about this experiment when I was on the *Holiday*.

To be clear, my cabin's vibration was not a good vibration. It was not at all soothing. It was a jarring shake. And to avoid further brain damage, I had to reduce it.

After landing in New Orleans, I took a taxi straight to Wal-Mart and had the cabby wait in the parking lot while I bought four pieces of bed foam. I stuffed them in the cab and had the cabby take me to the pier. As I unloaded my three giant pieces of luggage and four equally large pieces of rolled-up pink bed foam, I looked up and saw Greg standing by the curb with his bags.

"What the hell is all that?" he asked, holding a cigarette.

"Bed foam," I said and paid the cab driver.

"Nice color. Why do you have four of them?"

"To reduce the vibration in the bed."

"When the girls see this, you won't get any vibration."

"Very funny. Seriously, though, didn't the vibration annoy you?"

"It definitely shakes in there," he said, "but it doesn't really bother me. It certainly never made my tongue go numb."

"Well, it bothers the crap out of me and hopefully this will make it better."

I lugged my stuff up to the ship where I saw some familiar faces. One of the dancers I knew from the last contract gave me a big hug. She hugged everyone so it didn't really mean anything, and yet I was surprised at how it lightened my mood.

All day long I had more smiles and greetings from the people I knew before. Most of the people who'd been there two months earlier were still there. Florina was still there.

When we saw each other I acted as we had before and kept my distance. I just said hi. We had all but ignored each other after that one-night stand. But that day, she got all excited and ran up and gave me a big hug and said it was great to see me. Yeah that didn't make any sense.

I slept on my four pieces of bed foam that night and noticed that although the vibration was still unacceptable, there was definite improvement. At the next home port, I went back to Wal-Mart and bought four more pieces of bed foam. This time they were yellow. I put all eight pieces on top of the mattress.

"The sheets don't fit. How am I supposed to make this bed?" my cabin steward asked later that day.

My virtual mattress was two feet taller, and the sheets could no longer tuck under the mattress. They didn't even cover the bottom two pieces of foam.

"Just lay the sheet on top the best you can. Thanks," I said.

The yellow ones had a different raised pattern than the pink ones, and I thought that alternating the colors would be the most effective at reducing the vibration.

"Why you do this?" the steward asked, peeling back the corners and poking the colors.

"I don't want monkey brains."

"What?"

"Never mind."

The extra bed foam helped, and the vibration became almost tolerable.

When it came to vibration, my cabin had it the worst. When I stood in my corridor and in front of my cabin door, the intensity of the shaking was at its highest. A few paces in either direction and the vibration decreased dramatically. Ten cabin doors away, the vibration was nonexistent.

Everything rattled in my cabin, and I started stuffing socks in between the problem areas. One sock wedged in the frame kept my cabin door quiet, but it took eight socks, strategically placed in an apparently random pattern, to keep the ceiling quiet. I kept my desk drawer clear of noisemaking pencils and pens and coins. Along with the vibration, there was a loud grumbling noise. It was like a bad rap song with deep bass tones that I could feel in my chest. It gave me headaches. When the ship docked, my cabin became peaceful and calm. The absence of noise was noise itself, like how turning off the TV can wake someone up.

But otherwise the volume in my cabin was too loud to be white noise, and I couldn't ignore it until I came up with the glorious idea of sleeping with earplugs. I slept with them every night on the ship, and now I never leave home without them. I buy them in bulk and wear them on airplanes, on road trips, and when mowing the yard. I wear them to vacuum. I wear them when the ceiling fan shakes. I wear them when Mirka snores.

From an I/S standpoint, the *Holiday* was in great shape for my second contract. Two months had passed and Greg kept everything in good order and didn't leave any backlogged work.

My only complaint was the condition of my two 100-foot network cables. While rummaging through Mr. Temper's mess during my first contract, I had found two brand new cables, and used them every embarkation day to connect the ship to the pier-based network. After plugging them into the ship, I had to dangle my arm out the hull door, and throw them up to the pier without missing and throwing them into the water. Then I'd walk through the ship and out to the pier to plug in the other end of the cables. The cables Mr. Temper had used were covered with grime that got all over me and my white uniform. They were a tangled mess and had actual knots in them.

Those new cables were clean. They were shiny clean and I took great care of them. After every embarkation, I neatly wound them around my hand and elbow and taped the bundle in two places to keep it together. I was so proud of them.

I had shown Greg how to take care of them.

"So if you tape them in two places, then they won't get all knotted," I explained before leaving the *Holiday* on my first contract.

And Greg followed my instructions, but instead of masking tape (which peeled off without any residue), he used duct tape. The cables were now covered in sticky goo that turned black and got all over me and my uniform.

But otherwise, the ship only needed to be maintained. It was a more balanced work schedule. Some days were very busy like before. Some days were moderately busy. And some days my pager never went off and the only work I did was sleep in late, hang out at the beach, and be in the crew bar by 8:00 p.m.

I had been drinking heavily for a solid eight months. I drank through most of my first contract, all through Europe, with my friends at the campout, and then back to White Russians during the first month of my second contract. My stomach began to burn when I drank. One night I was playing darts with the ship's doctor, and asked him about it. He said the condition is called gastritis and among other things excessive alcohol consumption can trigger it.

"What should I do?"

"Stop drinking," he said as he took a sip of his vodka tonic.

"I'd like a second opinion."

"Sucks, doesn't it?"

"Yeah. Any other options?"

"Cut back on your drinking, or switch drinks."

"Now we're talking."

So I did both. I switched to Corona and cut back to three drinks a night, which was much less than the six to eight drinks a night I had grown used to. I did this for about two weeks until the gastritis went away. Then I went back to five drinks a night and got hammered plenty of times for the rest of my seven-month contract. I was drinking a little less than I had before, but still way more than I ever had on land. The gastritis never came back.

"If you drink or smoke," my hiring manager had said during my interview, "then you'll probably do more of that on ships."

It's one of the most accurate predictions anyone has ever given me, although I would probably amend that line to say, "If you drink or smoke *or have sex,* then you will probably do more of that on ships."

Luckily for the cruise line, passengers did lots of drinking as well.

Bob Dickinson, former CEO of Carnival, mentions in his book that on most ships, beverage sales bring in more revenue than any other onboard source. People usually think the casino generates the most onboard revenue, but only 30% of the passengers gamble. Almost every passenger spends money on drinks every day, and because the cruise lines purchase alcohol duty-free, it is far more profitable to sell alcohol on a ship than in a land-based bar. To take full advantage of this, bars are located everywhere and are never more than a few steps away. It's one of the key elements in the design of a cruise ship.

Twenty-one was the minimum drinking age onboard Carnival ships, but this is only enforced when the drink is purchased. Nobody went around looking for minors in possession. The cruise line actually sets the drinking age because a foreign-registered ship does not fall under U.S. jurisdiction. The drinking age on ships used to be eighteen, just like it was on land before the National Minimum Drinking Age Act of 1984, but Carnival later changed it to twenty-one because there were too many complaints about the youngsters getting too rowdy.

But the adults do the same thing. At one of the muster stations during boat drill, a mere five hours after embarkation began, there was often an unmistakably drunk passenger, laughing, singing, and sometimes puking. Sometimes passengers were too drunk to make it to boat drill and they passed out in their cabin before the ship even set sail.

I knew a gift shop manager who used to go to the spa at the beginning of each cruise to get a facial. The spa gave it to her for free as a way to advertise the service to passengers that walked by. It was a good selling tool, and passengers would often book appointments after seeing it, but the drunk ones would walk up and poke her to see if she was alive.

Excessive alcohol consumption is a curious phenomenon onboard cruise ships. Booze is often part of any type of vacation, but a cruise vacation conjures visions of fruity umbrella drinks and fine wine with dinner. Social settings often include alcohol, and a cruise ship, packed with 2000 other vacationers, is one of the most social environments you can be in.

Time onboard was limited, and to get their money's worth, passengers gained a collective six tons as they maximized their food intake. The same mindset, I think, is partly what made passengers drink more than they would on land. Many passengers binged for the entire cruise and this was especially true on the shorter cruises. Three-day cruises, like from Miami to the Bahamas, were almost always party cruises. The same held true—actually it was even more true—for the two-day cruises.

On a cruise, nobody had to work the next day or stay sober to drive home. It was an environment tailor made for heavy consumption. There were countless stories of drunken passengers taking their clothes off and streaking through the corridors or jumping in the pool naked. Drinking added to the fun of the cruise and didn't usually cause health problems for the passengers because once the cruise was over, the binge was over. But if you were a crewmember, the heavy binge continued with the start of the next cruise. And then the next one. And so on for the entire eight-month contract until you get gastritis.

☆ ☆ ☆

I had been on the ship—and on the hunt—for a couple of weeks, but didn't seem to have any options. Florina, the Romanian, would date me, but that would mean forfeiting the fun of the chase. But nobody wants to be in dry dock so I made a move one night and she accepted.

We had a lot of fun spending time together. When you are stuck on a ship, it's comforting to know that somebody is waiting for you to finish work and join her in the crew bar. It feels good to watch her smile when you do nice things for her, and it's more fun to go to the beach when you have companionship.

It's also fun to have someone you can make love to while wearing earplugs. They had become such an integral part of my life that after having a drunken thought about it, I had to. And with fluorescent orange poking out of each ear, I did.

On another occasion, I asked her to talk to me in Romanian while we made love. As I look back now, it feels like such a sleazy thing to ask.

"What do you want me to say?" she said.

"It doesn't matter because I won't understand it."

So she did. She was making solid eye contact as she spoke, and it was sexy as hell until I got the impression she was confessing her love for me.

I never asked her what she said. I didn't want that conversation. I had that lack of enthusiasm you get when the person you're dating likes you more than you like them.

We had been together for about two months when, because of some mechanical problems, the *Holiday* was scheduled to leave New Orleans at midnight instead of the usual 4:00 p.m. While the mechanics were installing new engine parts, many of the crew had a rare opportunity to party in New Orleans for the evening. Florina had to stay on the ship, but I went to Harrah's Casino and met a bunch of crewmembers and lost $600 while I got sloppy drunk.

I started walking back to the ship and made it to the long road that ran alongside the pier. It was about 11:15 p.m., and the road was completely deserted. There were three-story buildings on either side, and with all the shadows and dark corners, I felt exposed and vulnerable as I stumbled along by myself. I looked back and saw headlights coming from behind. Just as it passed me the car stopped, the door opened, and I was invited in.

It was a taxi, and the back seat was crammed with people. I stuffed myself into the back seat and sat on a girl from England, named Amy, who offered me a sip of her Hand Grenade.

Hand Grenades were sold at a bar called the Tropical Isle and marketed as the strongest drink on Bourbon Street. They were equivalent to 4.5 regular drinks. I slurped down half of her Hand Grenade as we passed it back and forth, and it was empty by the time we got to the ship.

Amy was a crewmember, and the taxi was full of other crewmembers heading back to the ship. She was attractive, with fair skin and reddish hair. She was friendly like the girl next door, but a total party animal. When Amy signed on, she was the talk of the ship, just as all attractive sign-ons are. About a week after she arrived, the ship's grapevine knew that she had slept with an Italian. Other guys were to follow.

I tend to ask questions that many people wouldn't ask. I like to hear the private things that people don't normally share. I'm especially interested in private things that pretty girls don't normally share. And Amy was a pretty girl.

A few weeks before the cab ride, we were in the crew bar together. It was a slow night, and I was shooting darts by myself when she came over to talk. It was her first contract, and we were talking about how fast relationships move on the ship.

"Dating someone for a month onboard is like dating someone for four months on land," I said.

"Why is that?"

"Because you see each other so often. Let's say that your first date on land happens on a Saturday night. Maybe you talk on the phone a couple times that week and go out again the next weekend. It might continue like that for a month before you start seeing each other during the week.

"On the ship, your first date is often the first time you sleep with someone. After that, you see each other every night. You probably eat with them at least once every day. You probably hang out in port together at least once a cruise."

"Assuming your work schedule permits it," she said.

"Yeah, that's true. I probably have one of the most flexible schedules on the ship."

"I bet you've slept with a lot of girls," Amy said, sounding a little contrived.

"Why do you say that?" I smiled and blushed. Sex makes for such great conversation.

"You just have that look. I bet you've broken a lot of hearts, haven't you?"

"Actually, it's quite a bit less than most guys my age."

"How old are you?"

"Twenty-nine."

"And how many girls have you slept with?"

"Eleven."

"That's it?"

"Yep. And at this time last year, my number was only two."

"What?"

I went on to explain that story, then turned the question on her.

"How many guys have you slept with?" I asked.

"Guess."

A low estimate was the only correct answer so I said ten.

"Higher," she said.

"Twenty."

"Higher," she said, this time in a slightly softer voice.

"Fifty."

"Higher," she said, a little quieter yet.

I kept going until she stopped talking and shook her head to tell me that the number was higher still. We stopped in the range of 400-500.

"I don't really know," Amy said, looking at the ground.

I closed my mouth and nodded, waiting for an explanation.

Then she raised her head and looked at me in silence. We just looked at each other for a moment. Then her look of guilt disappeared. "I used to be a prostitute," she said while staring me straight in the eye and taking a drag from her Marlboro Menthol.

My mind generated an endless list of questions, and I asked them all. Did she have a pimp? How much money did she make? Were her customers ever violent? How did she get into it? What did she do if her potential customer had a horrible, disgusting, fat body? We were both pretty drunk, and though I remembered most of the conversation, I don't remember her answers to these questions.

"I like sex," she said, "and so I figured why not get paid for it." I do remember that answer.

"Have you told anyone else on the ship about this?" I asked.

"No. Can you keep it between us?"

"No problem."

"So I have to ask," Amy said, taking another drag. "Are you turned off after hearing that?"

"Not really," I said, knowing that it was the only correct answer.

I was actually a little turned on by it. I wanted to know what it would be like to make love to a professional, a prostitute. Would someone with that much experience be better than a "normal" woman? Would the movements be more coordinated? I got better with practice, at least I thought I did, and so wouldn't that make an experienced prostitute one of the best lovers ever? And if she slept with me out of desire rather than money, then wouldn't she be more into it? Genuine passion, I think, is more intense than fake passion. Wouldn't my experience with her be even better than those who had paid?

I would never cross the moral boundary of paying for sex. But free love with a former prostitute was having your cake and eating it, too. Still, I wasn't sure about the moral boundary of sex with a former prostitute. If I loved her, then I could justify it. But this wasn't love, this was curiosity.

So back to the taxi ride, which was a couple of weeks after Amy had confessed to being a prostitute. We all got out of the taxi and walked up the gangway. One of the guys had to pee really badly, and since my cabin was close to the gangway he walked with me to use my bathroom. Amy followed. We went into my cabin, and I left my cabin door open. While the other guy was in the bathroom, the prostitute and I flirted.

"I want to see," she whispered in my ear while grabbing.

"Okay."

When the guy walked out of the bathroom, she took my hand.

"She wants to look at my schlong," I said to him as she pulled me into the bathroom.

"Yeah, we'll be right back," Amy said.

I went willingly. I closed the bathroom door.

For the last two weeks, my mind kept going back to the notion of being with her.

"So let's see," she said as she undid my button and pulled down the zipper.

She looked from different angles, kind of like the doctor did at the New York City STD clinic. She was silent. She had a frown on her face.

"There it is," I said proudly.

"Yeah. There it is," she said with zero enthusiasm.

I guess she had seen larger ones in her day. She validated the feeling of inadequacy I used to get when I stood at a urinal next to a guy who was taller and bigger built. Those were the times I peed with force to make it sound big.

And that was it. We walked out of the bathroom to see that the other guy was gone and had left my cabin door wide open. As I looked at the open door, I realized what had almost happened. Also, an open door put me at greater risk for getting caught by my girlfriend Florina or anybody who walked by, and it didn't feel good. I thought that this must be what it felt like for people who constantly hide something from the person they're cheating on.

It all happened very fast. I had to ask the other guy for the order of events the next day because I couldn't quite remember. It wouldn't have happened without the alcohol. Even though I was not emotionally attached to Florina and was just waiting for her to sign off, I'd always planned to be faithful out of principle. But I had lost my integrity and essentially cheated on her that night.

That is when I realized that cheating was easier than I thought. Maybe the ship's environment was partly to blame. Nothing happened beyond the hand grab. We didn't even kiss, but in my drunken state I would not have said no.

I didn't tell Florina. She was signing off in three weeks, and I was counting the days and trying to decide if I wanted to sleep with Amy after Florina left. Amy was scheduled to sign off one cruise after the Florina. That would give me a five-day window of opportunity.

Florina and I never talked about future plans until she brought it up during her last week onboard.

"So I was thinking we could stay together. You want to try to be on the same ship again?" she said.

"I'm sorry, but I'm not looking for that."

"So when I sign off, that's it?"

"Yeah I guess," I said as I shrugged.

She started crying and became angry. Then she started yelling. "This always happens to me with ship relationships," she screamed in between sobs as she turned away from me and crouched down to the floor.

This wasn't what I wanted. I didn't want her to feel bad. I wanted to comfort her, but I wasn't sure what to do. So I crouched next to her.

"Come here and give me a hug," I said as I put my arm around her.

That didn't go over well.

"Don't touch me," she said as she threw my hand off.

I didn't have much experience with breakups, and this was the messiest one yet. She got up and stormed off to her cabin. We had been outside at the front of the ship, and her cabin was all the way at the back. I followed her most of the way, but she had such long legs and was walking so fast that I practically had to jog to keep up. I finally broke off the chase and just let her go. I saw her the next day at lunch.

"I'm surprised you're still talking to me," she said when I went up and said hi.

"I'm surprised *you're* still talking to *me*," I said.

"Sorry about last night. The alcohol made me emotional," Florina said.

"It's no problem," I said, realizing that alcohol is mankind's most frequently used scapegoat.

We stayed together for the rest of her time on the ship. We even slept together a couple more times although we weren't the same couple as before. After that argument, there was tacit tension. An uncomfortable distance, really.

She signed off the ship and then emailed a lot. I always responded. A couple of months later she asked if I wanted to meet her for lunch in New Orleans. She was going to be there before joining her next ship. I was uncomfortable because I already had a different girlfriend, but I said yes. Then her schedule changed and we never met, and I never saw her again.

When Florina left, I still hadn't made up my mind about Amy.

"You know my friend wants to date you," Amy said to me on the first night of her last cruise.

"Yeah, I know."

I had known for a few weeks at that point, but never acted on it.

"So would you go out with her?"

"I'm not interested in dating anybody right now. I just went through a messy breakup." I made this blanket statement because I didn't want her friend to feel rejected.

"What about later? Would you date her later?"

"No."

"Would you *ever* date my friend?"

"No."

"Why not?"

"I have no interest in her. I'm sorry."

"Would you ever date me?"

"Maybe."

But other than that conversation, I didn't pursue her and didn't see her much during her last cruise. I think she was more interested in other guys. Guys with bigger schlongs, maybe. And it's just as well. Her past made me uninterested in a long-term future with her, and I was still worried about catching a disease, even though a year and a half of debauchery had tempered that fear quite a bit.

CHAPTER 11

WHAT YOU SHOULDN'T DO WITH A METAL DART ON A CRUISE SHIP

We had a lot of parties on the *Holiday*. About every two months the hotel director organized a ship-wide crew party complete with food and free drinks. One of the ship's large lounges would be sectioned off with posted signs that read, "Private Party," and a security officer would guard the door to keep the passengers out.

Sometimes the parties were more private. The casino manager often organized a party in one of the small lounges for his staff because they worked later than most departments and usually couldn't make it to regular ship parties. One of the doctors had a going-away party that the F&B manager catered with chicken and pig that had been alive earlier that day when he bought them in port. Because I worked with all the department heads, I was invited to just about every one of their private parties. I partied in the chief engineer's cabin for his girlfriend's birthday. I partied in the hotel director's cabin for a purser's birthday. The casino manager had a party in his cabin for no particular reason, and I went to that. These were in addition to the drinking and partying we did almost every night in the crew bar and during the day at the beach.

We also had a crew disco party in the *Holiday's* crew bar about once a month. The tables and chairs were moved out of the way to make a small dance floor, and the ship's DJ brought in the good speakers and a few colored lights to go with the disco ball. The officers and staff could go to the passenger disco every night of the week, but the crew-ranked employees didn't have that privilege and so the crew discos always had a good turnout.

There were Independence Day parties, but they never happened on July 4th. There were never enough motivated American crewmembers for that. Besides, the non-American crewmembers had to tolerate enough American immodesty and patriotic fervor from the passengers anyway. But I joined the Indians for their Independence Day and feasted on a buffet of Indian entrées while they blasted Indian pop music. They knew the words to every song. They danced with passion and showed how proud they were of their heritage.

I also went to a Canadian Independence party. It was a small gathering that one guy organized on the open crew deck. It was BYOB, and the organizer brought some Labatt Blue, a Canadian beer, which he bought in port. He asked everyone to show up wearing something that represented Canada. A couple of people had maple leaf stickers on their shirts or a water tattoo of the Canadian flag. I took a yellow Post-it note and in South Park fashion wrote, "Blame Canada" on it and clipped it on my ball cap.

When the ship was in port, we had yet another reason to party. If we weren't on a shore excursion, there were essentially two options: Go to a beach or go to a bar. It wasn't much different than being in the crew bar, really. We just drank someplace different. My favorite bar was a place called the No Name Bar in Cozumel. It was walking distance from the pier but well hidden from the passengers. Sometimes I'd play chess with the owner or play Connect Four with some of the other crew. One night I grabbed the microphone and started rapping Snoop Dogg's "Gin and Juice." There was no karaoke, no music. Only drunk Jay and a microphone. It was also the same night that the photography manager hit a small jackpot on the bar's slot machines. Instead of cash, he was awarded a bar gift certificate that he had to use that day. He cashed it all in and bought seventy-five Coronas. He handed two Coronas to everyone he knew and lined the rest up on the bar for anyone to take. It was quite a sight, but a bit anti-climatic because we drank dollar Coronas on the ship every night and we didn't even have enough time to finish the beers before we had to be back onboard.

With Carnival, every cruise included a talent show in which passengers performed onstage. It usually involved singing or playing an instrument. The crew had its own talent show about every four months. A few people sang or played an instrument, and sometimes the dancers choreographed a special routine. There was also a group of guys who always dressed up in skirts and stuffed balloons down their shirts to perform some kind of skit. Those always generated a lot of laughs.

The art auctioneer brought a CD with him one night to the crew bar and asked the bartender to play it. It was an album from the Hermes House Band, which became popular in Europe with techno versions of "I Will Survive" and "Take Me Home, Country Roads." Whenever that CD was played, the crew bar exploded. Everyone screamed and jumped out of their seats and bounced around and hugged and swayed as they sang along to the lyrics. For the next three months that song was played once or twice a night, and every time the reaction was the same. It was a phenomenon unlike any I had seen. They were like a cult and just couldn't get enough of that damn CD. After a few weeks I'd had enough, but everyone else kept bouncing and singing along.

The chief purser was a very likable girl from Ireland. After a few drinks somebody would put on an Irish tune and she'd start River Dancing in the middle of the crew bar. But the best crew bar antic happened when the Internet café manager took his pants and underwear off and moved his hips so that it swung around in circles.

"Dude! You did the helicopter in the middle of the crew bar!" I said to him when he told me about it.

"Yep."

"Did you get in trouble?"

"I got sent to the staff captain," he said.

"Then what?"

"I denied it completely."

"Did he believe you?"

"No, and so he ordered security to question people who were in the crew bar that night to corroborate my helicopter incident."

"Then you got written up, right?"

"Nope. Everyone covered for me and said that they didn't see anything."

✢ ✢ ✢

Just like with dating, one month of friendship onboard was equal to about four months of friendship on land. There was no distinction between friends and coworkers. We worked together and ate together and partied together seven days a week so there was never a need for a long goodbye.

I always thought it was cool—prestigious even—to know people from other countries, and while on ship, I knew people from all corners of the world. They weren't just acquaintances. These were close friends I came to know very well, and they had a great diversity of professions.

I used to sit in the F&B manager's cabin while he disciplined some of his staff. He had worked for Carnival for twenty years and told stories of the old days, when the regulations were more relaxed and having sex with the passengers was more the rule than the exception.

One of the production singers gave me some singing lessons. I'm an awful singer and there wasn't much she could do for me, but I still enjoyed the experience.

I drank with a fly-on performer who could swallow a sword that curved ninety degrees. I ate lunch with a guy who had a foot juggling act and had performed on the Ed Sullivan show thirty years earlier. I'd chat with the fly-on comedians, and sometimes our conversations turned into a monologue as they worked their craft and tested new material on me. They always had a pen and paper on them, and I liked being present when a new idea struck, and they wrote it down for later.

I got to know a couple of women from the embarkation staff in New Orleans. I used to smuggle duty-free Marlboros off the ship that the ladies would reimburse me for. I felt bad supplying the older woman with cartons of half-priced cigarettes. It was like helping her to her grave, but in return, they would bring me some Fruity Pebbles and Gatorade and other grocery items I couldn't get on the ship.

One day the older woman offered to let me borrow her car. I took her up on it and saved fifty dollars in cab fare that day as I drove to a specialty shop to buy some darts. I returned the favor by topping off her gas tank, and for the rest of my time with New Orleans as a home port, I was free to use her car any time I wanted. This was a huge advantage. Really huge. It saved me two hours of waiting for the crew bus, which only went to Wal-Mart or the mall. I could actually drive to my destination. It was like I was sixteen again and reliving that feeling of freedom that came from not having to wait on someone else to get somewhere. Sometimes I'd borrow her car simply to go to Jack in the Box and order a Sourdough Jack and curly fries just because I could.

I spent most of my free time in the *Holiday's* crew bar playing darts. You know you're lucky when you can hit the bull's-eye while you're drunk during rough seas. These were real darts with sharp metal tips instead of those imitation plastic ones. At no time did I feel that having darts in our drunken hands was dangerous. Except once when an arrogant guy, an American named Bobby, aimed a dart at Peter, a social host, who was sitting on a couch near the dartboards.

"Can I throw it at the wall above your head?" Bobby asked Peter half-jokingly.

Peter's girlfriend was sitting right next to him and she protested, but Peter didn't. With his head tilted up slightly and his eyes looking up to meet Bobby's eyes, he just shrugged his shoulders and gave a reluctant nod of approval. Peter's body language made it clear that he did not want this, but he wasn't going to back down. Bobby didn't expect it.

"You're sure it's okay?" Bobby asked.

Peter nodded again, even though his eyes were begging Bobby not to go through with it.

It looked like this was really going to happen, and Peter's girlfriend let go to jump away so that she wasn't in the line of fire.

"All right, this is the last time I'll ask," Bobby said as he took aim and pumped the dart. "You're sure it's okay, cause I'm going to throw it?"

Peter gave a single nod. Bobby leaned forward on his right foot, pumped a couple more times, and threw the dart.

Bobby was consistent and accurate and was probably one of the top five dart players on the ship. I had beaten him a couple of times, not because I was a top five dart player, but because there were some nights when he just wasn't on. He had been drinking this night.

Peter didn't flinch or even blink. The dart landed and stuck. It was perfectly centered about six inches above his head. I didn't think he would really throw it. And then without a pause, Bobby grabbed a second dart, leaned forward on his right foot, pumped a couple of times, and threw again.

It was mesmerizing. I stood there and watched the way you watch a police chase on television, never averting your eyes so as not to miss the impending disaster. Again Peter didn't blink. His girlfriend stood silent with her hands covering her mouth. The second dart landed right next to the first, again about six inches above his head. Then Bobby grabbed his third and final dart. He raised it up to aim.

"Okay, okay, that's enough," I said, jumping in and waving my hands.

Bobby immediately brought his hand down as if he were glad that someone had called this off. Peter didn't say anything and took a sip of his drink. His girlfriend sat down and hugged him. The tension immediately dissipated.

"Dude, don't do that again," I instructed Bobby.

He puffed up his chest and scowled until I added, "Please." Then he relaxed.

"Man, I know you're a great dart player," I went on, "but someone could've bumped into you. The ship could have hit a wave and then he could've been blind in one eye."

Bobby nodded and agreed. Then I sat down next to Peter and told him the same thing. He also nodded and agreed. And then I finished my game of darts with Bobby like nothing had happened. He beat me as usual, because luckily, he was on that night.

✵ ✵ ✵

There were gaping differences in the workload and quality of life among the different positions and departments onboard. I knew an assistant housekeeping manager who worked ten to twelve hours a day until he became a shore excursion manager so he could average working only five hours a day. His ranked dropped from officer to staff, but it didn't matter. The privileges were almost identical, and his new position had far less stress and gave him a lot more free time to be in the crew bar.

I watched a crew-ranked waitress get promoted to an officer-ranked purser. This jumped her from the lowest rank to the highest. One day she was serving food to the officers and the next day she was sitting with those same officers while her former peers served her.

When she first wore her officer duds, her speech and body language betrayed a lack of confidence both on the job and when hanging out with her new officer purser friends. But within a few weeks she grew cozy in her new role and her personality changed. She was less friendly with me. She was never rude, just less friendly. Instead of always smiling and being nice to me because I had a higher rank, she no longer bothered to hide her real attitude toward me.

She became somewhat pretentious and began ordering food in the mess hall instead of being extra polite in asking for it. She bought a $300 pair of sunglasses and made sure that everyone knew how expensive they were when she wore them in the crew bar. She often kept her officer's uniform on in the crew bar, whereas before she'd always changed out of her crew-ranked uniform and into regular clothes.

Her new uniform, her new rank, and her new confidence made her more desirable, at least to me. There it was again, my attraction to power. The affect her uniform had on me was particularly surprising because officer uniforms do not hang well on women. The pants are baggy and the shirts are loose and hide the female curves. The uniforms for waitresses were far more visually appealing because they were designed for women. But the waitress uniform represented a lower social status that was less desirable than an officer who wore the more prestigious officer uniform. At least to me anyway.

This girl's hair hadn't changed. Her physique hadn't changed. She was pretty, but I reminded myself that there were other women onboard who were probably more attractive. But her new level of sophistication induced a desire that was undeniable, though I never told her. It was obvious that she wasn't interested.

Female lions mate with males that physically dominate a territory. The male lions achieve their power through physical superiority, and that power is a status symbol. The more they have, the more they're desired. The same with humans. Power and high status are attractive. Not to everyone, of course, and I may be an anomaly in that as a guy, I'm attracted to women with power. I think a lot of guys are turned off by this. In any case, there was no better place to witness this phenomenon than on a ship, where kings and peasants lived so close to one another.

I felt it with a hotel director too, even though she was not my type. Although she was very pretty, she smoked, she weighed more than me—which wasn't that hard given than I only weighed 140 pounds—and she was a bit older. She was awesome to hang out with, but had she been a bartender, I wouldn't have been attracted to her at all. But because she had one of the most powerful positions on the ship, I found myself leaning in to kiss her on the cheek after partying in her cabin one night. Nothing else happened, but I was ready for it to. And all because of her rank.

I had never consciously realized that sex appeal is more than just genetics and fashion. There is a level of prestige involved similar to how the popular kids in high school weren't always the best-looking.

It wasn't until after I worked on ships that I realized just how much image affects the way others rate your attractiveness, or at least how I rated the attractiveness of others. It happened while I watched the movie *Bride and Prejudice*. There is a scene in which the bride-to-be is singing a song called *No Life Without Wife* with her three sisters. Some of the girls were better-looking than the others, but they were all cute. They were well dressed throughout the movie.

During this song, three of the girls danced with grace. One didn't. And that one became instantly less attractive to me once I saw her goofy movements and flailing arms. It reminded me of a girl I knew in college. She was pretty, but her style of dress left something to be desired. I had considered asking her out until I saw her dance. Her arms were out of control, and every movement she made was awkward. Then and there I knew I'd never, ever date her. She had lost any appeal she ever had to me.

As I thought about these two awkward-dancing women, I realized that I had undermined my own limited sex appeal countless times with my dancing. I used to jump in the middle and do a jig that rivaled the *Elaine Dance* from *Seinfeld*. My goal was to be as funny and ridiculous as possible. I usually got some laughs, but now I realize those were expensive laughs. Image-killing laughs. Weird Al Yankovic gets lots of laughs, but think about the image he portrays.

So maybe that's why I was never able to attract one of the ship's dancers. A dancer's career is based on image. Image is constantly on their mind, and it's why nearly all dancers love to have their picture taken. Thus I realized another mistake: a dancer will not date you if you look like you're having a seizure when you dance in front of her friends.

✿ ✿ ✿

I went to the pizza bar with some friends one night after the crew bar closed. There were a number of us sitting at a table when the crew bartender walked by. He had finished closing his cash register and was headed to the bar manager's office when he came to our table to chat.

"Hey, have a seat," I said after we'd been talking for a couple of minutes.

"No, no, I can't," he said.

"Why?"

"If I sit with you now, then tomorrow I sit with the staff captain."

I had forgotten how restricted the crew-ranked crewmembers were. They had no onboard privileges. Zero. They were allowed in passenger areas only when they were working. Besides getting off the ship while in port, they were confined to the crew areas in their free time. They could not go to the piano bar, or the disco, or the Vegas-style shows, or the fly-on acts, or the passenger bars, or the 24-hour pizzeria, or the Lido Deck buffet, or the musical acts.

Officers and staff could do it all. They were free to roam the passenger areas and enjoy every passenger amenity, with two exceptions: One, the casino was off limits. This kept the crewmembers from working together to steal from the house. And two, eating in passenger dining rooms was only permitted if a crewmember's family came on a cruise.

Nowhere else do members of a different class work and live so closely together. I didn't go to the disco every night, sometimes only once a month, and after watching the same Vegas-style show a couple of times, there was no reason to see it again. I did eat a lot of 24-hour pizza and a lot of food from the Lido Deck buffet. But even if I didn't use a specific amenity very much, the freedom to do so made living on the ship far more bearable.

One of the best reasons for working onboard was the travel. Passengers only saw each port once and had to choose just one or two things to do, but the crew visited each port repeatedly.

It was one of the few amenities in which the crew had an advantage over the passengers.

I was in Cozumel twice a week for a year, and I did everything there was to do on that island. Many of the crewmembers paid for their shore excursions, but because I kept the shore excursion manager's computer running, I always went for free. I went down the list of excursions and picked a different tour each week and the shore excursion manager would write me a free pass that I'd hand to the local tour operator. I swam with the dolphins and drove the speedboats. I sailed in the catamaran tour and rode a horse in the ocean. I hand fed the stingrays. Going through the excursions was one of the few things that kept me going during a contract.

There were other things that the crew did in port that most passengers would never do. Things like going to the movies or playing mini-golf were almost as much fun as any shore excursion because it made you feel normal again. Even going to the local grocery store was enjoyable because the package labeling and products–in Mexico, for instance—were unfamiliar, and I got to see the locals living in their element rather than faking an image for the tourists.

One of my favorite things to do was to go snorkeling and feed the fish. I'd grab some bread rolls from the staff mess and sneak them off the ship. I had an underwater case for my digital camera, and I got some great pictures and video of fish swarming around me like piranha.

✳ ✳ ✳

I was at the hotel director's meeting one day when he told us that in a few weeks we would have a theme cruise.

Theme cruises were initiated either by the cruise line or by some other company. Sometimes only some of the passengers would be there for the theme cruise. Other times, the entire ship would be charted. The basic premise is that people like to be with their own kind and so a cruise was structured to bring people with similar interests together.

Some of these cruises included seminars, like the "Chefs at Sea Cruise," which had hands-on cooking classes, or the "National Geographic Traveler Photography Cruise," which had classes on photography. Others, like the "Acupuncture at Sea Cruise" and the "Wine and Food Festival Cruise," offered services or events that you wouldn't normally find on a cruise ship. Some cruises centered around a celebrity guest, like the "Country Cruise Getaway with Tim McGraw" or the "Rusty Wallace NASCAR Cruise." There were cruises for people with disabilities, gay cruises, murder mystery cruises, singles cruises, and poker cruises.

Rosie O'Donnell chartered a cruise for 500 gay and lesbian families and had a documentary film made out of it called *All Aboard: Rosie's Family Cruise.* John Heald, a cruise director with Carnival, started a blog about his experiences on the ship, and he had such a following that he organized a theme cruise for his fans called the "Bloggers' Cruise."

Though not really a theme cruise, it's worth noting that some elderly people have been known to opt for living on a ship instead of a retirement community. They just book cruises back to back indefinitely and stay in the same cabin.

Some cruises circumnavigate the globe. These "Around the World" cruises visit about fifty unique ports and last up to four months on a single itinerary that is broken into segments that can be purchased separately.

You can even be a passenger on a container ship, although there isn't much to do since there are virtually no amenities onboard. In contrast, the most expensive way to travel on a cruise ship is to buy an onboard condo from a ship called *The World,* where prices range from one to six million dollars each.

The theme cruise that happened on my ship was called the "Christian Cruise." The hotel director explained how it would work during one of his weekly meetings. The entire ship was chartered, and the company that organized the cruise brought on their own preachers, Christian speakers, and Christian performers to provide all of the onboard entertainment. Passengers paid three to five times the regular price of a cruise to immerse themselves in a Christian environment. It was expensive because, in addition to paying for the Christian entertainment, the company that chartered the ship had to make up for all of the ship's normal revenue streams that were shut down during the cruise.

The hotel director went through the list of preparations that would convert the ship into an environment free of sin and temptation. Gambling was not allowed, and the casino was turned into a Christian bookstore. Every slot machine and gambling table had to be fully covered and out of sight. The bars served only non-alcoholic drinks, and all liquor bottles had to be hidden. The gift shop's liquor store was shut down, and its windows had to be blacked out to block the sight of alcohol.

Seductive perfume posters were removed from the gift shop. Cosmopolitan-type magazines with covers that said things like, "10 Ways to Touch a Man" or "Orgasms Incorporated" were taken down. There was a poster in the spa that revealed a woman's upper back and it had to be removed. Television was censored. Shows like *CSI* and *The Simpsons* were forbidden so that no violence, adult language, or sexual content showed on the cabin televisions. Instead, a special set of Christian movies and other G-rated family shows were aired. The Vegas-style production shows were cancelled and replaced with Christian entertainers. The crew was required to wear conservative clothing at all times. Instead of tank tops and shorts, long sleeves and pants were mandatory.

Despite all restrictions, the crew loved it. The casino staff, the dancers, and the musicians didn't have much to do, so they didn't have to wake up early or be sober for a shift. It was a vacation. So while the passengers were praying and studying the Bible, the crewmembers defiled themselves even more than usual.

It was an easy cruise, even for the crewmembers who had to work, because the deeply devout Christians were exceedingly pleasant and hardly ever complained. It was one of the smoothest cruises the pursers ever had. The other hotel departments also had far fewer complaints than on a normal cruise. And it was probably one of the few cruises in which not one crew member slept with a passenger.

✲ ✲ ✲

One of the more interesting theme cruises is the "Nude Cruise." Each year, a handful of cruises are chartered and filled with a couple thousand passengers who walk around the ship naked. Like a nudist colony or a nudist beach, the microcosm of a cruise ship is the perfect hideaway. My wife, Mirka, was a crewmember during a nude cruise that happened on the *Ecstasy*. From the casino cage, she had a great vantage point, and this story comes from her.

The passenger rules were simple. They had to be over eighteen and clothes had to be worn when the ship was docked and during the captain's party. If they weren't wearing bottoms, then they had to carry a towel and sit on it instead of directly on the chairs. Other than that, clothing was optional for the entire cruise. Boobs, butt, and schlong could be hanging and dangling all day long.

The charter was announced to the crew a month before the sailing date. After an overview of what to expect, the crew had the option to be temporarily transferred if they felt uncomfortable. About 2% took this option, and they were sent to a different ship at Carnival's expense. The crew that stayed had the option of working fully naked or being dressed in their normal uniform. 0% of the crew worked naked.

One of the problems was that passengers didn't always use their towels, and it just wasn't a pleasant sight to see someone's nether regions on a community chair. The housekeeping department was diligent about wiping everything down and security helped enforce the towel rule, but once the crewmembers witnessed bare skin touch a chair, they just didn't want to sit there anytime soon.

The passengers also sat at the dining tables and ate their food naked. Now I'm all for naked dining when I'm at home by myself, but I'm not about to share my bread basket with some hairy old guy who just scratched.

The crew mostly disliked the naked bodies. Only about 5% of these bodies were young and in shape. 10% were average. The other 85% were either old, or fat, or both. The average passenger age was fifty, and their flesh jiggled in the dining room as they danced the naked Macarena. Many of the women were obscenely overweight, and one woman had multiple rolls on her stomach, which her sagging boobs rested on. She started covering herself toward the end of the cruise, probably because of the tacit scorn of the eyes upon her.

The casino employees had no desire to look at these naked bodies, and since the assistant casino manager was married to the refrigeration engineer, the A/C was set to be really cold in the casino. This forced the passengers to wear robes. It made the casino staff cold, too, but they thought it was worth it. It worked for a couple of days until the passengers complained and the thermostat had to be raised.

One of the ports was a private island. A few of the crewmembers went to the island to check it out, but they reported that the passengers didn't act different than anyone else on a beach, they just didn't have their clothes on.

Although none of the crew worked fully naked, some of the crew did participate. By their own decision, the ship's dancers did one of their production shows topless, and they also partied in the passenger disco topless.

There was an overweight guy named Jack who worked in the casino, and he went to the disco completely naked. Ship's security wouldn't let him in because he didn't have a name tag, so he went back to his cabin and put on shorts so that he would have a place to pin his name tag. Security said no, you have to wear your name tag in the normal chest area position. So right there, while standing outside the disco as the security officer watched, Jack took the needle from his name tag and pierced it through his nipple and set the latch. Then he took off his shorts and danced his way into the disco completely naked and victorious.

It was all very entertaining for the crew. Mirka was in the casino cage when a male passenger walked up to her counter. He was tall and the countertop reached just below his waist, and when he leaned forward, it curled up like an inchworm on top of the counter. He wasn't trying to be offensive or even funny. He just wanted to exchange his chips for cash. She tried not to look, but as he talked about his bad luck at the tables, she couldn't help but notice that the cold granite counter caused just enough shrinkage to make it point directly at her.

Instead of a formal night, the nude cruise had a costume night. There were all types of costumes both erotic and funny. A brunette girl, who was beautiful and had a body in the top five percentile, wore an outfit that was made of black vinyl. The costume was snug fitting and wrapped around her neck with a low-cut back that tapered into a G-string from behind, and left her privates completely exposed.

One guy named Bill wore some suspenders that were covered in fluffy brown imitation fur. But instead of latching onto pants, the end of the suspenders had a stuffed toy monkey that wrapped its hands around Bill's parts. Because the casino was so cold, there wasn't much to grab onto, and when the Fluff Monkey lost its grip, the suspenders snapped up.

"Hey, watch your monkey!" one of the other passengers at the blackjack table would yell as everyone laughed and hollered.

The guy would stretch the monkey and put him back in place, and a few minutes later it would snap up again and someone would blurt out, "Run for your lives, the monkey is on the loose again!"

✷ ✷ ✷

A few weeks after Florina signed off I started dating a beautiful shoppie from Australia named Claire. She was very petite and had an amazing body. She was nineteen. I was twenty-nine. I didn't think the difference in age would be a problem, especially for a ship relationship. I know people with successful marriages who have a similar age gap, but Claire and I were not a good match. She was a lot like me when I was nineteen, but now that I was twenty-nine, her youth was annoying.

I've always been a science buff. It was my favorite subject, and I still love to know how things work. One day Claire and I were walking down the beach and looking at the ocean.

"Do you know what causes the waves?" Claire asked in an excited tone that suggested she knew the answer.

"What?" I asked, already knowing the answer.

"It's the moon. The moon causes the waves. I don't know how. I just know that the moon causes the waves. Isn't that cool?"

Then and there I knew that our relationship was over. But I just bit my tongue. Of course, the complete answer is that the gravitational pull of both the moon and the sun creates the tide, not the waves, and that wind is what mostly causes the breaking waves that hit the beach.

Okay I had to look that up before I wrote this, but at least I knew the moon's gravity played a part.

I'd been getting more and more annoyed with her as each day passed. I knew I was being pompous, but it seemed like all of our conversations went like that. She would say something as if it were the biggest revelation ever and I'd have to play along. It was always something that had been a revelation to me ten years earlier when I first learned it. She was such a nice girl, and if we had been closer in age, I'm sure I would have felt different.

I'd just had the messy breakup with Florina, and I wasn't keen to go through that again. So I hung on, not sure how to get out of it. Then I had a knock on my cabin door one night. I opened it and Claire was in tears.

"What's wrong?" I asked.

She held out a pink slip. It actually was a slip of paper, pink in color, and she had just been fired. Claire would be off the ship in less than ten hours. She fell into my arms for a hug, and once my chin cleared her shoulders, I let go of my sad face and let loose with a grin of relief as I comforted her in my arms. When the hug ended I put my sad face back on.

"What happened?" I asked.

"She said I had a bad attitude," Claire said as she wiped her eyes. "And that she was forced to let me go after I missed that meeting with the corporate manager."

"Oh yeah, I remember that."

I spent the rest of the night helping her pack. We had a bon voyage bone, and then she was gone.

The procedure for firing a crewmember could be pretty harsh. If she had done something flagrant like fighting or getting caught with drugs, then she would have been confined to her cabin until the next embarkation day. Security would have guarded the cabin door twenty-four hours a day to make sure she didn't leave. This prevented the problems that arose from a disgruntled crewmember who had no work and lots of free time. Even if she wasn't that upset, she would have been more likely to drink and party too much, so confining crewmembers to their cabins made the most sense.

Claire was lucky that her manager told her the night before. The normal process for getting fired for something that wasn't flagrant was a knock on the door at 6:00 a.m. on embarkation day. The crewmember would wake up to pack, sign some paperwork, and be off the ship by 9:00 a.m. Sometimes crewmembers were even escorted to the airport to ensure that they flew home instead of staying in the United States illegally.

✲ ✲ ✲

A few days after Claire was fired, one of the Italian engineers asked me to help him transfer pictures from his digital camera to his computer. He was on duty and said his cabin was unlocked and that I could just go there and do it. So I did. After copying the pictures to his computer, I opened one to make sure it worked, and that was the first time I saw all of an Italian's hair. It was a picture of him striking a pose on the bed, in the buff. I clicked to the see the next picture. And the next. There he was, naked in every picture. I called him back.

"Hey, I finished moving your pictures to the computer," I said.

"Thank you. Did you see the pictures?"

"Yes, they were wonderful."

"Sorry about that," he said laughing. "My girlfriend took them."

It wasn't the only time I dealt with nudity on the computers. I didn't have much storage space on my servers, and every couple of months I had to delete the .mp3 files and the movie files that my users had saved on the network drive. They took up the most space and they were never work-related and so I never bothered asking them before I hit delete. I just deleted at will. If they were songs I liked, then I would listen to them before deleting them. If it was porn, then I might take a peek before deleting it.

I didn't know the people involved, but there is a story of some crewmembers who met in the main lounge one night to watch a few porn reels on the giant movie screen. It was late, and they locked the doors so that no passengers would walk in. Everyone was drinking and having fun, and afterward they tidied up and took all the films with them and went to bed, but they forgot about the one that was still in the projector. In the morning one of the hostesses went to the main lounge to give her usual lecture and play her usual film about the next port.

"And here is a film about the fun you can have in Pago Pago," she said as she pressed play.

CHAPTER 12

HOW TO DECONTAMINATE A CRUISE SHIP

For me, there was social evil onboard the ship. I'm speaking, of course, about the rampant infidelity. On land, I'm probably surrounded by more unfaithful people than I realize. After all, lovers tend to cheat in private. But there was no hiding it in the ship's small-town atmosphere. I witnessed multiple affairs in progress every day. It bothered me not just because it existed, or because I witnessed it; what bothered me was that it was so commonplace and so frequent that it came to be considered normal behavior. Fidelity was an aberration.

As physical beings, we like to indulge in physical pleasures. Land-life and society tend to keep our morals and inhibitions in check. But ships don't do that. The detachment from family and land-based friends gave everyone the freedom to act on their lust with little chance of getting caught.

Before my wife Mirka worked on the *Holiday*, she worked on a different ship and lived with a roommate named Ellen from Hungary. Ellen kept pictures of her hometown boyfriend all over the wall of their cabin. She even hugged a framed picture of him at night while she slept. Ellen talked about how they were a perfect match and how she couldn't wait to marry him.

But it was her first ship contract, and after a month onboard, she slept with the production singer. It was a one-night stand, and two weeks later she started dating a guy from the gift shop named Ben. They slept together in her bed while the framed picture of her hometown boyfriend was perched a few inches away. That was okay because Ben was crazy in love with a girl from a different ship and he talked about her constantly, even in front of Ellen.

After a couple of weeks of Ben telling Ellen how excited he was to see his girlfriend when their ships were going to be in port together, Ellen stopped seeing him. A week later she started dating an Italian bridge officer whose wife was taking care of their six-month-old twin girls back in Italy.

There was a housekeeping manager whose wife and kid came on the ship to cruise. The housekeeping manager put his ship relationship on pause while his family was onboard. It always blew my mind when the unfaithful brought their hometown sweetheart to the ship. I just never understood how you could parade her around in front of everyone who knew you had been unfaithful. Even if nobody told your sweetheart directly, wouldn't you be at risk of them learning it through the eyes of the people they met?

The housekeeping manager's ship mistress was nowhere to be seen during the cruise, but she came out of hiding after his family left and they resumed their affair as if nothing had happened. Then the mistress signed off and the housekeeping manager briefly dated a gorgeous 6'3" blonde Croatian stewardess. She had been pursuing him for awhile, and he said he tried to resist her advances.

"I have my limitations," he told me one night in the crew bar after he'd finally succumbed. A few weeks later his original mistress came back onto the ship and they started dating again.

There was no shame in being promiscuous. The best example I saw of this was when a girl from the gift shop started dating the staff captain. Four days after the staff captain signed off, she started dating the doctor. When the doctor signed off, she looked all over for her next guy and even gave me the let's-get-it-on eyes.

I don't know if she found anyone, but two weeks after the doctor left the staff captain came back to the ship and they started dating again right away. Then the gift shop girl signed off. Within a week the staff captain was dating a girl from the casino. Then the staff captain signed off for vacation again. After visiting his wife and two kids in Italy, he came back to the ship and started dating the casino girl again. This all happened with no drama and no confrontations that I ever saw.

But there was big drama with the casino manager from South Africa named Alan. He signed on the ship two months before his wife, a gorgeous casino cashier from Slovenia named Mila, was scheduled to sign on. Three weeks before Mila arrived, Alan started dating a Bulgarian dealer.

We didn't think much of it and expected the affair to end when Mila arrived. It was business as usual. But a week before Mila arrived, Alan emailed to say he had found someone else and didn't want her to come to the ship.

It was too late for Mila to change her plans. She also hoped that they could work through it and stay married so she signed on the ship, and instead of staying in her husband's cabin, Mila was assigned to her own cabin. She spoke with him a couple of times and tried to talk him out of leaving her, but Alan wasn't having it.

"I don't want to know you," he finally said to her.

It's difficult to avoid someone on a ship and if you both work in the casino, it's impossible. Not only did they both work the casino floor, but their positions meant that they shared a small office. The Bulgarian mistress, who also worked in the casino, was always around, and it was heartbreaking to watch everything unfold.

I walked into the crew bar one night and saw Mila sitting with tears streaming down her face. In fact, every time I saw her, she was either crying, about to cry, or had just finished crying.

Alan emailed the corporate office and explained the situation, and a manager from Miami flew to the ship to make an assessment. The manager did her best to console Mila, but finally let her go home on medical leave.

Mila left the ship at the next homeport. A couple of months later, Mirka talked to Alan.

"Why did you leave Mila?" she asked.

"I never loved her."

"Then why did you marry her?"

"I was getting old and thought that it would be my last chance to get married."

Everyone agreed that Mila was a better catch than the Bulgarian mistress. Mila was friendlier and much better looking. The only thing the Bulgarian mistress had, maybe, was slutty sex appeal. Mila had sex appeal, but it was wholesome and the kind that I would think most guys would prefer in a wife. Maybe the Bulgarian was better in bed. But it didn't matter because four months after Mila left, Alan was transferred to another ship and had to leave his Bulgarian mistress behind.

Stories of infidelity were endless. Every crewmember at sea could tell you one. It happened on every ship, in every department, and in every rank. Had I stayed on ships long enough, I likely would have been involved in more infidelity either from my own weakness or from someone cheating on me.

I have a friend who was a virgin when I met him in college. Like me, he was saving himself for the right girl. He wasn't ready, but one night his girlfriend seduced him. He told me about it the next day.

"So how was it?" I asked.

"Dude, it was freaking awesome, and now that I know what it feels like, I just want to bang every girl I see."

Over the next few weeks and years I watched him become a lewd mass of sexual energy. His first taste infected him with an insatiable appetite that manifested in the way he looked at and treated women. For him, it seemed there was only one topic worth discussing.

"Dude, there are so many hot chicks here," he would say.

"Dude, that girl was so freaking hot," he would say five minutes later.

I was in my abstinence phase during all of this, and at times I was disgusted with his new personality. And then on the ship, without realizing it, I started acting the same way. The environment crept on me. My morality began to rot, and I didn't seem to care.

I began to say indecent things. One of the musicians was dating a youth counselor and one day he told me that one of the dancers came on to him.

"What did she say?" I asked.

"She said she wanted me and said she would wait for me to break up with the youth counselor."

"Are you going to do it?"

"I don't know."

"Dude," I said, still fascinated with the prestige of the dancers, "that's like trading in your old Honda for a new Lexus."

He didn't like that.

Sex was always on my mind. I sat next to the crew trainer one day during the crew talent show, and she was wearing a skirt that went halfway up her thighs. She had beautiful, toned legs. Maybe I was cold and maybe she had just worked out, but I could actually feel the heat radiating from her legs. I couldn't keep my eyes off of them, and all I could think about was how I wanted to be with her.

I hit on one of the girls who worked at the corporate office in Miami. She was a programmer, and I saw her a couple of times when I was passing through. Her skin was soft and dark and flawless. She had puffy lips and pretty eyes. She had a graceful walk and a relaxed and peaceful voice, and I imagined her to be very sensual.

We talked a couple of times when I had problems with one of the programs she wrote. I flirted with her over the phone the first time we talked, but she ignored it. She flirted back with me the second time. I decided that I would ask her out if I was ever in Miami again though it never happened.

Since that girl reacted so favorably to my flirt, I flirted with a different girl in the IT department over the phone. She was married, but I ignored that because marriage never mattered on the ship.

"Hey, thanks for your help," I said to her as she was looking something up for me. "I always enjoy hearing your sexy voice."

She ignored my comment and started talking about how to fix the problem with the servers.

"Okay, I'm trying that now," I said, typing in the command she had told me to try. "It's working now. Excellent. It must have been that sexy voice of yours that fixed it."

"Listen, I'm a married women, and I'd appreciate it if you wouldn't talk to me like that."

"I'm so sorry. It won't happen again."

As I look back now, I can't believe I did that.

But at the time, that encounter wasn't enough for me to change my ways. There was a band that mostly performed in a lounge at the back of the ship, and the lead singer was beautiful. I've always been especially attracted to girls who can sing. She had a great body, too, and I usually saw her in full makeup and wearing fashionable stage clothes that showed off her figure.

She sat down next to me in the staff mess one night as the rest of her band joined us. The conversation was friendly.

"How long have you guys been playing together?"

"About seven years now," she said, answering for the rest of them.

"How long have you been on ships?" I asked as I checked her finger and saw a wedding ring.

"This is our second contract."

"It's my second contract, too."

"What do you do?"

"I'm the I/S manager. I fix the computers."

"That's cool. I always envied people that could work with computers."

"So I see your ring there. You're married?"

"Um, yeah. That's my husband right there," she said, pointing to the guy sitting across from her.

"Boy, you're a lucky guy," I said to him.

"Thanks," he said with caution that I ignored.

I looked at her.

It disgusts me to put down on paper what I said next.

"If you weren't married, I'd be chasing you." I took a sip of my water. "In fact," I continued, "you should be careful because I might chase you anyway," I said laughing and thinking I was so funny.

She gave a disapproving chuckle and the table went silent. My grin faded as I glanced at everyone. Then I realized what I had just done: I had changed the mood from friendly to uncomfortable—practically hostile—and had come across as a total dirt bag. I took one more bite and left the table with much of the food still on the plate. I never got to talk to them much after that since they all avoided me for the rest of the contract.

Maybe I was more susceptible than most to the negative influences of the ship environment, but I wasn't the only one this transformation happened to. Mirka witnessed it with one of her friends. She saw him for a few days in Miami while they were waiting for their ship assignments and didn't see him again until a few contracts later when they went to a hockey game together. It had been two contracts since she'd seen him, and the only thing he talked about was how piss drunk he got on the ship and how many women he and his maître d' friend had scored. Then he looked out at the ice rink and talked about how #22 was sleeping with a famous model and how #43 could get almost any girl he wanted. When Mirka first met him, he could carry on a normal conversation, but after two contracts, he talked about nothing but sex and alcohol.

Sex was truly the lifeblood of the ship environment. It rarely, if ever, affected the level of service that the passengers received. We all acted like angels around the passengers, but we were very different around one another. Sex was so easy to find and nearly everyone was doing it. It is, after all, hardwired into our very existence. Without a sex drive—or put another way, without a desire to act in ways that lead to offspring—our species couldn't exist.

Family and land friends were so far away that you never had to answer to them and they never knew what you did. Society wasn't there with its watchful eye. And because everyone else was doing it, it was easier to ignore your own morals.

So there I was, ignoring my own morals. I wasn't the nice, considerate guy I'd always thought myself to be. All I wanted was sex, and I didn't really care if that made people uncomfortable.

Your environment shapes who you are and how you act. Although I didn't realize it at the time, I resented the ship because of this. Looking back now, I can't believe how repulsive I had become.

✳ ✳ ✳

A couple of weeks after I offended the back lounge band, there were bulletins posted around the ship asking crewmembers with B positive blood to contact the infirmary. One of the crewmembers—someone I didn't know—was in need of a transfusion. After giving blood in the afternoon, I went to the crew bar that night and caught an exceptionally nice buzz off of two beers.

I was standing near the entrance when this beautiful girl walked in. She had just signed on the ship. New faces were always welcome, especially pretty ones. I followed her with my eyes as she walked toward me on her way to the bar.

"Well, hello," she said in response to my staring.

"Hi," I said back.

As I played darts that night, I kept glancing over to the table where she was sitting.

A couple of days later, my pager went off. It turned out a girl from the casino cage was having problems with her printer. It was the same girl from the bar. Her name was Mirka.

After fixing her printer, I went back to the computer room and looked her up in the A-Pass system. She was two years older than me and from the Czech Republic. We had a few passing conversations over the next few days, and then she invited me to join her and some casino friends in Cozumel.

The plan had been to rent Jeeps and drive around the island, but we woke up late and all the Jeeps were gone. There were five of us. Three decided to go to the beach, and Mirka and I took a taxi downtown to get massages.

The massage parlor doubled as a hair salon, and it was in a rundown building with no air-conditioning.

"Hi, we'd like to get massages," I said to the hairdresser, who was in the middle of cutting hair.

"Okay, wait here," she said, walking to the back and disappearing around a corner.

"Here is the lady that does massages," she said, motioning to a short, overweight Mexican woman who was especially unattractive.

"Hi," I said to the masseuse. "We'd like to get massages."

The masseuse looked at the hairdresser.

"She doesn't speak English," the hairdresser said and then translated for me.

The masseuse nodded her head and said something back.

"Which one of you wants to go first?"

Mirka and I looked at each other and then she asked me to go first. The masseuse led me to a small, square room with dingy stucco walls that stopped short of the thatched roof. Since daylight came in through this space, they had decided the room didn't need a light fixture. In the middle of the room was a massage table covered with a dark green sheet, but instead of a headrest that extended from the end of the table, there was just a semi-matching green pillow lying on top of the bed. It was a U-shaped travel pillow like you see at airports. It was made of cloth and had no pillow case.

It looked clean enough so I lay down on my stomach and placed my face on it. It didn't smell too fresh, and my face began to sweat immediately. I wondered how many other greasy faces had been sweating into this pillow. I pushed it away a few minutes later when I realized how ridiculously uncomfortable it was. It was too high, and I was slightly more comfortable without it. I was there for a massage, but my neck continued to cramp as I alternated between turning my face to the left and right.

The door to this room was not a typical door. It was a hard plastic collapsible curtain door that slid across its top railing to divide the room. When closed, there was very little space between the front of the bed and the curtain. It was certainly not enough space for this lady. She ooched pass this space a number of times during the massage, and each time the folds in the curtain flapped across her butt while the folds in her belly slid across my head.

After thirty minutes, my session was over. I peeled away from the sheet that was now visibly soaked in sweat.

"How was it?" Mirka asked.

"Interesting—and I'm not sure you want to go," I said.

"Ah it's a massage. It can't be that bad," she said as she went in for her turn.

After her session, we walked over to La Choza, my favorite restaurant in Cozumel.

"I don't think I'll ever go there for a massage again," I said.

"What a stupid pillow," she said.

"Yeah, and it didn't even have a towel to cover it. That sheet was so sweaty by the time I finished that I thought I should wring it out."

"I wish you would have because it was still wet when I lay down."

"They didn't give you a fresh sheet?"

"No."

"So this is our first date and we've already shared sweat. I think we're moving too fast."

"Who said this was a date? I'm paying for my own lunch."

After eating we went to the beach and met the other three from the casino.

"Can you put some sunscreen on my back?" I asked, handing her the bottle.

"Put sunscreen on you?" she said, taking the bottle. "I think we're moving too fast."

From the beginning I could see myself in a long-term relationship with her. But when we first tried to make love, I wasn't able to perform. Few things are more humiliating, more degrading, than being unable when you're about to sleep with a girl for the first time. I was ready, but during the delay of finding the condom, I lost it and couldn't get it back. The problem was that I was thinking too much. Mirka had told me about her last boyfriend, and I felt like I had to meet or exceed his performance. I also really wanted a future with her, and all the pressure just got to me.

"Well, this is awful. I can't think of anything more embarrassing," I said.

"It's okay. Don't worry about it. It's probably from the alcohol."

We tried again the next night.

"Just relax and don't think about anything but the touch and the feeling," she said.

That helped. But I was so worried that as soon as I was ready, I started.

Without protection.

And that was how I discovered that sex is simply better without a condom. I mean, like, way better. Latex insulates the sensation and you miss out on so much. It's like wearing a glove to pet a kitten and never knowing just how soft it is.

This no-condom thing was a major discovery for me. It was as if I had been a virgin all along, never realizing how pleasurable it could be. From then on, I didn't want to use them at all. After having been terrified of disease and pregnancy for so many years, my first experience, my first *real* experience made me ignore the risks. I craved that unprotected sensation.

And so we continued, unprotected, and it was working out great until Mirka said she was late.

"What do you mean *late?*" I said.

"I haven't had my period yet."

Oops.

These consequences of sex were becoming a real inconvenience. They spoiled everything. The next couple of days were unnerving. She was five days late when she walked into the crew bar. I had just thrown my set and handed the darts to Bobby.

"Hey," I said as she walked over.

"I have something to tell you," she said, leaning in to whisper in my ear. "I'm not pregnant."

"Hooray!" I belted out with my hands in the air.

"Dude," Bobby said. "You made me jump right as I was throwing. I missed the dartboard completely."

What a relief. I mean, seriously, that was a close one. But once I thought about it, I knew that I needed proof. Either one of us could have been transferred to a different ship or sent home at a moment's notice. I could have woken up the next day to see that she had flown home to have our child without ever saying goodbye or even telling me about it. I had to be sure, and only after seeing the toilet could I fully relax.

With that crisis behind me, I was happy to see my parents on their next free cruise. It had been scheduled a couple of months earlier, before I had met Mirka, but I didn't tell her about it until the night before. We had only been dating for three weeks and it was a bit awkward at first, but my folks loved her. We all spent time in port together, and ate in the passenger dining room.

On the last night of the cruise mom once again did a huge favor and took $6,000 in cash to deposit in the bank for me. I said goodbye to my parents and went to the crew bar.

After shooting darts all night, I went back to my cabin. I had just pulled the sheets over me when I got a page from one of the accountants who shared my office.

"Our office is flooding," he said.

All of the ship's servers were in that room. I wasn't in the mood for this.

"Is it just a little bit of water or a lot?"

"Not too much right now, but it's getting worse."

"So you're saying that it's bad enough that I should get out of bed."

"Yeah, I think you should come up here right now."

The *Holiday* had been flooding quite a bit in recent months. One day the swimming pool on Deck 10 started leaking down to the casino on Deck 9. The water was running down the walls and dripping onto the slot machines. Mirka saw sparks shooting out of them. That side of the casino was roped off, and the swimming pool was drained for the rest of the cruise. In the next home port, when all the passengers were off the ship, the welders fixed the bottom of the swimming pool by climbing up into the ceiling of the casino.

There were a number of times on the *Holiday* when a pipe broke and flooded some of the passenger cabins. It was a nightmare for the pursers who had to deal with moving upset passengers to a different cabin, or worse, had to deal with irate passengers who were forced to stay in the wet cabin because there weren't any empty cabins to move them to. It was one more new experience and so I never minded when the ship flooded. That is, until I had to clean up the mess.

I/S managers were responsible for sending a weekly status report to the shore-side management in Miami. In that week's report, I wrote up a description of the flooding and copied the other I/S managers in the fleet. I kept a copy for myself, and with only a few grammatical changes, here it is:

It was Saturday September 13th at 4:30 am when I got a page that the computer room was flooding. Fortunately I had not gone to bed yet and headed up to check it out. Hot water was coming from a broken pipe in the laundry room and seeped into the computer room from one of the drains beneath the carpet. The plumbers were paged to stop the leak. Housekeeping arrived with wet vacs to soak up the water. After ten minutes, I noticed that the water was rising faster than one wet vac could suck it up, so I had them bring another wet vac to help.

In the meantime I radioed the bridge to send an electrician to cut all power to the computer room. All power was cut and the servers ran on battery power for another ten minutes until the battery bank ran out. Unless the servers did it on their own, they did not have a proper shutdown as I was not about to stand in potentially electrified water to go through a proper shut down sequence.

The additional wet vac brought the flooding under control and the water level eventually receded but not before spilling into the passenger area. The noise from two wet vacs and twenty crewmembers talking and walking up and down the corridor woke up the nearby passengers and they were poking their heads out to see the action.

The plumbers disassembled the ceiling in the laundry to locate the faulty pipe and to cut the flood's water supply. One of the two sets of battery backup units was on the floor in the computer room and it shorted out. The sparks were pretty cool.

When the electrician arrived to cut the power, he just stood in the water and used his bare hand to unplug the battery units which were still sparking. I don't understand how that could have been safe. I had to track down a power strip to replace the one that was floating. I removed the fried battery units from the power loop and had the electrician turn on the power to the computer room. It was like a nuclear reactor coming online as everything electrical revved up and hummed to life at the same time.

Most of the servers came back with no problem, but a few took some extra effort. This was the day we were in home port so in the middle of all this I had to set up embarkation.

One of my network switches died after the power was restored so I swapped it out with my spare. Otherwise everything is working fine and the only major damage was losing the battery banks and all of my backup tapes as they were soaked.

It was noon before I had everything cleaned up. After being up all night and through the morning, I lay in bed and had just pulled the sheets up when my cell phone rang.

"Hello?"

"Hey, dude," my friend Foy said, "I'm here at the embarkation terminal. What now?"

"Goddamn it, Foy."

"What!"

"I'll be right there," I said, putting my uniform back on.

I had offered free cruises to all my friends and family, and Foy was ready to cash in. He was listed as my stepbrother for the cruise that started that day. I got him checked in at the gangway and took him to the purser's desk to get his cabin keys. I told him about the flooding as we walked to his cabin.

"All right, dude," I said as he threw his bags on the bed of the passenger cabin I had secured for him, "lunch is on Deck 10, and I'm going back to my cabin to go to bed now. I'll meet you in the dining room for dinner."

"Where's the dining room?"

"Just go to Deck 5 and ask around. You'll find it."

"Cool."

Because I had to work and carry the pager during that cruise, I didn't party quite as hard as I had when my friend

Ryan came to cruise. We still got drunk every night, but we were always in bed by 3:00 a.m. Separate beds, that is.

I waited until the next to last night of the cruise before asking Foy what I had been planning to ask for months. By then he'd been partying non-stop for three days with people from all over the world. He'd been shagging a beautiful British girl for two days. We were in the dining room and had just ordered our food and were enjoying the bottle of wine that the maître d' gave us for free. Having connections on the ship was awesome.

"So I have a question for you," I said.

"What's that?"

"When my contract ends, I'm going on a backpacking trip through Asia. You want to go with me?"

"You mean like you and Ryan did?"

"Yes."

"Hmm. When does your contact end?"

"Three months."

"Interesting. Tell me more."

"Well, when Ryan and I went, we had no pre-booked lodging. And, except for our short flight from Athens to Cairo, all we did was buy roundtrip airfare from Dallas to Rome. Otherwise, we had no itinerary. We stayed in hostels and avoided taxis whenever possible."

"Why didn't you take taxis?"

"Ryan had this weird goal of using public transportation whenever possible. He thought it would add to the experience if we used buses and subways instead of taxis."

"Did it?"

"Actually, it did."

"Did you guys have fun?"

"Have you had fun on the cruise so far?"

"Oh hell yeah."

"Well, backpacking is a lot like this. But in addition to all the partying, you get lots of eye-opening cultural experiences. The whole trip through Europe was awesome, and he and I agree that it was the coolest thing we've ever done."

"How come you didn't ask Ryan to go again?"

"I did. But he's only been at that startup company for a few months and can't get away. He might be able to meet us for a couple weeks at some point, but he can't be gone the whole time."

"How long would you want to go?"

"How about two months."

"I don't know if I could take that much time off from work." He worked for the same small consulting company in Dallas filling the same IT position that I'd been laid off from.

"Yeah, I don't know if they would let you do that or not."

"Well, let me think about it, and I'll check with my manager when I get back."

"Cool."

✵ ✵ ✵

About a month after Foy left, our ship was infected with the Norovirus. It's the most widely reported ailment on cruise ships. Victims suffer diarrhea, vomiting, and abdominal pain for a couple of days. Most of the outbreaks on cruise ships happen when the virus is brought aboard by someone who got infected in port, either from person-to-person contact or from contaminated food or water. It's extremely contagious, and once onboard it spreads like wildfire. One infected chef can contaminate hundreds of meals. One infected passenger can contaminate the handrails and elevator buttons that hundreds of passengers will touch.

248

Sea-based Norovirus outbreaks receive far more media coverage than the land-based outbreaks. The Centers for Disease Control agree that outbreaks on ships are just as common as outbreaks on land. Any confined space with lots of people incubates the disease whether it's a cruise ship or a movie theater or a school. But there is no organized system to track the number of people that get sick after eating contaminated popcorn from a movie theater, and so that story would likely not get any media coverage.

The confined environment of a ship makes it easy to track the number of infected people. The infirmary is actually required to keep a running total of passengers who complain of diarrhea or vomiting. When 3% of the onboard population report the same ailment, it's considered an outbreak. The CDC gets notified, and the media outlets pounce.

Outbreaks are inconvenient even for those who stay healthy. For passengers, a sick family member affects the whole family and the vacation they paid for. Healthy crewmembers don't have it easy either. The workforce is already spread thin, and losing even 3-10% of the workforce is crippling. The long hours get longer when you have to cover for those who get quarantined.

The outbreak on the *Holiday* lasted three consecutive cruises. The infirmary took notice when on one cruise a handful of passengers and crew got infected. It got a little worse on the second cruise and worse still by the third cruise.

The captain called a meeting. Every onboard department head and high-ranking assistant manager was required to attend the meeting. They needed to be able to communicate and enforce a plan to everyone in their department. Although I was a department of one, I got to be there. This was the first time I'd been involved in an epidemic, and I was eager to know how these things were handled.

There were about fifty people in the room, and the atmosphere was lighthearted as we took our seats and chatted and joked. It felt no different than the hotel director's weekly meeting. The captain started things off.

"Okay, we have a serious situation," he said, although I didn't think his body language matched his words. "We will need everyone's cooperation here. Please, give full attention to the doctor now."

"Listen, guys," the doctor said. "This is a very serious situation. To get this under control, we will need to follow my plan to the letter."

The doctor's body language matched his words, which abruptly changed the atmosphere. Everyone was now taking it more seriously. This power of poise has always amazed me. The combination of body language and the way you talk determines how others respond. Thoughts and beliefs don't always stand on their own. The key to making them powerful is in the way they are presented.

"Carnival reported that six percent of the passengers and eight percent of the crew are infected," the doctor continued. "If we don't get this under control, it will continue to get worse.

"Sick crewmembers will be quarantined to their cabins at the first hint of a symptom. No exceptions. Everyone must wash their hands frequently, especially after using the restroom and before eating.

"Housekeeping will have the brunt of the extra work. They will begin sanitizing twenty-four hours a day. Every handrail, every elevator button, every door handle, and anything else that people touch will be wiped down with a bleach-based disinfectant multiple times a day. Every casino chip will be cleaned. If we follow this exactly, we can wipe this out in one cruise."

Mirka helped clean the casino chips. The casino crew dropped in a handful of denture cleaning tablets into buckets of warm water. After the bubbling stopped, they dumped in the chips and let them soak for about ten minutes before drying each one by hand. Not only did the denture cleaner disinfect, but it also was good at dissolving the dirt and grime that had built up on the chips.

Cabin stewards and dining room staff, infected before the regimented sanitation program began, were dropping like flies, and the shortage of personnel was a real problem. Some of the healthy crewmembers who normally served the crew were moved over to help serve the passengers. Most of the officers and staff didn't have cabin stewards for that cruise.

We also didn't have any waiters in the staff mess. Instead of ordering our food off the menu and having it brought to us, we just grabbed a plate and served ourselves from the kitchen's buffet line. The only person working the staff mess was a girl whose only job was to squirt self-drying sanitizer into everyone's hands as they walked in.

When a crewmember was quarantined, someone was assigned to bring him food, but with all the chaos, some people were simply forgotten about. Mirka's roommate had to call her boyfriend to bring her some food.

Because we were so short on staff, passengers probably received a slightly lower level of service than normal. But disease is a fact of life, and there is only so much that can be done to keep it off of a cruise ship. Metal disks are placed on the mooring lines to keep rats from boarding, but you have to let the passengers on.

The plan worked just like the doctor said it would. The number of sick people dropped to one percent on the next cruise, and it was completely gone on the cruise after that.

Shortly after the outbreak, a sanitation officer from Latvia named Tatiana boarded the *Holiday*. I'd first spoken to her during my first contract back on the *Triumph*, when she paged me one day.

When I called the number from my pager, she picked up and introduced herself. "Can you help me with my computer?"

"Sure. What's the problem?"

"Difficult to describe. It is in my cabin. Can you meet me here?"

"Sure, I'll see you in a few minutes," I said.

I knocked on the cabin door.

"Come in," she said.

She had the overhead fluorescent cabin lights turned off and instead had a couple of smaller lamps in use that made the room slightly darker. She was wearing her officer uniform and sitting on the bottom bunk with her computer on her lap. I sat down next to her, making a conscious effort to not sit too close or too far away.

"So what's wrong with it?" I asked.

"I'm running out of space."

"You're hard drive is full?"

"I think so. How do I tell?"

"Let me see," I said.

I put the computer in my lap and started poking around. She leaned in close to watch.

I thought of Tatiana as one of the most desirable girls on the ship. She had light-colored blue eyes and blond hair and a beautiful European complexion. Her best feature was her lips. They were naturally pouty and perfectly shaped. On top of all that, she always wore an expression of confidence.

"Actually, you have plenty of space. Four gigs, to be exact."

"What does that mean?" she asked, turning her head so that our faces were very close together.

"It means that you have plenty of space. Why did you think you were low?"

"I was trying to copy something and it didn't work."

"If you have it with you, I can try."

"No, it was from a different ship. I do not have it."

It felt like she just wanted a reason to get me to her cabin.

"So what does a sanitation officer do?"

"I go to a ship and stay for three weeks. I evaluate the sanitation, make changes if needed, then go to next ship in the fleet."

"For an entire contract you only stay on each ship for only three weeks?"

"Yes."

Though it didn't occur to me at the time, her brief stay on each ship meant that she had probably been with many guys. There was sexual energy between us as we sat on her bed with her computer working perfectly fine. But I had a girlfriend on the *Triumph* at the time so I didn't make any moves.

Mirka and I were dating when I saw Tatiana again, this time during my second contract on the *Holiday*. I sat down with Tatiana in staff mess one day.

"Hey, how are you?"

"Okay," she said. She didn't really remember me, but I had not forgotten her.

"I met you on the *Triumph* about a year ago."

"Okay," she said, taking another bite of food.

"How long are you staying on the *Holiday*?" I asked, struggling to get some conversation going.

"Three weeks."

Maybe I was smiling too much. Maybe I was staring. Whatever I was doing, she noticed it. After a couple of minutes she finally responded.

"Did we have sex?" she asked, dropping her hand on the table.

"No," I said, laughing, but probably still staring.

"Well... do you want to?"

I wiped my mouth with a napkin.

Mirka and I had only been dating for about a month. We were having a lot of fun together, but hadn't yet made a deep connection, nor had we officially agreed that we would be exclusive. In fact, she kept asking me if I was married.

Living on ships for eight years had negatively affected her as well. She had a hard time trusting people because during her eight years on ships, she had had four ship boyfriends, all of whom had cheated on her. Her last boyfriend turned out to be married. She expected me to cheat. And with its dark spurs prodding me along, the ship urged me to sleep with Tatiana, who would be off the ship in a few days.

"Well do you?" Tatiana asked again.

"No," I declared. "I have a girlfriend."

CHAPTER 13

WHAT YOU SHOULDN'T
SAY TO THE CAPTAIN

I ordered Michael Gelb's *How to Think Like Leonardo da Vinci* and had it shipped to the home address of one of the women who worked the embarkation terminal. She brought it to me during the next homeport and after reading it one night, I set the book down and closed my eyes. One of the book's suggestions was to pay special attention to what your senses perceive.

I concentrated, but all I could hear was that headache-inducing thunder of the engines. Then I focused on what I was feeling. All I could feel was that monkey brain vibration. Wait. I could also feel that engine thunder in my chest. I opened my eyes and left the cabin.

I looked down the cabin corridor. There was that wavy linoleum that unevenly reflected the light above. There was that light above, in all its low-hanging harshness. I walked down the corridor and past the smelly ashtray bolted to the wall.

I stepped onto the I-95 and paused. It was about 1:00 a.m. and yet there was still plenty of foot traffic. Crewmembers looked at me as I stood staring at the walls with no apparent purpose.

The walls were flat, and painted solid white. I looked up. That overhead jumble of pipes and wires, which had disappeared from my normal awareness, came back. I looked at the floor. The metal was fatigued, and you could make out where the crossbeams were beneath the floor. Red paint had been replaced with a think layer of clear lacquer. Wire brushes had been attached to power tools to strip the paint beginning at 8:00 a.m. every morning the week before. I couldn't sleep through that even with earplugs. The paint-stripping marks were uneven and fanned out in all directions. An entire floor of scratched steel was ugly even by crew standards.

Except for the pretty girls walking by, I couldn't find anything that was pleasing. So I went up on deck. I took a slow breath of the salty night air through my nose. Continental air was never this clean. It was a clear night, yet the moon was nowhere to be found. The ship was far away from the city lights, and I'd never seen so many stars. With my hands dangling over the rails, I listened to the waves splashing against the hull and wondered when I had last been in a traffic jam.

For the next few months I paid special attention to everything and realized that I constantly alternated between diametrically opposed environments. The crew areas were miserable, but everything else was awesome. I'd force myself to swallow lukewarm bites of hamburger in the staff mess one night, while the next night I'd eat fish that the F&B manager caught and prepared himself and served to a privileged group in the dining room. While smelling the suntan lotion on the beautiful bodies next to me, I'd dig my feet into the sand while sipping a beer, and then a few hours later I'd board the ship and smell motor oil as I stepped over broken pieces of the engine and pallets of bundled trash on my way to another crappy staff mess dinner.

This increased awareness made it more difficult to sleep because my cabin was like a never-ending earthquake with the equivalent magnitude of 4.5 on the Richter scale. I could stand in front of the mirror and watch my body shake. Passengers on the decks above me even complained to me about it.

"I promise you," I'd tell them after apologizing for their inconvenience, "it's not nearly as bad as my cabin."

The worst part was trying to sleep. Alcohol was mandatory, but that bed shook me awake even from a drunken slumber. I'd lie there, trying to get back to sleep. My body would gradually tense up until I became aware of it and then I consciously relaxed. Then I would gradually tense up again, notice it, and consciously relax again. I do the same thing when the dentist picks my teeth. When I did get back to sleep, I stayed tense through the night.

The eight pieces of bed foam made the bed too soft, which gave me chronic back pain like never before. I tried to switch up the foam pieces. I put four underneath the mattress and four on top. I tried putting all eight pieces underneath the mattress.

I asked the ship's carpenter for a piece of plywood. I was hoping to put eight pieces of foam on the bottom, then a piece of rigid plywood, and then the mattress on top of the plywood. The foam would absorb the vibration and the plywood would keep the mattress from sinking in the middle. The carpenter ignored me for a couple of weeks before telling me that he couldn't get a piece of plywood that big. So I dropped down to just two pieces of bed foam, one underneath the mattress and one on top.

Sometimes I lay on my side to minimize the amount of flesh that made contact with the vibration. It helped in that my body shook less, but it made my head shake more. Monkey brains. Gotta avoid the monkey brains. I tried to sleep on my back as much as possible and when I did roll to my side, I hung off the edge of the pillow so that less of my face would touch the vibration.

The next day I'd watch the sun drop right into the water as a postcard perfect cloud would cover just a sliver of it. Then I'd stay up all night partying with Mirka and we'd watch the sunrise. And no matter how many times I had seen it before, I'd catch myself standing there in the middle of the day and gazing at the open ocean. On rare occasions, I'd see dolphins swimming alongside us. More often, I'd see the flying fish scatter from the ship or I'd watch the sea birds swoop down to pick up the remains of fish that took a ride through the ship's thrusters.

257

Then I'd think of my living conditions. It was like an extended hotel stay. I'd lived out of three suitcases for two years. I would have moved nine times in two years when I finally left the *Holiday* for good. Signing off a ship was like moving because you have to pack everything and say goodbye to friends and familiar surroundings and go reestablish yourself someplace else.

My hiring manager was right. I did reach a point where I wanted nothing more than to be off the ship. It had become a floating prison.

As a comparison, imagine working in a cubicle seven days a week, always eating in the company cafeteria. Coworkers are your neighbors and the only people you can be friends with. You're only allowed to leave the building during scheduled breaks that happen four times a week, and you sleep in a space about the size of a master bathroom.

Even the captain's cabin is only the size of a one-bedroom apartment, but the captain doesn't have a full kitchen and he doesn't own his furniture and he's bound by the same schedule as everyone else. On land, my standard of living in a one-bedroom apartment was higher than that of every cruise ship captain at sea.

Speaking of captains, one day I needed to install a patch on the captain's computer. I had been on ships for about a year at this point and had found that the best time to work on the captain's computer was right as the ship sailed because he was always on the bridge and not sitting at his desk. I would ask if it were okay to work on his computer, he would say yes, and then I'd walk a few steps to his cabin and do what I needed to do.

"Bruno," I said with a slow, friendly tone as I walked on the bridge and headed toward the captain. About fifteen people were on the bridge. They were all silent because the captain had his hands at the controls and was guiding the 46,000-ton ship delicately away from the pier. The captain didn't seem to acknowledge me and kept looking out the windows and down at the pier.

"Bruno," I said again. "Would it be all right if I worked on the computer in your cabin?"

He turned his head away from what he was doing, looked at me for half a second, and shooed me away with a flipping motion of his wrist. No one else said anything and just watched me as I turned around and left the bridge, completely pissed off.

I didn't understand. I had tried this same tactic with the previous captain and it worked like a charm. Of course, he and I had a good relationship, and I don't think the ship was actually in motion or that he had his hands on the controls when I had done this before.

Bruno woke me up the next morning with a page at 8:00 a.m. I called him back.

"Hi, this is Jay," I said with morning frog voice.

"I would like you to take a look at my computer," the captain said.

"Is this something you need to have fixed right now?"

"Are you too busy to come right now?"

"No, but I was sleeping."

"It is eight o'clock, and that is when the workday begins."

"We all have different schedules and my girlfriend works late in the casino. I didn't go to bed until 5:00 a.m."

"You were working until 5:00 a.m.?"

"No, I stayed up to spend time with her."

"I would prefer you to come to my cabin now."

"Okay, I'll see you in a minute."

I couldn't be bothered with my uniform so I put on a T-shirt and my most comfortable and favorite pair of jeans—the ones with gaping holes on each knee and loose threads dangling all over. I slipped on my sandals, put on a ball cap, and went to his cabin.

"Bruno," I said with that same slow, friendly tone that had worked so well on the previous captain.

My attire seemed like a good idea when I put it on in my cabin, but I felt a little underdressed next to his clean uniform and fully striped epaulets. I poked around on his computer with something that was clearly not urgent and then went back to bed.

Later that day, the captain paged me again and asked me to come to his cabin. I shared an elevator ride with the hotel director, who had also been paged by the captain. We entered the captain's cabin together and saw that the staff captain was also in attendance. I knew I was in for it.

"Thank you everyone for coming," the captain said after we all sat down on his couches. "I have a number of complaints with you, Mr. I/S manager. The first is that if I page you, then you should not protest about the things I ask for."

"I am always happy to help you at any time for urgent requests," I said. "I only ask that if it is not urgent, then you send me an email."

"If other computer problems are more urgent, then I understand. Otherwise, I expect you to do what I ask when I ask."

"Yes, but everyone has a different schedule on the ship. If your problem isn't urgent, then I don't know why I should have to be here if I've only been asleep for three hours."

"I do not care if your girlfriend works in the casino. I expect you to do what I ask."

I repeated myself. He repeated himself. We went back and forth for fifteen minutes until both the hotel director and the staff captain chimed in and took the captain's side. It was clear that my position was indefensible.

"Fine. I will come up here whenever you ask," I said, just to end this. I sat with my face in my hand. I slouched on the couch. I full-on pouted. It was all I had.

The captain rambled on and repeated himself yet again. I simply agreed.

"And next," he said, "you will wear your uniform whenever you are on duty. I do not want to see you working in jeans that have holes."

I agreed.

"And finally, you will not call me Bruno. You will address me as captain."

"Yes, captain," I said.

The meeting ended. I walked out with the hotel director. He took the stairs, and as I waited for the elevator, the staff captain walked up and waited with me. During busy times, crew elevators often stopped on every floor, so we were likely to be there awhile. We exchanged friendly looks, and I could tell that he sympathized with me.

"Listen," he said, "he is the captain, and the best thing you can do is to just go along with whatever he wants. I've worked with many captains, and trust me, your life will be much easier if you do this. There was one time when—"

He went silent as the captain walked up. I made eye contact with the captain and then looked away with an expression of contempt.

"Oh, come now, don't look so sad," the captain said. "It wasn't that bad." Then he reached over and started pinching my cheek as he made baby sounds. "Boo boo moo moo boo?"

I raised my arm to break the grip he had on my cheek. He started laughing as he turned to the staff captain. In that moment I could have punched him in the nose, but later I wished I had pinched his cheek in return. Either action would likely have gotten me fired.

A few days later I was summoned for a drug test that I don't think was entirely random. I passed. A few days after that, Carnival awarded me my one-year anniversary pin in a ceremony along with fifty other crewmembers who had been with Carnival for one year. Each person's name was called to have their picture taken with the captain as he shook their hand and gave them the anniversary pin.

I put on a goofy smile for my picture. After it was developed, I took a marker and defaced it by giving the captain a uni-brow, extra chest hair, and a pint-size penis. I put a caption next to his mouth that read, "Hello, my name is Mr. Asshole," and a caption next to my mouth that read, "Why do I have to shake hands with this douche bag?" I stuck the picture on my cabin wall for the rest of the contract.

Now don't get me wrong. There are worse jobs than being an I/S manager on a cruise ship, and relative to other sea jobs, I had a great gig. Consuming alcohol onboard a NAVY ship is generally not permitted, and the crewmembers of cargo ships don't usually visit sandy paradises. Also, neither of these types of ships has unlimited quantities of beautiful women onboard. I don't know how those mariners do it. I don't know how the crew-ranked people on a cruise ship do it.

I knew a crew-ranked waiter from Thailand who had just started his first contract. As time passed I watched as the life got sucked out of him. He smiled and joked a little less each week, each month. He was barely twenty.

"I never smoked before working here," he told me one day.

I didn't ask, but I knew he didn't smoke for conformity. He didn't smoke to improve his image. He worked eighty hours a week, and smoking was his only onboard privilege.

Nonetheless, every job has its downsides, and toward the end of my second contract, I couldn't help but focus more and more on the things I disliked about the job and the people I had to interact with.

There was this spa manager. I loathed the sound of her voice and the sight of her pretty face, and she knew it. She was always friendly and nice, but she could barely use a computer. Any I/S manager would agree that it doesn't matter how nice or how pretty a girl is because, if she bothers you with questions like, "How do I email a file?" and when you demonstrate it she doesn't write it down and then forgets and beeps you the next day and says, "Can you show me that email thingy again?" then you will hate her.

In the same way that people with a truck get tired of helping everyone move, I got tired of helping everyone with their computer problems. You can always sell a truck, but once an IT guy, always an IT guy. Even after changing careers, everyone still came to me for computer help. On the ship, all 1,000 crewmembers saw me every day and knew that I was the computer guy and thus their personal computer consultant. They even asked for favors with their non-work-related electronics.

"I bought a new printer. Can you hook it up for me?"

"Can you help me put songs on my iPod?"

"Can you burn the pictures from my camera onto a CD?"

I started accepting payment. One guy gave me twenty dollars after I reinstalled programs that weren't working. Another guy bought me a bottle of Johnnie Black and a bottle of amaretto after I'd spent five hours backing up, re-imaging, and restoring his laptop. But I only got paid from people I didn't know very well. Close friends expected it for free, and I could never demand money from them.

But I did say no to stupid requests.

"Can you fix my cell phone?"

"No."

"Can you come with me to Best Buy and help me pick out a laptop?"

"No."

"Can you give me a free copy of Microsoft Office?"

"No."

☼ ☼ ☼

With all the heavy drinking, it was like a college dorm with different rules. But it became boring because there was nothing to do except drink and chase women. Some people loved that about ships. I sure did, at least for a while, but it got old.

I took a lot of pictures during my two contracts. So did Mirka, but by her third contract she took very few because they were all the same. Here's the beach. Here's the ship. Here's the beach. Here's the ship. If I'd stayed longer, I probably would have taken fewer and fewer pictures as well.

The lifestyle took its toll. With the work schedule and heavy alcohol and tobacco use, bodies aged quickly. I didn't smoke, but I always thought I looked older when I woke up with a hangover. Daily alcohol use took its toll on me, but even more on those who had been on ships many years. A defiled thirty-year-old could pass for forty.

The final straw was the pager. That stupid pager. Initially, it felt good to have a pager. After all, they only give pagers to important people, right? But when the warm fuzzies of eminence wore off, all I had was a noisy piece of plastic. Actually, the noise of the pager became like fingernails on a chalkboard, so I switched it to vibrate mode. Then it was like wearing a piece of my vibrating cabin.

The pager was bearable on the large ships because I was only a few days away from getting a break. The large ships had multiple I/S managers so pager duty was broken up in shifts, with a few days on and a few days off.

But on the *Holiday*, the smallest ship, there was only one I/S manager. So for ten months, I was the only one who carried the pager. The only time I didn't have it on me was when I was off the ship in port. Otherwise it was always with me. Always there. And relentless. It woke me up at night, interrupted me during dinner, or when I just wanted to sit down and rest for five minutes.

I didn't mind having to work. What I hated was the fact that my whole day was a series of interruptions. A normal eight-to-five job means that you start work with a list of things to do, and with a small amount of interruptions, you work on that list until the day is over. But my workday on the ship was never over, and each time the pager went off it chipped away at my patience.

Toward the end of my contract, I started throwing the pager across the room when it went off. One day I flung my cabin's cordless phone into the wall and broke it when someone woke me up with an urgent request. I thought back to a story Dana, the pro wrestler, had told me about when her pager went off one day near the end of her contract.

"Without even looking at who it was," she said, "I just tossed it over the edge and down it went, making that horrible beeping noise until it plunked into the water."

As tempting as that idea was, I couldn't bring myself to do it. Bad for the environment and all. Plus, getting a new pager would be one more thing I'd have to add to my work list.

In retrospect, maybe I should have thrown that pager over-board. I got to the point where, after yet another untimely interruption, I would stand in the middle of my cabin, clench my fists, look at the ceiling, and yell at the top of my lungs. I was waiting for my skin to turn green and my muscles to bulge and rip my uniform. I'd imagine turning into The Incredible Hulk and rampaging through the ship to break every computer and to beat up everyone who annoyed me.

"How do you like my holey pants now, Mr. Asshole Captain?" I'd yell while lifting him off the ground by the neck and tossing him overboard.

"I'm so glad you're using the angle grinder outside my cabin at 8:00 in the morning," I'd say to the painter and then explode a can of white paint in his face.

"Yes, I actually live on the ship. Can you believe it?" I'd say to a passenger and then push them down the stairs.

I was in my office printing the Sail and Sign cards one day and talking to one of the accountants that shared my office.

"You know, I absolutely hate the sound of this card-printing machine," I said as I put in earplugs. "I'm sorry you have to put up with it, too."

"It doesn't bother me," he said.

"Really? 'Cause I have extra earplugs."

"Doesn't bother me at all."

"You know, earplugs are my saving grace on this ship," I told him. "Alcohol helps a little with the other senses, but not enough. I think I'd be much happier if I could deaden all of my senses."

He stared at me with pity. "Jay, is that really how you feel?"

I thought for a second. "Yeah. It really is. That's pretty bad, huh?"

His question made me realize how unhappy I had become. I even caught myself kicking some of the PCs when no one was looking. I was becoming Mr. Temper and realized that most people would lose their temper if you gave them a pager and stuck them in a vibrating cabin long enough.

It was the end of my contract and once again, I did as little work as possible and left everything else for my successor. I made an enemy of the new chief purser after ignoring him when he asked me for computer help. All the rapport I had built with the previous chief purser went with her when she signed off the ship.

Once again I arranged to stay in a passenger cabin for my last cruise while my successor moved into the vibrating cabin. On my last night, a group of us went to the comparatively spacious passenger cabin to drink and play poker.

About twenty minutes into it, our neighbor started pounding on the wall. We were quiet for about two minutes until the neighbor banged on the wall again. After the third wall pounding, we heard a knock at the door. I knew it was going to be security and that our night of fun was over. But it was my neighbor, a passenger, and she was in her pajamas.

"What are you guys doing?" she asked, squinting her eyes as they adjusted to the light.

"Playing poker," I said, stepping into the corridor with her. "I'm so sorry that we're loud."

"How long are you guys planning to be up?"

"Pretty late, I think." She didn't know that my cabin was full of crewmembers, and I wasn't about to tell her.

"How many people are in your cabin?" I asked.

"My mother, my daughter, and a couple friends."

"There are five of you?"

"Yeah. And we're all trying to sleep. Can you guys please be quiet?"

"Well, probably not. But hold on a second—I'll be right back."

I rushed back in the cabin, grabbed my suitcase, and threw it on the bed. I rummaged around until I found what I was looking for. I went back to the corridor. The woman was still standing there in her pajamas, leaning against the door frame. I held out my hand and she uncrossed her arms and cupped her hands together to catch the pile of the individually wrapped packets I dropped into her hands.

267

"These work great, and there are enough for everyone in your cabin."

"What are these?" she asked.

"Earplugs. You have to roll them between your thumb and index finger like this before putting them in your ears. If you wear these, you won't hear a thing, I promise."

She nodded, and I couldn't believe she didn't get offended. She went back to her cabin and we didn't hear from her again.

I had arranged for my second contract to end right before our ship entered a three-week dry dock. Dry dock policies had changed, and this time the crew was not allowed to remain on the ship unless they were working. Some of the crew stayed in New Orleans the whole time, some flew home to be with their families, and some made extra money by joining the dry dock painting crew.

Screw that.

I signed off the ship with $10,500 in cash. I was flying with a one-way ticket, and after the Twin Towers went down, one-way tickets guaranteed that airport security would check your bags. They pulled me aside to search them.

"Excuse me," I said, whispering to the guard, "I have a large amount of cash in my bag and don't want everyone in line to see it."

"Okay, follow me."

He took me to a private room where two guards and a supervisor went through my stuff.

"Where's the cash?" the supervisor asked, trying to act intimidating and important.

I pointed to the zipper pocket where the envelope was.

"How much is this?" he asked, pulling out the giant stack of bills.

"Ten thousand, five hundred dollars."

"You know the limit is ten thousand."

"Yeah, I know," I said and wondered if these guys had the authority to just take the cash. One of the guys started counting while the other picked through the rest of my bag.

"Why do you have so much cash?"

"Well, I work on a cruise ship and I just finished my contract."

"Oh, a cruise ship. You guys actually live on the ship, don't you?"

"Yes."

"What do you do onboard?"

"I fix the computers," I answered, trying not to sound annoyed.

"We had another guy come through here yesterday who also worked on a cruise ship. He said he was the maître d'."

"Was he British and unmistakably gay?"

"Yeah," they all said, chuckling and finally relaxing.

"Yeah, I know him. He was the maître d' from my ship."

"He had a big a wad of cash, too."

"How much?"

"Twenty-two thousand."

"Did you guys let him fly with that much?"

"Yeah."

"Did he have to pay a tax or fee or something?"

"No, we just let him go."

By then, the other guy had finished counting my money, and they let me go.

☆ ☆ ☆

I was falling for Mirka and in the process had become a relatively nice guy again. It's amazing what happens when you meet the right one. She had to return to the ship after dry dock, but during dry dock she came home with me and stayed at my parents' house, where my folks made us sleep in separate rooms. They had just bought a top of the line Sleep Number® bed, and my mom wanted to show it to us.

"So go ahead and lay on it, both of you, and I'll show you how it works," mom said as she held the remote control in her hand.

Mirka and I lay down on either side.

"Now, see, you can adjust the firmness of each side like this," she said, pushing a button.

"Not bad, Mom. That's pretty cool."

"And I can adjust the mattress up and down like this," she said, pushing another button.

"Kind of like a hospital bed. Not bad for sitting up and watching TV in bed."

"Exactly," she said. "And it's perfect for reading in bed, too. But I saved the best part for last."

"All right, let's see it," I said.

She pushed another button that turned on the bed's vibrating mechanism. Mirka and I leaped out of the bed at record speed.

"What's wrong?" she asked.

"Mom, you actually *paid* for a bed that vibrates?"

"Yes, and it's wonderful."

"No, it's awful, and I don't ever want to feel that again."

I spent the next two weeks hanging out with Mirka and getting ready to backpack through Asia. Working on ships was the perfect job for taking these kinds of trips. I always had money in my pocket and time at the end of a contract.

Foy had asked his manager about a two-month leave of absence. They said no. So he quit. And off we went.

After seeing how folks in Thailand and Cambodia lived, I realized that as uncomfortable as ship life was to me, an American, in many ways it was an increase in the standard of living for crewmembers from Third World countries, where things like hot showers and flush toilets didn't exist.

I bought a one-dollar package of muffins in China, and after eating half of it, I was ready to throw the rest away.

"You must be rich," a Chinese guy said to me after freaking out when he saw that I was going to throw it away.

"No, not at all," I said, handing him the muffins. "Why do you think that?"

"Because you throw away food."

It was a perspective I had never considered, especially after seeing all the giant trash cans full of wasted food from the ship.

The whole trip through Asia was amazing and changed the way I thought about many things. We spent ten weeks visiting six countries and twenty-seven cities. Ryan, not wanting to miss out entirely, took some vacation days and met us in Hawaii for the last week of our trip.

CHAPTER 14

YOU WON'T BELIEVE
THE THINGS PASSENGERS DO

Every cruise included at least one boneheaded passenger who revealed himself by asking something like, "Does the ship have its own generators?"

Of course, the only alternative was a giant extension cord that plugged in at the Miami pier. With so many passengers on each cruise, there was bound to be a few that lacked common sense, but the ship seemed to engender more brainlessness than expected. On every cruise, and I mean every cruise, at least one person asked,

"What time is the midnight buffet?"

Here are some other gems from the passengers:

"Did this ship ever sink?"

"What do you do with the ice sculptures after they melt?"

One lady called the purser's desk and said, "I've been trapped in my cabin for over an hour now. My cabin has only two doors. One is to the bathroom, and the other says do not disturb."

"I don't understand why my stateroom steward keeps leaving packets of butter on my pillow."

"Do these stairs go up or down?"

Two ladies were standing near the pool and asked a crew-member, "Is that sea water that you put in the pools?" The crewmember said yes. Then one lady turned to the other and said, "See, that is why there are so many waves in the pool."

While in the photo gallery: "How do we find our pictures if our names aren't on them?"

A fan of the *Love Boat* went to the purser's desk and said, "I'd like to meet Captain Stubing, please."

"If I fell off the ship without anyone knowing, would the ship still come back for me?"

"Can we use U.S. dollars in Alaska?"

"Will this elevator take me to the front of the ship?"

"What religion are those people with the patches behind their ears?"

And finally: "Can I cash in my food stamps for casino chips?"

Cruise ships were also great at showing how bad many Americans were at geography. Mirka, being from the Czech Republic and wearing a nametag that said "Czech Republic," still had passengers refer to her country as Czechoslovakia. That country hasn't existed since 1993, when it split to become the Czech Republic and the Slovak Republic. Ten years had passed and yet most Americans, including myself, didn't know that.

My geography was horrible before ships and so I bought a world map and hung it on the wall in my cabin. That way I didn't have to ask crewmembers where their country was. I just looked it up. But most passengers didn't do this and would say something like, "Where *is* Macedonia?"

This either offended the crewmember, who was proud of his country, or made him think the passengers, and thus all Americans, weren't all that smart.

I was in the back of the purser's office when an Australian purser named Cathy walked in, leaned back against the door, and stared at the ceiling in disbelief.

"Oh my God," Cathy said. "You'll never believe this one."

"What happened?" I asked.

"So you know how we have framed pictures of the social hosts and pursers and band members hanging in the display cases out here, right?"

"Yeah," I said.

"And below each picture the crewmember's name and country is listed."

"Yeah, I know what you're talking about."

"Well, this lady, an American, of course, was looking at the pictures and the country names and stopped me to say, 'Excuse me, where is the USA?'"

"I said 'What do you mean?' "

"That country," she said, pointing to a framed picture. "Where is it?"

"You mean the USA?"

"Yeah, where is that?"

"Ma'am, that stands for the United States of America. You know where that is, right?"

"Oh, okay, now I get it."

I also heard another story about a woman who was upset with the itinerary of her cruise when she realized that she was going to Grand Cayman. She thought she had booked a cruise to the Grand Canyon.

One of the spa girls was a Scot, and passengers constantly asked her, "How long have you been speaking English?"

English is the native tongue of Scotland, of course, but I had to sympathize with this one because even after hearing the ship's different accents for a year, I still had trouble understanding that Scottish girl.

I often avoided the passenger areas because 95% of all passenger encounters were the same.

"How long is your contract?"

"Do you live on the ship?"

"Can you get off in port?"

I'd take a crew corridor or crew elevator even if it meant that it would take me longer to get where I was going.

Then there were the complaints. Cruises were booked with the expectation of perfection, and most of the time the cruise delivered. Sometimes it fell short and warranted a complaint. Yet even when the cruises ran smoothly, some passengers still whined. The purser's desk is where most of the complaints went. Here are some of those encounters:

"The towels aren't soft enough for the price I paid."

"I'm very sorry, ma'am," the purser said. "We'll try to use more fabric softener."

One time the purser couldn't calm a passenger and so he called the chief purser over.

"Hi, I'm the chief purser. What seems to be the problem?"

"Another passenger just called my daughter a slut."

"I'm very sorry, sir," the purser said, "but we have no way to control the comments of others."

"I'd like to talk to your boss, please."

The chief purser called the hotel director, and eventually the captain had to get involved to help calm down that passenger.

In another case, a passenger complained about his cabin.

"I paid for an ocean view cabin, but I did not get one."

"Okay, I'm looking at your cabin number now," the purser said, "and actually you do have an ocean view. If you open your curtains you'll see that you do have a window."

"I opened my curtains, and all I see is a parking garage."

"Yes, ma'am, we're still docked. You will see water when we set sail."

Many passengers got upset when the ship couldn't make it to a scheduled port. The cruise line often gave a partial refund to all passengers when that happened, but that wasn't good enough for some. I was on the *Holiday* during a four-day cruise that had only one scheduled stop in Cozumel. But before the cruise could start, the engines had to be repaired and this delayed our sailing time by nine hours. It meant that we didn't have enough time to make it to Cozumel so we sailed to Key West, instead.

Carnival gave everyone a 25% refund, but the pursers still had to deal with lots of unhappy passengers. The chief purser talked to me in the crew bar that night and told me about two girls she had to talk to.

"We'd like a full refund, please."

"I'm sorry, but we're only giving a twenty-five percent refund," the purser said.

"That's not good enough. We'd like a full refund, please."

"And why is that?"

"Because going to Cozumel was the whole reason we took this cruise."

"I understand that you wanted to visit Cozumel, but we were only scheduled to be there for eight hours. This is a four-day cruise, and if you do the math, Cozumel is only eight percent of your trip, and we think a twenty-five percent refund is very reasonable."

Sometimes no matter what the cruise line did, it couldn't please everyone. This was the case with automatic tipping. By default, Carnival automatically charged the recommended tips for the cabin stewards and the dining room staff. Passengers could remove the automatic charges and tip in cash to their preference. Carnival tried it both ways, and whether or not tips were automatic, passengers complained that it should be the other way around. So picking the lesser of two evils, Carnival stuck with automatic charges as a convenience for passengers and as a way to help keep the crew from getting stiffed.

Sometimes complaining worked against the passengers.

"We'd like to upgrade our cabin," two women said while checking in at the embarkation terminal.

"I'm sorry, but the ship is fully booked," the embarkation woman said. "You can check with the purser's desk after the ship sails to see if there are any cabins available."

Any time the ship was fully booked, the only way to get an upgrade was if there were no-shows, as in passengers that paid for the cruise but didn't show up to take it, and the pursers didn't know if there were any no-shows until the ship sailed. This wasn't good enough for these two women. So before they even boarded the ship, they made a scene until the embarkation manager was called over. They were rude and argued for fifteen minutes before finally giving up and boarding. I stood there as the embarkation manager told the chief purser about it.

"Those passengers in cabin E96 were total bitches," the embarkation manager said. "Do not give them a cabin upgrade even if you can."

"You got it," the chief purser said without hesitation.

Most of the time the cruise line was very accommodating, and unfortunately, the ones who complained the most usually got the most compensation. The compensation wasn't much and usually consisted of a free bottle of champagne that was worth about ten dollars on land. A passenger might spend thirty minutes waiting in line, another ten minutes complaining and spoiling their vacation mood, until the purser, now miserable, finally caved and offered the champagne. In my opinion, a ten dollar bottle of champagne just isn't worth all that.

Some passengers complained just to get that bottle of champagne. Sometimes it was a bottle of wine. A chef from Norwegian Cruise Lines said that on about every other cruise a passenger stuck something in their food and then complained and asked for compensation. The maître d' knew it was a scam but usually gave them a free bottle of wine anyway.

One guy took his complaining a little too far and was kicked off the ship for an attempted mutiny. It happened on a Renaissance ship when he and his wife paid for a cruise with an apparent guarantee that the ticket prices would not drop. But when they talked to the other passengers, they found out that there was a wide range of ticket prices, many of which were lower than what they had paid.

The husband then typed up a leaflet with the title, "Are You Entitled To A Large Refund On Your Cruise?" He had copies made and began distributing them throughout the ship. He rallied passengers to be part of a class-action lawsuit he was planning against the cruise line.

The captain saw the leaflet and then summoned the husband and told him to stop his actions immediately, citing that he had violated the conditions of his ticket. After a second warning, the husband continued his efforts, and then the captain ordered the husband and wife off the ship. The couple ended up paying an extra $5,500 in airfare to get them from the Caribbean back to their home in London.

One gift shop manager emailed me a story of a passenger on her ship who was kicked off for bringing a gun onboard. She said he dismantled it to get it through security at the embarkation terminal and later, with two bullets in it, he took it with him when he got off in the first port. Ship security found it when he tried to get back on the ship. Within an hour he and his family were kicked off the ship, and he was arrested at the pier by the local authorities.

Some passengers thought the ship would wait for them if they were running late in port. But let there be no mistake: the ship will leave without you. It only waits about fifteen minutes past the scheduled sailing time. If you aren't onboard, then adios. The exception was for any shore excursions purchased onboard. The company that ran the shore excursions was in constant contact with the ship's shore excursion manager, and if a tour was running late, then the ship would definitely wait. The ship might also wait if late passengers had a way to communicate to the ship that they were running late. But the captain never waited for missing passengers if he had no idea when they might stroll on back to the ship.

278

I was standing by the gangway when a couple nearly missed the ship during a rainy day in Cozumel. They were the only two missing passengers, and as soon as they boarded, the gangway was pulled and the ship immediately set sail.

"You guys nearly missed the ship," the security officer said to them.

"But we were waiting for the rain to stop so we wouldn't get wet," the wife said, brushing the water off her clothes.

"Doesn't matter," the security officer said. "The ship will leave you even if it's raining."

On another occasion, I was at the front of the *Triumph* as the ship sailed away from the pier in Saint John, Nova Scotia. Fifteen minutes after we sailed, when we were about a quarter mile away, I saw a man on the pier waving his hands and jumping up and down. The ship did not return for him. But I did wave back.

Some passengers behaved differently in front of the crew, especially the officers. When I was dressed in white, they often tried harder to be noticed and to be funny than when I wasn't wearing my uniform.

"Hey, who's driving the ship?" I would hear countless times as they saluted me.

"Shouldn't you be on the bridge, captain?" was another passenger favorite.

I generally gave the passengers a courtesy laugh, but not always.

One day I was alone in an elevator when it stopped and a husband and wife walked in. The husband broke the silence.

"Capacity: thirty-five hundred pounds," he said, pointing to the sign and looking at his wife. "I guess we're exceeding the capacity of the elevator since you're here."

Then he started laughing. It was an exaggerated hillbilly laugh, and his eyes darted back and forth between his wife and me. I made no sound and just looked at him while his wife shook her head and sighed with disgust. I'm pretty sure he didn't get any romance that night.

✵ ✵ ✵

As funny as the passenger stories were to the crew, it was tough to make them funny to the passengers. I once listened to an assistant cruise director go onstage and read a list of "Top Ten Silly Passenger Stories." She only got a couple of chuckles. It's mostly about timing, I think, but it's tough when the audience was the butt of the joke. I mean, passengers don't exactly spend a lot of money to come onboard and be told how stupid they are.

As with any group of 2,000 or more people, there will always be instances of stupidity. Almost everyone has left his common sense at home at some point, and even if only one percent of the passengers do something laughable, that's twenty laughable things the crew witness and talk about per cruise. Because both complaints and a lack of common sense seemed so ubiquitous, Americans got a bad rap. Many crewmembers thought of Americans as nothing but rude, stupid, overweight hamburger-chasers. Even the American crewmembers began to agree.

There weren't too many European or Asian crewmembers that were overweight, but many of the American passengers were. And hamburgers were so quintessentially American that some of the crew avoided them just so they wouldn't appear Americanized.

My wife had a friend named Jean who came to visit us for a week after we'd quit ships and moved to Dallas. Jean was from Wales and had also worked on ships. We had a lot of friends over, and for lunch one day we cooked some burgers and sausage and I saw Jean put a burger on her plate.

"Jean, I'm surprised to see you eating a burger," I said.

"Well, you know, when in Rome," Jean said.

One of my American friends asked, "Don't you like hamburgers?"

It would have been too hard to explain so we just skirted around it.

The crew constantly made fun of me as they generalized about the perceived inadequacies of Americans. I wasn't the only one. Just about every American crewmember heard the same thing. I talked to an I/S manager who worked on the *Holiday* after me, and one of his biggest complaints was how the crew gave him a hard time for being American.

I took it in stride and often played along, but it got old. As I learned more about the wars, the people, and the living standards of the rest of the world, I became a more humble American, but it was still unpleasant to listen to constant negative comments about your home. Home is home and we're all proud of our homes. And most of the crew only knew America from the ports and from the passengers on vacation, which gave such an incomplete picture of the United States. If these same crewmembers had a chance to see America's land-based life, then I'm sure they would feel differently.

The United States is so big and diverse that you don't need to leave the country to travel, and this, I think, contributes to why Americans are so bad at geography. Getting to know a family on land might reveal that Americans weren't so stupid after all. Besides, seafaring stupidity wasn't unique to Americans. Crewmembers who worked on other lines had the same laughable stories about European passengers.

Whether good or bad, the more unfamiliar something is, the more of an impact it has. This is partly why cruising is so enjoyable. Everything about a cruise is unfamiliar to people who live on land. It's why I wanted the job. And I think it is why many passengers lose their common sense when they step onboard.

Nowhere else can you be in a closed environment with 2,000 other vacationers and another 1,000 multinational people who are there to serve you. Passengers are awestruck with all the food, the people, the sights, the sounds, and the activities. They get so overloaded with unfamiliar sensory experiences that they do and say boneheaded things. Things like:

"How far above sea level are we?"

CHAPTER 15

WHEN IT'S OKAY TO
QUIT YOUR DREAM JOB

"So, you're quitting ships," Mirka said, buying a round of shots for a Greek guy from the casino who had worked on ships for nine years. "And this is your last night in the crew bar."

"Yes."

"Are you going to miss working for the passengers?"

"No," the Greek said, shaking his head. "I can't do it. I just can't do it. I can't work for those muppets anymore."

People ask if I miss working on ships. I do. A little bit. When I look at pictures of the *Triumph* or the *Holiday* now, it's like looking at pictures of an old house I used to live in. I get that feeling of long-lost familiarity. At night I sometimes picture the crew bar in my mind. I can see everyone drinking and partying and having the time of their lives, and sometimes I wish I were there. And though the environment had some negative effects on me, there was an enormous amount of positive cultural learning experiences. If given the choice, I would do it all over again.

Johnny Vancouver is back in Canada now as a deejay. Bud now lives in Vegas and works as a technician for one of the shows. I keep in touch with only a couple of the girls onboard, all of whom are back in their home countries and living a normal land life again.

I don't hear from JB very much these days. I know he stayed on ships a couple years longer than I did. I heard from a mutual friend that he nearly got fired after an especially intense seven-day binge in which he went around telling everybody on the ship, "I just can't get sober." He was going to bed drunk, waking up drunk, and drinking throughout the day. He eventually quit working for Carnival, and I suspect that like most people, he didn't drink nearly as much on land as he did on the ship.

I had always thought of my heavy consumption on the ship as temporary. All along I didn't like the unhealthy feeling that accompanies heavy drinking. But there was just something about ships and alcohol. Once I was back on land, I drank less. Immediately.

Still, I miss the ship parties and the ship friendships. I miss the beaches and shore excursions. I miss the lack of responsibility. I miss the privilege of my rank and the officer prestige. And as snobbish as it sounds, I miss being in a group in which I felt elite.

Like when I went to the crew purser because I lost my crew ID.

"Normally this would cost you twenty-five dollars," she said.

"Yes, but of course I could just make one myself in the computer room. I have one of those card printers, you know."

"Yeah, I guess that's true," she said, clicking the mouse to set the card-printing machine in motion.

I would have printed it myself if I'd known how to. I had never needed to do it myself, and I wasn't in the mood to poke around and learn yet another specialized software program. Besides, it felt good to know that I could get it for free, when most everyone else would have to pay twenty-five dollars.

But the novelty of ships had worn off long ago. All the things that make cruising such an addictive vacation for the passengers, and such a fun place for the crew, had become commonplace and there wasn't anything new to experience. Watching the propeller shafts spin from inside the engine room? Who cares. Standing on the bridge and looking through binoculars at the oil platforms in the Gulf? Big deal. Spending the day on a beautiful beach? Whatever.

Even so, I was ready to do another contract as long as I didn't have to sleep in that vibrating bed. But I needed to know if Mirka and I were compatible for marriage, and there was no way to determine that on a ship.

"If you want to work on a cruise ship just to meet lots of girls," my stepfather had said, "I wouldn't count on it."

In his defense, he made a different prediction after my first contract.

"Just watch," he said. "You're going to marry a girl from Europe and probably even live over there at some point."

He was spot on with that one.

I knew that Mirka and I needed to know each other on land before we could decide on marriage. Another contract would just delay that. I was thirty and she was thirty-two, and if we were going to get married and have kids then we had to get moving. Her contract finished when I got back from Asia, and we both quit Carnival and lived in the Czech Republic for a year. Turns out we were a perfect match so we moved to the States to get married.

Again I knew from the beginning that I wanted something long-term with her. I had felt the same way about other girls, but because I always took it so seriously, I was never able to relax and have a long-term relationship. Most people probably don't need casual relationships the way I did, but had I not spent two years with a relaxed attitude about sex and relationships, I don't think I would've ever been marriage material for anyone.

After I describe the rampant infidelity onboard, people who don't know Mirka often ask why I married a girl from ships. The truth is that although there were far more instances of infidelity than faithfulness, Mirka and I both knew many successful ship couples.

I had always imagined that the first person I loved would be the person I married, and for me, that's what happened. But now I can't decide if that's an entirely good thing or not. Maybe I missed out on some things by having only loved one woman. Things like the wisdom that results from a broken heart or knowledge of how love can be a little different with each person. Mirka thinks it's a good thing and says it's one of the reasons she married me.

And I'm thankful to say that I survived ships with a clean bill of health. No herpes. No AIDS.

"Your future wife will be mad if you don't take this opportunity to sleep with all these women," that friend of mine had said when I got the job.

So I put that question to Mirka one night a few weeks before our wedding.

"Would you agree with that statement, honey?" I asked her.

"Yes," she said.

Although my friend's prediction was true, it was not for the reasons he had envisioned.

"Is it because it made me a better lover?" I asked Mirka.

"No," she said. "You couldn't even make love the first time we tried."

"You didn't have to bring that up."

"And anyway," she continued, "lovemaking can be learned in a relationship."

"Then why do you agree with that statement?"

"Because I think that if you hadn't experienced all that, then you would have always wondered what it would have been like. And that type of curiosity can destroy a marriage."

✷ ✷ ✷

I had been disconnected from my typical American life for three years—two years living on ships and one year living in the Czech Republic—and when I finally returned, it was like time travel. Suddenly there were new TV shows that I'd never heard of and new TV stars I didn't recognize. Half of all songs from the radio were brand new to me. Cars looked different because so many new models were out.

My friends and family had different hairstyles. Some had gotten married in ceremonies I hadn't been able to attend. They looked a little older, as did I, and had carried on with their lives the way they would have if I had died. How dare they. The universe went on about its business. It did not revolve around me. How dare it.

Experiencing a lower standard of living changed me, too. I was less spoiled. After living in a closet on ships, I lived on a low income in Czech. When I came back to the States, many things seemed excessive and unnecessary. A three-bedroom house for two people felt huge. I didn't crave gadgets like before. I tried to avoid throwing away food. Driving a nice car no longer seemed a necessity. I had a better appreciation for the luxuries and creature comforts that I'd known all my life. And now that I've readjusted to them, I don't ever want to give them up.

So should the day ever come when it's possible to live on the moon, count me out. I might visit for a couple of days, but I'd never live there. If I were offered the chance to be one of the first astronauts to take a six-month trip to Mars, I'd decline. Neither sounds exciting anymore. It sounds like sub-par living, with little space, bad food, and little to do. Like being a cruise-ship crewmember, but much worse.

I learned that different cultures can get along just fine and people of the world are more alike than they might realize. I lived with over fifty nationalities, and we all partied the same. I never saw a nationality that didn't drink, laugh, party, have sex, or cheat on a spouse.

Ships may attract certain kinds of people, but more than that, I think they create a certain kind of person. People adapt.

Our environment shapes us. It's why our choice of friends and occupation is ultimately a choice of who we will become.

✻ ✻ ✻

The instant the double doors opened, my throat tightened and my eyes began to water. It was all I could do to hold it back. As she walked toward me, dressed in white and holding her father's arm, I could see that she had tears in her eyes too. We held hands and wept our way through the vows.

"Alright babe," I said as we drove home from our wedding reception. "I have a surprise for you."

"What surprise?" she said.

"I booked a cruise for our honeymoon."

"Oh perfect," she said, knowing that I was joking.

"Yeah just think, we could be passengers this time instead of crewmembers."

"Does that mean I have to go to Lido Deck and eat a hamburger?"

"Yep. If you're going to be a passenger, then you have to act like a passenger," I said.

"Well then I just have one question," she said.

"What's that?"

"Will I get wet if I go snorkeling?"

See pictures from my time at sea, and watch video of what happened inside the ship during the hurricane. Just go to Facebook and search for "The Truth About Cruise Ships."

Companion ebook called *"Cruise Like a Master: How To Save Money And Be Completely Prepared For Your Cruise Without All The Stress!"* It's a result of the research in the writing of *The Truth About Cruise Ships.*

Available now at: www.CruiseLikeaMaster.com

Made in the USA
Lexington, KY
10 April 2012